a r

Youth, Multiculturalism and Community Cohesion

Palgrave Politics of Identity and Citizenship Series

Series Editors: **Varun Uberoi**, University of Oxford; **Nasar Meer**, University of Southampton and **Tariq Modood**, University of Bristol

The politics of identity and citizenship has assumed increasing importance as our polities have become significantly more culturally, ethnically and religiously diverse. Different types of scholars, including philosophers, sociologists, political scientists and historians make contributions to this field and this series showcases a variety of innovative contributions to it. Focusing on a range of different countries, and utilising the insights of different disciplines, the series helps to illuminate an increasingly controversial area of research and titles in it will be of interest to a number of audiences including scholars, students and other interested individuals.

Titles include:

Derek McGhee
SECURITY, CITIZENSHIP AND HUMAN RIGHTS
Shared values in uncertain times

Nasar Meer
CITIZENSHIP, IDENTITY AND THE POLITICS OF MULTICULTURALISM
The rise of Muslim consciousness

Ganesh Nathan
SOCIAL FREEDOM IN A MULTICULTURAL STATE
Towards a theory of intercultural justice

Michel Seymour (*editor*)
THE PLURAL STATES OF RECOGNITION

Paul Thomas
YOUTH, MULTICULTURALISM AND COMMUNITY COHESION

Palgrave Politics of Identity and Citizenship Series
Series Standing Order ISBN 978–0–230–24901–1 (hardback)
(*outside North America only*)

You can receive future titles in this series as they are published by placing a standing order. Please contact your bookseller or, in case of difficulty, write to us at the address below with your name and address, the title of the series and the ISBN quoted above.

Customer Services Department, Macmillan Distribution Ltd, Houndmills, Basingstoke, Hampshire RG21 6XS, England

Youth, Multiculturalism and Community Cohesion

Paul Thomas
University of Huddersfield, UK

First published 2011 by
PALGRAVE MACMILLAN

Palgrave Macmillan in the UK is an imprint of Macmillan Publishers Limited, registered in England, company number 785998, of Houndmills, Basingstoke, Hampshire RG21 6XS.

Palgrave Macmillan in the US is a division of St Martin's Press LLC, 175 Fifth Avenue, New York, NY 10010.

Palgrave Macmillan is the global academic imprint of the above companies and has companies and representatives throughout the world.

Palgrave® and Macmillan® are registered trademarks in the United States, the United Kingdom, Europe and other countries.

ISBN 978–0–230–25195–3 hardback

This book is printed on paper suitable for recycling and made from fully managed and sustained forest sources. Logging, pulping and manufacturing processes are expected to conform to the environmental regulations of the country of origin.

A catalogue record for this book is available from the British Library.

A catalog record for this book is available from the Library of Congress.

10   9   8   7   6   5   4   3   2   1
20   19   18   17   16   15   14   13   12   11

Printed and bound in Great Britain by
CPI Antony Rowe, Chippenham and Eastbourne

Contents

Acknowledgements

This book is the culmination of a long-term involvement in researching understandings and impacts of community cohesion practice with young people, and young people's experiences of cohesion and identity in Oldham and Rochdale, Greater Manchester, and I would like to thank all the youth workers and their agencies in those areas who have participated in the research. Youth work professionals around the country continue to work, often in very challenging circumstances, towards a more tolerant, diverse and equal society, and they deserve great praise for their efforts, especially at a time when politicians mistakenly tell us we need less publicly funded work with young people and communities. I have tried to highlight the voices and experiences of those youth workers and the young people who took part in the research processes as much as possible, but the conclusions are inevitably mine. My hope is that, in drawing on real experiences at ground level to suggest what the new policy approaches of community cohesion in Britain do and could represent, this book and its arguments can be of use to policymakers and educational practitioners, as well as academic colleagues and students.

In particular, I would like to thank Oldham Metropolitan Borough Council Youth Service for the considerable access that facilitated both my original doctoral research and the Youth Identity Project, and thank the Rochdale Pride Partnership for the funding that enabled the Youth Identity Project to be extended to Rochdale. The positive involvement of a range of youth workers and agencies from Rochdale in that research was a credit to them and their area. I would also like to thank Kirklees Metropolitan Council in West Yorkshire for funding my evaluation of the initial 'Preventing Violent Extremism' (PVE) work in their area. I'd also like to thank my institution, the University of Huddersfield, and my School, the School of Education and Professional Development, for their consistent support of my research, with this support including study leave and initial funding of the Youth Identity Project that generated much of the data utilised here. Thanks to my colleagues for all their encouragement, in particular to Pete Sanderson, who has worked with me on the Youth Identity Project and generally inspired me, to Helen Jones and Ann Harris for all their help as my research confidence developed, to Jenny Armitage for all her transcription work, to Andy Mycock for his advice and to my dedicated colleagues in the Youth and Community Work Team. I would also like to thank Paul Bagguley and Yasmin Hussain of the School of Sociology and Social Policy, University of Leeds, for all their encouragement and guidance as excellent doctoral supervisors.

I would like to thank Palgrave Macmillan and their staff for supporting this book, and the anonymous reviewer selected by Palgrave, whose constructive comments on the proposal were invaluable in helping me to shape my approach. I would like to thank the editors and anonymous referees of *Youth and Policy* and the *Journal of Social Policy* for their comments on articles that included aspects of what has become Chapters 1 and 4; Jaap Tanja of the Anne Frank Stichting in Amsterdam for his comments on the draft of Chapter 2 concerning developments in the Netherlands; the editors and anonymous referees of *Sociology* for their comments on the article that included aspects of what has become Chapter 6; and the editors and anonymous referees of *The Political Quarterly* and the *British Journal of Politics and International Relations* for their comments on articles that included aspects of what has become Chapter 8.

Above all, I would like to thank my family for all their love, support and patience during the writing of this book and during the preceding years of research. Thank you so much to my wife, Bev, my sons Rhys and Matthew, my sister Marie, and especially to my parents, Mel and Meryl, for everything.

Introduction: Community Cohesion – A New British Policy Agenda

At times over the past decade it was felt as if Britain's media and politicians have talked about little else but the interrelated issues of youth, multiculturalism and community cohesion. The violent disturbances in the English northern towns and cities of Oldham, Burnley and Bradford in the summer of 2001 saw Pakistani- and Bangladeshi-origin young people clash with the police, as well as with white young men, and led to media fears that Britain was witnessing the development of a violent and oppositional 'Asian gang' (Alexander, 2000) subculture. These events prompted a significant re-shaping of government policy approaches to 'race relations' (Solomos, 2003), the meaning and impact of which is the key focus of this book, with the emergence of 'community cohesion' (Cantle, 2001; Home Office, 2005) as both an explanation for existing problems between different ethnic communities, and as a goal for future progress. All public bodies in Britain now have a duty to promote community cohesion, and public support for cohesion is regularly measured at the local level (DCLG, 2008b). This cohesion analysis of 'parallel lives' suggested that profound physical and cultural ethnic segregation in many parts of the country had led to racial tensions and to separate and oppositional identities that urgently need to be overcome in favour of common identities and values if Britain's multi-ethnic society is to operate successfully and peacefully.

The dangers of such separate, particularly Muslim, identities were apparently confirmed by the horrific events in London on 7 July 2005, when four young British Muslims killed themselves and 52 commuters from a variety of ethnic backgrounds in four co-ordinated suicide bombings on public transport. The fact that this was not an aberration was confirmed by further botched attacks two weeks later, an attack on Glasgow airport in 2007, and a number of very serious foiled plots leading to convictions. The reality that the large majority of these Islamist attacks and plots have involved young Muslims educated and mostly born in Britain has suggested that Britain indeed has a 'Muslim problem' (Masood, 2006), with government responding through the 'Preventing Violent Extremism' (PVE) agenda (DCLG, 2007b) as part of the overall CONTEST counter-terrorism strategy (Home Office, 2009). Blame for this emerging and home-grown terrorist threat and for the broader problem of ethnic segregation and separate identities in many towns and cities that is arguably causal has been squarely laid at the door of 'multiculturalism', not only from perspectives historically question-ing of the relativity of values and identities implicit in multiculturalist policy approaches and its effects on national solidity (Parekh, 2006), but from apparent liberals (Goodhart, 2004) and even equality campaign-ers, who suggested that multiculturalism had left Britain 'sleepwalking to segregation' (Phillips, 2005) through its one-sided focus on differ-ence. The accusation here is that too great a policy focus on the needs of individual ethnic minority communities, and on their distinct and fixed ethnic cultures, has fatally weakened overarching identities and concern for commonality, with the result being separate and opposi-tional identities within specific ethnic and religious communities. Some evidence in support of this analysis of failed policy approaches to eth-nic relations comes in detection of a 'white backlash' (Hewitt, 2005) against equality policies seen to favour non-white ethnic minority com-munities, whilst ignoring the lives and concerns of white working-class communities experiencing profound changes relating to economic re-structuring (Collins, 2004). Some of this white discontent has taken a political form, with a rise in support for far-right groups such as the British National Party (Eatwell and Goodwin, 2010), alongside con-cerns that overtly racist and oppositional identities are growing amongst white young people in some areas.

These developments, both events and policy responses, in the first decade of the twenty-first century suggest that what has previously been seen across Europe as the relatively successful 'British model of multiculturalism' had failed and is now of necessity being replaced. In the 1960s, Britain accepted that assimilationist approaches to post-war non-white immigration, which had tried to force new migrants to abandon their own cultures, language and traditions, had failed, and instead started to promote forms of multiculturalism within public policy (Solomos, 2003). A key figure in this move was Labour Home Sec-retary Roy Jenkins, who linked multiculturalism with integration, the approach to which he defined in 1966 as:

Not as a flattening process of assimilation, but as equal opportunity, accompanied by cultural diversity, in an atmosphere of mutual tolerance.

(Cited in Solomos, 1988: 165)

Such approaches subsequently strengthened, both through legislation and resource allocation, as well as very significantly through practice at the local level (Joppke, 2004), into a concern with equal opportunities, and the need to celebrate ethnic diversity, with significant progress in challenging racism and reducing ethnic inequalities resulting (Modood et al., 1997). This context explains why the troubling events since 2001 outlined above, the blaming of multiculturalism (Phillips, 2005) for them, and the apparent replacement of multiculturalism with community cohesion as the policy priority for government around ethnicity and race relations have proven so controversial. It is beyond dispute that a significant policy shift has occurred, with a new term, community cohesion, emerging to become the priority and this being accompanied by a new emphasis on commonality, on common values and identities, rather than the previous concern with diversity and equality. This change has encompassed English language and citizenship tests for new migrants, a focus on the importance of promoting 'Britishness' as a shared form of identity (Brown, 2007) and the questioning of continued public funding for individual ethnic or religious community facilities and organisations (DCLG, 2007a). The community cohesion discourse has also utilised 'integration' but the focus here has apparently been much more on commonality, rather than the diversity seen as integral to successful integration by Roy Jenkins in 1966.

Therefore, the change from pre-2001 policy approaches represented by community cohesion, at least in terms of language, emphasis and stated priorities, is significant. What this shift towards community cohesion really means and represents, and how it is actually being understood and operationalised at ground level, is a key focus for this book. To some commentators, the simple fact that cohesion is emphasising commonality, rather than diversity, and is doing so at the same time as overt attacks on multiculturalism, means that it should be understood as a retrograde, backwards step towards coercive assimilationism (Back et al., 2002), the 'death of multiculturalism' (Kundnani, 2002) encouraged from a perspective that wants to deny both the continued reality of racism and the importance of ethnic diversity in British society. Other perspectives agree that community cohesion represents the end of multiculturalism, seeing it as a policy approach that *should*, and must, die because of its damagingly counterproductive impacts on national solidity (Goodhart, 2004) and its role in promoting reactionary, separatist identities based around essentialised understandings of ethnicity or religion (Malik, 2009; Phillips, 2005). Such debates and tensions are not uniquely British, with a profound re-thinking of policy underway in other European states similarly pursuing pluralist approaches in the past, such as the Netherlands (Sniderman and Hagendoorn, 2009). The aim of this book is to contribute to making sense of these British changes and debates, and in so doing, to argue that both the perspectives identified above on the post-2001 policy shift are significantly wrong. In short, it is argued here that, rather than representing the 'death of multiculturalism', community cohesion represents a helpful and necessary reorientation of multiculturalism's priorities and approaches in order to positively engage with modern complexity, and that it is certainly not a retreat to assimilationism. At the same time, the book argues that attacks on multiculturalism and diversity from supposedly progressive quarters (Phillips, 2005) have been unhelpful and misleading in that they have given credibility to critiques unsympathetic to ethnic diversity and the need to respect and defend it per se.

Such a positive interpretation of what community cohesion has the potential to be and represent in Britain is out of step with most academic analysis (Flint and Robinson, 2008; Wetherell et al., 2007), but this book's perspective is that much discussion of community cohesion has been completely free of empirical evidence, resting instead on analysis of national governmental reports and accompanying national political discourse (Ward, 2001; Wetherell, 2008) that sheds little light on events on the ground. This book suggests a more positive understanding of what community cohesion can be, and what it might represent for the direction of Britain's policy approach to 'race relations' and ethnic diversity, and it does so by drawing on significant empirical evidence from areas of the country seen as witnessing the sort of profound ethnic segregation, and the separate, oppositional and potentially dangerous ethnic and religious identities that this policy shift is concerned with.

Empirical research data

In particular, this book draws on empirical evidence from young people, and those who work with them, in Oldham and Rochdale, two distinct local authority areas within the large Greater Manchester conurbation in the north-west of England. This book is *not* a case study, but grounded evidence around the understanding and implementation of community cohesion, the forms of ethnic, national and religious identity prioritised by young people, and the reality of ethnic tension from these areas helps to illuminate the meaning and relevance of the national policy developments and challenges analysed here. Such evidence will help to shed light on the reality of community cohesion policy implementation, and on associated policy developments, such as 'Preventing Violent Extremism' (DCLG, 2007b), as well as the identities, experiences and tensions that these policies have attempted to engage with. The book's aim is that this grounded approach can shed light on how we might understand the community cohesion-related national policy developments of the past decade, and what this tells us about the state of British multiculturalism.

Oldham witnessed the first of the 2001 urban disturbances that prompted this national change of policy direction, with four days of unrest that attracted unwelcomed national attention on the town (Ritchie, 2001). The neighbouring borough of Rochdale was assessed at that time as racially tense but avoided riots (Travis, 2006). Historically based around the textile industries, industrial employers in Oldham and Rochdale, as they did across the north of England, recruited labour from Pakistan and Bangladesh in the 1950s and 1960s, just as migrant labour had been recruited in previous times from Eastern Europe and Ireland. Both of these local authority areas now have significant ethnic segregation:

> Cities in the north and west dominate the group of places with the highest levels of segregation. The top eight cities on White/ Non-White segregation are all from here. All the places with high or very high segregation are Pennine towns crossing from West Yorkshire into Lancashire, north of Greater Manchester.
>
> (ODPM, 2006: 148)

This ethnic segregation is shown in housing and schools (Burgess et al., 2005), with both areas also having high levels of economic 'social exclusion' (Byrne, 1999). The decline and eventual disappearance of the once-dominant textile industries has had a profound impact on the socio-economic position of Oldham and Rochdale. Oldham was the 38th most deprived Local Authority out of 354 in England at the time of the 2001 disturbances (Oldham MBC, 2004), with both Oldham and Rochdale having electoral wards amongst the most deprived nationally: as a district Rochdale Borough is ranked 25th most deprived (out of the 354 Local Authorities in England) in terms of the average scores of its Lower Super Output Areas (LSOAs) (Rochdale MBC, 2009: 7).

Issues of ethnicity and youth are highly relevant to wider discussions of poverty, inequality and life chances in areas like Oldham and Rochdale. Demographic trends mean that young people in Oldham are disproportionately of ethnic minority origin. One in eight (13 per cent) people in Oldham as a whole are of ethnic minority origin, but that proportion rises to almost one in four (23 per cent) among young people aged less than 25 years. In a series of detailed population forecasts produced for Oldham Metropolitan Borough Council (MBC), Manchester University highlighted the extent to which this demographic balance will change the face of Oldham in the coming decades. With the number of white 'under 18s' in Oldham expected to decrease between 2001 and 2028, and the numbers of Pakistani- and Bangladeshi-origin 'under 18s' expected to grow, these forecasts show the non-white section of Oldham's under 18 youth population rising from just under 25 per cent in 2001 to almost 40 per cent in 2021 (Oldham MBC, 2005, 2006). Rochdale has similar ethnic demographic disparities amongst its youth population (Rochdale MBC, 2009). Young people in Oldham and Rochdale, especially the most marginalised, and the professional youth workers working with them, are a particular focus for this empirical evidence and discussion of it, not only because of the role of young people and young adults in the 2001 urban disturbances, racial tensions and extremist activity outlined above, but because of their centrality to the future of Britain's multi-ethnic society. Too little academic discussion of the change of policy direction over the past ten years heralded by community cohesion has drawn on empirical evidence around the lives, opinions and identities of young people, or of the reality of policy impacts on those young people and their communities. This book aims to contribute to a process of correcting that deficit.

The book draws on a number of pieces of field research, and uses them to discuss and analyse how we might understand national policy developments around community cohesion and multiculturalism, and the issues that they aim to impact on. This field research evidence includes in-depth research around how community cohesion has actually been understood and implemented by youth workers in Oldham (Thomas, 2006, 2007a), and the community contexts in which it has been operationalised, with the experiences and opinions of youth workers from a variety of youth and community work agencies in both the statutory/local authority and voluntary/community sectors quoted. In all cases, youth workers, the agencies they work for and their geographical base have been anonymised. That process was consolidated by research with young people across Oldham and Rochdale on their experiences of segregation and cohesion, the forms of identity that are important to them and their feelings about diversity (Thomas and Sanderson, 2009). That research project was funded by the University of Huddersfield and the Rochdale Pride Partnership, and utilised action research approaches whereby youth workers used a variety of collaboratively devised qualitative research approaches to gather research data from young people. The key aim here was to utilise the existing relationships of trust between youth workers and the young people they were already working with. Whilst being fully aware of the dangers of compliance and conformity in such group-based research approaches (Albrecht et al., 1993), the belief here was that more meaningful data could so be gathered, and the openness and honesty of young people in expressing their views maximised. Youth work's historic concern with disadvantaged youth has been sharpened by the 'social exclusion' focus of the Labour government (Mizen, 2004), meaning that any youth work-based research process would over-represent socially excluded young people. This might be seen to skew any data, but arguably issues of ethnic segregation and of exclusive and essentialised identities oppositional to the 'other' are precisely related to young people and communities who have lost from the economic re-structuring of post-industrial globalisation (May, 1999b), and on attempts to engage with young people at risk of attraction to racism or even 'violent extremism' (Thomas, 2002, 2008, 2009, 2010). The fact that the Rochdale element of the Youth Identity Project was funded by the 'Prevent' PVE strategy and that the author carried out evaluation of the initial 'Pathfinder' pilot year of PVE activity (Thomas, 2008) with young people in the Kirklees area of West Yorkshire (Kirklees was the home of two of the four 7/7 suicide bombers) also contributes to the empirical grounding of the book's arguments.

Making arguments about real and important social issues and policy responses is all that any sociological research process can aim for (Mason, 2002), and that is what this book aims to do: use empirical evidence and a reading of a range of academic and policy documents to make some clear arguments about what analysis of community cohesion in practice, and the experiences and identities of young people it engages with, tells us about both the reality and future possibilities of this new direction in 'race relations' policy. In doing so, the book hopes to be of help to policy-makers and practitioners, as well as academic researchers and students. My role as a Youth and Community Work lecturer at the University of Huddersfield means that I am in daily contact with youth workers based across Yorkshire and Greater Manchester, many of them working with marginalised young people for whom ethnic segregation, racial tension and feelings of social marginalisation are a lived reality, with such attitudes often reflecting the feelings of wider communities. Much of the empirical research outlined above has been carried out in conjunction with youth and community work agencies, although the conclusions and judgements are entirely mine. The key events and policy developments, and the associated debates around how we can understand the purpose and impact of these policy approaches, are discussed in the various chapters of the book, the content of which is briefly summarised here.

Chapter summaries

Chapter 1 discusses the key themes and concerns of the community cohesion policy agenda. The chapter provides a context for this discussion by briefly analysing the 2001 riots, and the national (Cantle, 2001; Denham, 2001) and local governmental (Clarke, 2001; Ritchie, 2001) response process and associated reports (Ouseley, 2001) that led to the emergence of community cohesion as a new priority, a position confirmed and operationalised by subsequent strategy documents (DCLG, 2007a; Home Office, 2005; LGA, 2002). This enables the chapter to analyse the key themes of this discourse, which are the apparently damaging effects of ethnic segregation and 'parallel lives', problematic 'bonding' social capital in the absence of forms of 'bridging' social capital (Putnam, 2000) between different ethnic communities, and the role of agency and individual and community responsibility, both in hardening segregation and in overcoming it (Etzioni, 1995). This analysis can all be seen as consistent with themes and approaches of wider New Labour social policy (Levitas, 2005). Underpinning this whole community cohesion analysis is a focus on the negative consequences of previous, pre-2001 'race' relations' policies that have focused only on equality for each separate ethnic group whilst neglecting commonality and the need to nurture good relations between groups (Cantle, 2005; Malik, 2009).

Chapter 2 puts this post-2001 British policy development in context by looking at two European comparators. France's tradition of colour-blind republican citizenship has traditionally been seen as a polar opposite of Britain's multiculturalism (Flavell, 2001) but the book challenges the stability and longevity of that 'tradition'. The significant urban disturbances of 2005 (Waddington et al., 2009) have brought the tensions inherent in this French policy approach to the surface. These approaches and debates are discussed, as are the significantly different assumptions and experiences of the Netherlands. Historically seen as a highly successful multiculturalist society through its 'pillarisation' approach to pluralism (Bagley, 1973), the Netherlands has more recently experienced significant political convulsions linked to 'race', immigration and an apparent backlash against the problematic reality of this Dutch multiculturalist society. This has involved the election of overtly anti-Muslim and anti-immigration politicians and a rescinding of some multiculturalist policies (Sniderman and Hagendoorn, 2009). These developments are analysed in order to identify any similarities and differences with the British post-2001 experiences.

Chapter 3 summarises and discusses the widespread criticisms of community cohesion and what it apparently represents. Its approach is to relate these critiques to the key themes outlined in Chapter 1. Here, community cohesion's suggestion that ethnic clustering and segregation is inherently problematic or causal to wider social problems is discussed (Flint and Robinson, 2008; Kalra, 2002; Kundnani, 2007), as is the implicit suggestion that ethnic segregation is actually getting worse (Burgess et al., 2007; Carling, 2008; Finney and Simpson, 2009). Similarly, the contention that communities have used their agency to separate (Ouseley, 2001) and that the 'bonding' social capital of communities is the driver of segregation and racial tension is viewed by many commentators as a 'racialisation' of social problems and tensions – a blaming of the cultures, values and attitudes of non-white communities for issues whose roots actually lie in social structures and processes of profound social class and racial inequalities (Alexander, 2004; Burnett, 2004). This perspective suggests that community cohesion's concern with agency and social capital is a 'blaming the victims' approach, a reversal of causation around ethnic segregation and racial tension (Kundnani, 2002). Such perspectives imply that community cohesion represents a backwards step from previous progress on equal opportunities and ethnic inequality (Solomos, 2003), by the then Labour government (Back et al., 2002; Wetherell et al., 2007). The direct attacks on multiculturalism in the wake of cohesion's emergence, both from the right of centre (Grieve, 2009; Prins and Salisbury, 2008) and liberals (Goodhart, 2004; Phillips, 2005) are examined in the light of such critiques, enabling the chapter to summarise the overwhelmingly hostile academic response to what community cohesion arguably represents.

Given that much of these critiques of community cohesion are entirely free of any empirical evidence as to how community cohesion is actually being understood and operationalised on the ground, Chapter 4 focuses on community cohesion in practice. The chapter outlines how cohesion has been put into practice by national and local government (DCLG, 2007a; Home Office, 2003b, 2004, 2005; LGA, 2002, 2004), including guidance to Local Authorities and their partners, and experimental 'Pathfinder' pilot work funded by central government. The chapter then goes on to detail the in-depth research carried out in Oldham as to how community cohesion has actually been understood and practised in community-based work with young people. The chapter suggests that on the ground, cohesion enjoys significant support amongst youth workers, and the young people they work with, and outlines significant changes, and arguably improvements, made to professional educational practice in the name of community cohesion. This includes significant re-prioritisation and reorganisation of work to promote 'direct contact' between young people of different ethnic and other backgrounds. This direct contact in the name of cohesion is shown to be about the creation of safe spaces to promote understandings and respect in informal circumstances that fulfil the key principles of 'contact theory' (Hewstone et al., 2007), work that enables a 'rooting and shifting' (Yuval-Davis, 1997) in young people's attitudes and identities. Here, it is suggested that cohesion in practice is working with and respecting existing ethnic and other identities, augmenting them, rather than replacing in an assimilationist sense, with an overarching focus on common identities and experiences. This cohesion practice is not only working with ethnic identities and tensions, but also engaging with wider forms of identity and experience, including the importance of geographical 'territory' for young people, economic and social changes and divisions, and gender.

Chapter 5 further develops discussion of such wider social structures and forces by examining the extent to which community cohesion is, or should be, concerned with wider understandings of 'social cohesion' rather than just 'narrowly' focusing on relations between different ethnic groups. Here, the experiences and understandings of identity for young people are discussed in relation to issues of territory and 'turf' (Back, 1996; Kintrea et al., 2008; Webster, 1995), with a questioning of how far 'race' can be separated from place in young people's experiences. Similarly, economic changes and the rapidly developing reality of 'social exclusion' (Byrne, 1999; Levitas, 2005) for many young people of all ethnic backgrounds is discussed, as is the role of gender, with both forces related to the apparent reality of youth racial tension and segregation that the book is concerned with. It is suggested here, supported by empirical evidence, that a potential strength of community cohesion is its ability to address ethnicity, as well as other forms of identity and experience, holistically, rather than through the 'silo' approach of past policies. Based upon this, it is argued that cohesion practice is operationalising 'intersectional' understandings of 'identity' (McGhee, 2006), an approach vital and unavoidable in an increasingly diverse and fluid society.

Chapter 6 builds on this evidence by examining the suggestion that young British people of Pakistani and Bangladeshi origin are increasingly embracing separate, oppositional and problematic 'Muslim' identities that underpin the growing Islamist terror threat to the UK. Empirical field research evidence from Oldham and Rochdale is presented and discussed, focusing on key issues such as whether Muslim young people are antagonistic to national identity, how important religious identity is to young 'Muslims' and the role of Muslim young people in the creation of such strong faith-based identities. This data is used to challenge claims of young Muslim hostility to national identity and values (Prins and Salisbury, 2008), but also to discuss how we might understand a strong prioritisation of faith identity amongst young British Muslims (Abbas, 2005, 2007b; Lewis, 2007; Malik, 2009). It is suggested here that the strong prioritisation of faith revealed by this data can be understood as a dialectical response by young Muslims to profound global developments (Roy, 2004), as well as to generational tensions and changes within communities (Din, 2006; Macey, 1999, 2007).

Chapter 7 takes a similar approach to the identities, views and experiences of white young people and the feelings of all young people about the current reality and future prospects for a multi-ethnic society. White young people, especially those from working-class backgrounds, have been increasingly portrayed as problematic, and even as the 'real' victims of racial inequality (Collins, 2004; Runnymede Trust, 2009). Empirical data is presented and discussed in relation to other academic work (Hewitt, 2005; Nayak, 1999) to suggest that policy approaches that have prioritised ethnic inequality in the context of a widespread modern downplaying and denial of the relevance of social class as a force in society have led to highly racialised, and, at times, racist, understandings of identity amongst white young people, a development increasingly exploited by far-right political groups (Eatwell and Goodwin, 2010). What is clear is that there has been a 'white backlash' (Hewitt, 2005) from some young people and their communities to previous anti-racist policy initiatives, and that support for far-right political groups offering racialised explanations of inequality in society has grown in recent years (Copsey, 2008; Eatwell and Goodwin, 2010). In discussing the identities, opinions and media portrayals of white young people and their communities, the chapter directly addresses allegations and concerns that community cohesion represents a retreat from accepting the reality of, and opposing, racism (Pilkington, 2008). The chapter draws on empirical evidence and analysis of academic discussion to consider such claims. Here, it is suggested that community cohesion represents a significant re-thinking of the assumptions, methods and priorities of previous policies of 'political multiculturalism' or 'anti-racism'. It is acknowledged here, however, that this represents a difficult balancing act, with a danger that a re-working of language and priorities in relation to racism might be understood as a diminution of concern in general, especially within a policy context that has seen threats to 'single group' funding (DCLG, 2007a) and the replacement of race equability bodies with overarching human rights agencies (McGhee, 2008).

Chapter 8 examines a significant policy development that has emerged and been operationalised alongside community cohesion, but which is arguably fundamentally in conflict with the aims and principles of community cohesion, namely the 'Preventing Violent Extremism' (PVE) initiative (DCLG, 2007b; House of Commons, 2010). Intended as a 'hearts and minds' preventative programme as part of the government's wider CONTEST counter-terrorism policy agenda (Home Office, 2009), PVE has proven hugely controversial in both its focus and methods. Empirical evidence from PVE work on the ground (Thomas, 2008) is drawn on to suggest that PVE's monocultural focus on Muslims has proven damagingly in conflict with community cohesion in practice (House of Commons, 2010), and so questions how consistently the new cohesion perspective has penetrated central and local government. This has arguably left PVE 'falling between two stools' (Thomas, 2009), neither working constructively in tandem with community cohesion nor engaging effectively with the Islamist terrorist threat that is undoubtedly represented by a small number of young Muslims.

Chapter 9 provides the conclusion, where a summary of the preceding empirical evidence and discussions leads the book to suggest that, contrary to the overwhelming bulk of academic analysis, community cohesion, as it has been shown to be understood and practised, has the potential to offer positive and holistic ways forward around diversity and equality. In particular, the book clearly concludes that community cohesion does *not* represent the 'death of multiculturalism' (Kundnani, 2002) but instead a significant re-working of it. Here, the language and priorities of British policy approaches to ethnic diversity and 'race relations' (Solomos, 2003) have clearly changed, but the empirical evidence suggest that there is very significant continuity, with ethnic differences and identities being respected and worked with in processes that attempt to utilise the principles of 'contact theory' (Hewstone et al., 2007) to build mutual trust and respect and so augment existing identities with overarching common identities and experiences. This, the book argues, is the only viable way forward in an increasingly diverse society, an approach that has the potential to encourage a 'convivial cosmopolitanism' (Gilroy, 2004) that can help young people get 'race' further out of the way and focus on their common needs and shared humanity in a societal situation of significant and entrenched social inequality.

1
The Emergence of Community Cohesion

Introduction

The Introduction chapter outlined how UK government policy towards 'race relations' (Solomos, 2003), how government responds to and manages the reality of identified ethnic groups within society and how those groups interact, has changed markedly since 2001 with the emergence of the new policy priority of community cohesion. Not only was community cohesion a new term with little previous social policy pedigree (Robinson, 2005) but it has heralded a marked change in language, emphasis and stated policy priorities, and the nature and meaning of those changes remains highly controversial (Flint and Robinson, 2008; Wetherell et al., 2007). This chapter explores this new policy of community cohesion by analysing the 2001 urban disturbances that provoked this significant policy shift, the process of national (Cantle, 2001; Denham, 2001) and local (Clarke, 2001; Ouseley, 2001; Ritchie, 2001) governmental Inquiries and reflection that led to the emergence of community cohesion, and the key themes and concerns that can be detected within community cohesion.

Those themes and concerns are ethnic physical and cultural segregation and the separate and oppositional identities, rather than commonality that results from such segregation; a communitarian concern that the agency of individuals and communities has maintained ethnic separation and is not currently sufficiently utilised to overcome ethnic barriers; the analysis of problematic 'bonding' social capital in the absence of forms of 'bridging' social capital implicit in this segregation analysis; and an underpinning critique of the 'race relations' policy priorities of previous decades that arguably delivered greater equality for each separate ethnic group but badly neglected relations *between* groups and forms of common identity and experience, so inadvertently hardening those separate ethnic identities. The justification for, and the logic of, each of those themes and concerns is discussed in this chapter, and this significant shift in British policy is then contextualised by discussing the parallel experiences of two other Western European states, France and the Netherlands. Given how highly contested each of these themes and the overall thesis of community cohesion is in the UK, Chapter 3 then summarises and discusses key criticisms of community cohesion and its key concerns.

Petrol bombs and policy change

The violent disturbances that occurred in a number of towns and cities in the north of England during the summer of 2001 was the most serious outbreak of rioting in Britain since the inner-city disturbances of 1981 and 1985, with those earlier events seen as linked to large-scale youth unemployment and heavy-handed policing of multi-racial inner-city areas (Solomos, 2003). The 2001 disturbances have been frequently described as 'race riots' and have apparently led directly to a significant change in government's approach to race relations policies as the Introduction outlined. The actual events of 2001, the causal factors and the extent to which the term 'race riots' is in any way appropriate are discussed here, drawing on the published academic sources that have analysed the actual events of 2001 and their meaning (Bagguley and Hussain, 2008; Farrar, 2002; Kalra and Rhodes, 2009; King and Waddington, 2004; Waddington, 2010; Waddington et al., 2009). In so doing, this section also raises the question of the relationship between the 2001 disturbances and subsequent policy approaches. This section first provides a brief factual overview of the 2001 disturbances, and then discusses how we might understand these events and their subsequent impact through discussion of a number of key issues.

The 2001 riots

The 'official' governmental understanding (Denham, 2001) is that three separate outbreaks of violent urban disturbances occurred in the summer of 2001 – firstly in Oldham, Greater Manchester, from 26–29 May, then in Burnley, Lancashire, from 23–25 June, and finally in Bradford, West Yorkshire, on 7–9 July. All of these disturbances involved Asian young men of Pakistani and Bangladeshi origin clashing with the police, as well as with white men in the case of Oldham and Burnley. In each of the three areas, the violence was significant; Bradford witnessed the most serious events, with damage estimated at over £7 million, and 326 police officers injured (Denham, 2001), whilst in both Oldham and Burnley significant numbers of individuals from different communities clashed violently, as well as with the police. All three areas saw pubs, businesses and other buildings burned out, and police in full riot equipment attacked with a variety of weapons that included petrol bombs and cars (Bagguley and Hussain, 2008). In Oldham, an initial racial confrontation escalated to street disturbances that saw as many as 200 white and Asian people clash violently before a slow police response led to prolonged violence between large numbers of Asian young people and the police (Kalra and Rhodes, 2009). Burnley similarly saw direct violence between white and Asian groups, involving an escalating series of tit-for-tat racist incidents including an assault on an Asian taxi driver, a large-scale racist incursion into Asian areas and retaliatory attacks on white pubs that saw one pub burned down (King and Waddington, 2004). The scale and directness of these violent confrontations between white and Asian groups in both Oldham and Burnley, with both sides armed with weapons, means that the term 'race riot' can be seen as relevant, an echo of the Notting Hill and Nottingham riots of 1958 which saw violent clashes between whites and African-Caribbean migrants in an era of uncontrolled racial discrimination and prejudice (Sivanandan, 1981). In contrast, the Bradford riot, whilst linked to fears around racist incursions as discussed below, involved a straight confrontation between Asian young men and the police, a prolonged bout of anti-authority violence that was much more reminiscent of the inner-city disturbances of the early 1980s (Solomos, 2003).

The aftermath of these events has been difficult both for the towns and cities themselves, with national perceptions negatively altered, and for the communities involved, with draconian prison sentences impacting especially on the local Asian communities (Burnett, 2004; Kalra and Rhodes, 2009). Whilst these were undoubtedly the most serious outbreaks of violence that summer, the 'official' understanding (Cantle, 2001; Denham, 2001) itself is contentious, as it largely ignored similar outbreaks of violence in Leeds, West Yorkshire, on 5 June, and Stoke-on-Trent, Staffordshire, on 14–15 July. The lack of focus on those other events in government accounts suggests that they were viewed simply as 'copycat' incidents, a questionable judgement, and leaving those events in Leeds and Stoke badly under-scrutinised. As highlighted in the Introduction, the actual triggers and events in Oldham, Burnley and Bradford were not discussed in any real detail by the subsequent government-commissioned Community Cohesion Report Team (CCRT) process (Cantle, 2001), or by the governmental response (Denham, 2001). Similarly, the local Oldham review (Ritchie, 2001) did not focus significantly on the actual events, concentrating instead on what are seen as long-term problems of ethnic segregation, racial tension and economic marginalisation. The most significant and revealing focus on the actual triggers and conduct of the violence came in the Burnley local report (Clarke, 2001), which does devote more attention to the events, and amplifies it by including evidence submissions, including one by Lancashire Police that stresses the role of criminality and disputes over drug-dealing and territory within the disturbances.

This lack of an official scrutiny of the actual events is in stark contrast to the forensic examination of the triggers and events of the 1981 riot in Brixton, south London (Scarman, 1981), that is widely understood as having prompted the subsequent and widespread rioting across British inner cities. This analytical gap has only partially been filled by academic commentators, with only one full-length study of the Bradford riot (Bagguley and Hussain, 2008), and that thoughtful contribution limited by its lack of empirical evidence from actual rioters or direct witnesses (Waddington, 2010). Actual eye witness evidence from Bradford, including that of police officers, is drawn on elsewhere (Bujra and Pearce, 2009), whilst analysis of the Oldham and Burnley disturbances (Kalra and Rhodes, 2009; King and Waddington, 2004) has attempted to make sense of the eye witness and journalistic accounts available. These are all drawn on here, alongside community-based research sources (Sutcliffe, 2003), and the perceptions of youth work-based informants in Oldham of the triggers and events there. The aim here in the limited space available is to make sense of the 2001 events in relation to the way they were 'officially' portrayed and understood, and to the subsequent change of policy direction apparently carried out in direct response to these violent events.

Common factors?

A number of important themes can be detected in this analysis of the 2001 disturbances and their meaning. The first is the actual location of these disturbances. A common factor uniting Oldham, Burnley and Bradford is their past and present economic profile (Kalra and Rhodes, 2009). All three areas had been dominated by the textile and associated engineering industries, with recruitment of extra staff to the textile industries being the direct reason for the substantial Pakistani and Bangladeshi communities resident in each area (Modood et al., 1997). The subsequent decline and disappearance of that industry has left Oldham, Burnley and Bradford with poverty and unemployment rates above national averages, and with high levels of unskilled, poorly educated individuals seeking work in what has increasingly become an 'hour glass' economy that has little space in between the mass of minimum-wage, low-skill jobs and the highly paid professional roles of the emerging 'knowledge economy' (Mizen, 2004). Comparatively few of the latter well-paid jobs have yet to develop in post-industrial towns and cities like Oldham, Burnley and Bradford. As is the case nationally (Modood et al., 1997), this unemployment impacts disproportionately on the Asian communities of these areas:

> For those aged 16–24, the core group with which much of the post-riot debate was concerned, in each of the three towns, but especially in Oldham, Bangladeshi and Pakistani males in this age group had much lower levels of full-time employment, higher levels of unemployment and involvement in higher education than white British men of the same age.
>
> (Bagguley and Hussain, 2008: 41)

The resulting social exclusion (Byrne, 1999) in each area is significant, and, despite growing economic polarisation within each separate ethnic community, takes spatial forms that harden any existing patterns of ethnic segregation through severely constrained employment and housing options. The CCRT Inquiry process involved visits to other multi-ethnic areas of Britain not experiencing racial tensions, such as Leicester and Southall in west London. The suggestion here (Cantle, 2001) was that ethnic diversity had been managed better in those areas. Whilst it is undoubtedly true that good 'race relations' work has happened in those areas, the reality is that physical ethnic segregation of some minority communities in Leicester is as great as that of the 2001 riot areas (Finney and Simpson, 2009), so, arguably, the real difference is that these 'peaceful' areas have been much more successful in generating viable post-industrial economies that have produced jobs and the possibility of economic progress for all ethnic groups in their areas than have areas like Oldham (Kalra, 2000). Government has acknowledged the unevenness of ethnic diversity and of the settlement patterns of new migrants (DCLG, 2007a), but the great unevenness of economic prosperity and of social exclusion also needs to be acknowledged here when considering the causes of, and attempts to prevent, racial tension.

Closely allied to this understanding of modern economic dynamics in each of the 2001 riot areas is a reality of significant ethnic segregation. Whilst the implicit community cohesion suggestion that this ethnic segregation is getting worse is highly contested (Carling, 2008; Finney and Simpson, 2009; Ouseley, 2001), it is beyond dispute that Oldham, Burnley and Bradford, and other ex-industrial areas of Yorkshire, Lancashire and Greater Manchester, are amongst the most ethnically segregated local authority areas of England. Here, housing areas are significantly segregated by ethnicity, and schools even more so (Burgess et al., 2005). Originally created by racist practices in housing markets (Kundnani, 2001), this significant segregation has arguably been maintained by poverty, the lack of suitable alternative housing (Phillips et al., 2008) and demographic pressures within different ethnic communities (Finney and Simpson, 2009). It is clear that this local segregation and associated ethnic tensions had been growing for years, if not decades, without any effective action, suggesting a clear failure of local political leadership (Ouseley, 2001; Ritchie, 2001). The initial rejection by Oldham Council of the main recommendations of the local report following the 2001 riots (Ritchie, 2001) suggested both a denial of the local authority's own historic role in fostering ethnic segregation and a reluctance to show that political leadership (Bagguley and Hussain, 2008). One issue highlighted has been that in the period leading up to the 2001 disturbances, the Race Equality Councils (RECs), local agencies charged with addressing racial discrimination and promoting good race relations at the local level, and which had their roots in the 1976 Race Relations Act (Solomos, 2003), had collapsed in each of the towns subsequently experiencing riots. To some commentators (Bagguley and Hussain, 2008) this might a be a causal factor, but it can arguably be seen as symptomatic of the problematic ethnic relations in the area and of the corrosive long-term impacts of policies of ethnicism that focused on the needs of each separate ethnic community (Malik, 2009). Here, these RECs experienced the withdrawal of local authority funding and support because of the fundamental lack of agreement and cooperation between different ethnic minority community groups, a lack of united common purpose around race equality initiatives that could be seen as a product of past policies (Sivanandan, 2004) and which made their demise inevitable.

The impact of the combination of largely monocultural housing and economic marginalisation on youth identities is the subject of detailed discussion in Chapters 6 and 7, and this can be seen to accentuate a retreat to essentialised and oppositional identities for 'losers' in an increasingly globalised, neo-liberal economy (May, 1999b), a 'neighbourhood nationalism' (Back, 1996) stronger than that always demonstrated by working-class young men (Cohen, 1988) because life has not offered young men of Asian or white backgrounds the possibility of any other sort of identity in towns like Oldham or Burnley. Arguably, this analysis allows a direct comparison between the 2001 riots and those of 1991 that saw serious disorder on (almost entirely white) socially excluded British social housing estates on the edge of cities like Cardiff, Oxford and Newcastle-upon-Tyne, and which has been understood as a violent, gendered response to generational economic marginalisation in ex-industrial areas (Campbell, 1993). The long-term racial tensions and youth violence around perceptions of 'borders' and territory in ethnically segregated Oldham (Thomas, 2003) and similar ex-industrial northern towns (Webster, 1995) can be seen as a parallel here, with tensions over racial attacks and claims, amplified by sensationalist media coverage, of 'no go' areas for whites in parts of Oldham central to the pre-riot build-up of tension there (Kalra and Rhodes, 2009).

   This analysis of geographical economic marginalisation and closely associated ethnic segregation and tensions suggests that the 2001 riots can be seen as inevitable, but the 'flashpoints' model of public disorder (Waddington, 2010) rightly suggests that it is the complex interplay of factors at a number of levels that enables problematic, long-term social, political or economic problems to result in outbreaks of violence at specific places and times. This is illustrated by the fact that a number of other northern towns and cities, such as Rochdale, Blackburn and Dewsbury, share all the economic and social characteristics outlined above, and were viewed as being 'at risk' of violence during 2001 (Travis, 2006) but did not witness disorder in the way that Oldham, Burnley and Bradford did. A number of specific factors can therefore be detected in understanding the outbreak and conduct of the 2001 disturbances in Oldham, Burnley and Bradford, and consideration of them challenges the notion that these disturbances were in some ways 'inevitable'. They are far-right agitation and the role of local media in fanning this; clumsy and ineffective policing that had the effect of increasing tension and violence; allegations of criminality within the specific trigger incidents; and the accelerant role of new technologies within the disturbances and the bitterness of their aftermath.

Far-right agitation

Local agitation and inflammation by far-right groups like the British National Party (BNP) and the National Front can be seen as central to the 2001 disturbances, despite little focus on them in the community cohesion national reports (Bagguley and Hussain, 2008), a failure that echoes official analysis of early 1980s disturbances (Solomos, 2003). This was particularly evident in Oldham, with several marches or rallies, often largely made up of racist activists from other parts of the country, in the months leading up to the riots, with the last held on the day the riots started. The impact this persistent agitation had on Oldham's Asian communities, including the eve of the riot, was obvious to Johnson, a white youth worker with experience of work in Asian communities:

> There was a real fear of the BNP coming and doing this and that...they were turning up and we were saying, 'are they going to be here this weekend?'. The night before the disturbances they were in the pub up at Primrose Bank (a white area), which is on the edge of Bankside (Pakistani area), and if you've got a pub full of right-wing extremists, the community is going to say, 'hang on, they're only 200 yards up there.' There's going to be fear there.

One of the key incidents seen as increasing tension in Oldham some weeks before the riots was an incursion by football fans into Westwood, a mainly Bangladeshi area, before and after a game between Oldham Athletic and Stoke City, with far-right activists seen as influential on this fan behaviour. Similarly, BNP leaflets and websites were used to exploit and further inflame the mugging of a white pensioner by Asian young men, a job made much easier by it being termed a racist attack by local police and the *Oldham Chronicle* newspaper despite clear denials by the victim's family (Kalra and Rhodes, 2009). The reactionary role of local media can be seen as important here, with local newspapers in both Oldham and Burnley persisting in publishing incendiary and often racist letters, some of them anonymous and emanating from the BNP, in the months leading up to the riots. This, and the biassed press coverage of issues around claims of racial attacks, made the press culpable in the eyes of the local inquiries (Ritchie, 2001).

Similarly, the Bradford riot can be linked directly to racist political activity, with a far-right rally scheduled for Bradford on Saturday, 7 July, leading to a ban by the Home Secretary, an associated ban on a previously scheduled city centre multicultural music festival aimed at families of all ethnic backgrounds, and the holding of an anti-racist rally instead in the centre in case any far-right activists gathered. The context here can be seen as being a historical one of large-scale fascist rallies in Bradford in the late 1970s and substantial, violent responses by anti-racists, and a recent one of fascist agitation locally that included BNP leader Nick Griffin speaking at a rally held in a white suburb of Bradford the night before the riot (Copsey, 2008). This racialised context, built on increasing ethnic segregation within the city (Carling, 2008), the febrile atmosphere created by recent 'race riots' in Oldham and Burnley, hot weather and persistent rumours that far-right activists had appeared in central Bradford all provided the conditions for 'flashpoints' (Waddington, 2010) that led to and escalated the rioting. Arguably, the Bradford riot meant that a far-right 'strategy of tension' had achieved exactly what it hoped for (Copsey, 2008), with negative national media coverage of Asian young people fuelling popular fears and moral panics around 'Asian gangs' (Alexander, 2000), and resulting in significant political progress for the BNP at the local level, including elected councillors in areas of the north of England like Burnley, Bradford, Calderdale, Kirklees and Leeds (Copsey, 2008). This electoral upswing only subsequently started to decline with the 2010 national and local elections, and the election of a right-of-centre national coalition government.

The role of technology

The far-right agitation outlined above, in the context of long-term ethnic segregation and associated tensions, helped to create a highly racialised and tense atmosphere in Oldham, Burnley and Bradford, and in other similar towns and cities, prior to the riots. Arguably, 'technologies of information flow' (Kalra and Rhodes, 2009) were an important component in this growing tension and in its rapid escalation once the initial incidents of violence occurred. Relevant here is the use of far-right websites, both national 'official' ones and, more importantly, those of local 'front' organisations to spread false and misleading information about the nature and reality of racial incidents. Second was the role of mobile phone technology in mobilising large numbers of people rapidly on the basis of a rumour or claimed threat. Here, mobiles can be seen as a crucial element in the cycle of violent incidents in Burnley, and in the rapid escalation of the initial incident that sparked the Oldham riots (Kalra and Rhodes, 2009), as confirmed by white youth and community worker David, who has long experience of working with Asian young men in Oldham:

> The other thing about the Oldham situation is there are a lot of young Asian men around so suddenly, quickly, there are a lot of people in one place and the distances are not big, and the mobile phones are effective and suddenly everyone's there.

Similarly, the spreading of false information rapidly by community-based pirate radio and mobile technology were both crucial to the escalation of the 2005 Birmingham disturbances (King, 2009). Above all, modern technologies also played a crucial role in the large number of arrests made and convictions achieved in the wake of the riots in Oldham, Burnley and Bradford (Bagguley and Hussain, 2008). High-quality photography and video footage taken during the riots, some of it by dedicated, front-line information-gathering police units now formally known as 'forward intelligence teams', successfully captured clear images of many of the rioters, with subsequent media campaigns used to identify those involved. The clarity of such evidence partially explains the severity of the sentences received by many, especially those involved in the Bradford disturbances, and despite the fact that many had handed themselves in to the police following family pressure (Burnett, 2004). The length of these sentences following events arguably provoked by far-right agitation and police mishandling has left bad feeling in some parts of the Asian communities affected (Burnett, 2004), a feeling exacerbated in Oldham by the lower sentences given to the white men regarded as responsible for the trigger incident as a slow police response prevented the sort of detailed technology-based information gathering that subsequently convicted many of the Asian young men who had reacted (Bagguley and Hussain, 2008).

Police mishandling?

Clumsy and questionable policing is also an identifiable issue in relation to both the longer term causes and the immediate triggers of the 2001 disturbances. An identifiable longer-term policing issue is the role of Greater Manchester Police (GMP) around racial incidents and attacks within Oldham. Prior to the 2001 disturbances, Oldham had consistently recorded the highest number of 'racial incidents' in the Greater Manchester area and was one of the few locations nationally to show a larger number (but not proportionally, given the much larger white population) of racial incidents with white people as victims, rather than the reverse situation common elsewhere. Arguably, such data showed both the confusion following the Stephan Lawrence Inquiry (Macpherson, 1999) which emphasised that the victim's perception was crucial to the definition of a 'racial incident' and the highly racialised atmosphere in Oldham, whereby whites felt they were the real victims of racism in an echo of what has been termed the 'white backlash' (Hewitt, 2005). GMP's decision to present these raw racial incident statistics without any contextualisation of population size and proportionality of likely risk, and their silence as sections of the media and public used these to claim that whites were indeed the 'real' race victims, greatly increased racial tensions in the town, arguably setting the scene for the reporting of 'no go' areas and the racialisation of the attack on pensioner Walter Chamberlain (Kalra, 2002; Ray and Smith, 2002) by the local press. Indeed, Rafiq, a Bangladeshi-origin, Oldham youth project co-ordinator felt that the Oldham division of GMP were giving their own response to the Lawrence Inquiry's finding of 'institutional racism' within the police through this action:

> It doesn't surprise that the policeman in charge at the time (1999–2001) is no longer a policeman. I think they retired him off early or something, but he's no longer a policeman. At the time I think he had a political agenda of trying to undermine some of the Stephen Lawrence Inquiry recommendations.

The resulting bad feeling towards GMP amongst Oldham's Asian communities was compounded when the rioting broke out on 26 May. Having failed to prevent racist football fans marauding through Asian areas in the weeks previously, GMP's response to the large gathering of Asian young men prompted by the incursions of white racists, some of whom had earlier attended a BNP march, was to hem them in and effectively cordon off the mainly Pakistani area of Bankside. Local youth worker Habib commented that:

> The Police made mistakes, major ones and minor ones, in the sense that the way they policed was poor. The strategy of trying to hem Bankside in from blowing up actually caused more of a hassle than they needed.

Accusation of police mishandling of public order situations was also made in Burnley, where Lancashire Police were seen to be very slow to control large groups of white men from gathering and moving towards Asian areas, a failure compounded by allegations of brutality in their treatment of Asian men later in the events (King and Waddington, 2004). Perhaps the most serious criticisms of policing came in Bradford, with the suggestion that the violent escalation of the rioting on 7 July can be seen as a failure of policing at certain key 'flashpoints' during the day, such as the surrounding of a peaceful anti-racist rally with police officers already in riot gear, their failure to anticipate and deal with racist behaviour by a small group of white fascist sympathisers before they attacked an Asian man, and the arguably unnecessary chasing of Asian young men back towards the Pakistani-dominated area of Manningham that fundamentally altered the nature of the confrontation from polit-ical protest to a perceived community defence (Bagguley and Hussain, 2008). This latter tactical approach might directly be traced to criticisms made of the police for not defending the city centre against damage following earlier rioting by Asian young people in Bradford in 1995, a decision that arguably prolonged the 2001 rioting and greatly increased its intensity (Bujra and Pearce, 2009). This perception of being a commu-nity under police attack, coupled with the view that the racist agitation of far-right groups was not being taken seriously by the police, created the belief for some Asian young men in Bradford of the 'right to riot' (Jan-Khan, 2003).

Criminality?

The consistent police response in 2001 to such allegations of misman-agement was that violent and unjustifiable criminality lay at the root of such disturbances, giving the police little room for manoeuvre. Here, there are clear parallels to long-established perspectives of urban riots that portray them as inherently criminal, the 'madness of the mob' led by manipulative agitators. The immediate aftermath of the Bradford riots saw a range of political figures, including the city's Labour MPs, implying little sympathy for the cause or motivation of the rioters and suggesting that drugs 'turf' and criminality had played a large part in the actions of a criminal and unrepresentative minority (Bagguley and Hussain, 2008; Ward, 2001). A similar perspective was put forward in Lancashire Constabulary's submissions to the Burnley Inquiry, where they suggested that violent disputes between white and Asian drugs gangs which had lain behind a recent murder in the area had reignited, so sparking the Burnley riot in an already tense and racialised environ-ment (Clarke, 2001; Kalra and Rhodes, 2009). This perspective found support in the official Burnley report: 'I am convinced that what was described as a "race riot" was in fact a series of criminal acts perpetuated by a relatively small number of people' (Clarke, 2001: 8). This suggestion of criminality as a key cause for the 2001 riots was summarily dismissed by central government (Denham, 2001: 9), just as far-right agitation and police mishandling of ethnic relations were marginalised. Here, government's position implied that 'triggers' of criminality should not be confused with the profound racial tensions between communities, and between Asian communities and the police, both in these 2001 disturbances and in the preceding years. Nevertheless, interviews with active participants in the Bradford riot show that 'Many rioters acknowledged that they had histories with the police and that a desire to get even played a part for some of them' (Bujra and Pearce, 2009: 66).

Certainly, the suggestion that outside agitators were responsible for the 2001 riots seems misplaced. The riot in Leeds on 5 June, sparked by a very heavy-handed police arrest of an Asian motorist in the context of the recent events in Oldham, largely involved young Asian men, either from the immediate Harehills area or other areas of inner-city Leeds, with a local 'gang leader' quoted as saying 'The police are trying to turn this in to a race issue, but it's not. It's about police intimidation' (cited in Farrar, 2002: 12), and evidence that non-Asian young people were involved. Similarly, the vast majority of those arrested and charged for the events in Bradford were resident in Bradford, or the neighbouring town of Keighley (Bagguley and Hussain, 2008).

Summing up the 2001 riots

The necessarily short summary presented above of the 2001 riots in Oldham, Burnley and Bradford has attempted to summarise the evidence available and to pinpoint key issues. In doing so, it has tried to emphasise the local specificities and histories that have arguably been downplayed in the subsequent policy discourse (Kalra and Rhodes, 2009). It can be seen here that any suggestion that the riots were 'simply' about ethnic segregation was inevitable, or even that they were 'race riots' is somewhat simplistic. Whilst racial conflict between different communities was central to events in Oldham and Burnley, conflict between Asian young men and the police was central to all the outbreaks for a number of reasons, as shown by the under-reported events in Leeds

that focused on heavy-handed policing (Farrar, 2002). Police misman-
agement of multicultural communities and their inevitable tensions was
clearly a causal issue, as was persistent and cynical far-right agitation
that was not effectively countered at the local level. Underpinning
all this was the geographical reality of economic marginalisation and
social exclusion in all areas, with each area having spatial hotspots
where relative poverty combined with ethnically segregated communities to provide a reality of persistent, low-level tension and violence,
both between different ethnic groups and with the police, so making the 2001 riots less of an aberration for such areas than they first
appeared (Kalra and Rhodes, 2009). Here, rather than the riots being
simply about criminality, or being a rejection of British identity and
values, these violent disturbances were arguably more about frustration at that very British citizenship being denied to many Pakistani-
and Bangladeshi-origin young men, through economic marginalisation,
housing deprivation, and policing that seemed more interested in controlling them than dealing with racist violence (Amin, 2003; Kalra,
2002). Nevertheless, direct conflict between different, often spatially
separated, ethnic communities was a key factor, a reality re-emphasised
by the events in the Lozells area of Birmingham in 2005, where several days of violence between African-Caribbean and Asian communities
involved murders and serious inter-communal violence (King, 2009).
Those events seemed to confirm some of the key issues present in the
2001 riots.

The governmental response: community cohesion

Predictably, following the 2001 disturbances discussed above, local
inquiries produced reports focusing on specific circumstances in
Oldham (Ritchie, 2001) and in Burnley (Clarke, 2001), with a report
on ethnic segregation and tension in Bradford produced before but published shortly after the Bradford riots (Ouseley, 2001). The outbreaks
of violent disorder in Leeds and Stoke-on-Trent did not result in any
local inquiry process, and barely warranted a mention in subsequent
national government publications. Less expected was a central government Inquiry and its two resulting reports (Cantle, 2001; Denham,
2001) which looked more broadly at the state of national ethnic relations, offering a new national policy priority, community cohesion.
Following the 2001 disturbances, the Community Cohesion Review
Team, under the chairmanship of Ted Cantle, a former Chief Executive

of Nottingham City Council, was asked by the Home Office to produce an analysis of the causal factors and recommendations for future governmental action. This remit was addressed through a series of visits to the areas experiencing disturbances, and to other multicultural areas, holding evidence-gathering sessions at each location (Cantle, 2001). This methodical process would 'appear to be evidence-based policy making in action' (Robinson, 2005: 1412). Unlike inquiries into previous urban disturbances (Scarman, 1981), which had examined the 'trigger' incidents and resulting events of riots in detail, the resulting report (Cantle, 2001) did not, as discussed above, examine the actual events of the 2001 disturbances in any depth, confining themselves to restatement of the brief facts. In so doing, this inquiry process and the resulting long-term policy shift thus made only a very limited acknowledgement of the local specificities and causal processes discussed above. The clear implication was that these 2001 disturbances were symptomatic of much wider and deeper realities around race relations (Solomos, 2003) within Britain's towns and cities, and that these violent local events had provided an appropriate opportunity for central government to review and alter national policy approaches and priorities. Here, debates already underway, such as through the Commission on the Future of Multi-Ethnic Britain (CFMEB) (2000), were important. The independent CFMEB process, under the chairmanship of distinguished academic expert on multiculturalism, Lord Bikhu Parekh, included a number of key national academic and political commentators on ethnic diversity. The resulting report received considerable media criticism, particularly centred on what was perceived to be its anti-British tone in suggesting that Britishness 'has largely unspoken, racial connotations' (CFMEB, 2000: 38). Whilst such media attacks were predictable, the report's focus on Britain being a 'community of communities' struck Joppke (2004: 250) as a 'reassertion of orthodox multiculturalism', just as it was being seriously questioned in wider society, with comparatively little focus on the wider meta community. However, within its concerns with the proper and constructive balance between ethnic diversity and societal unity, the CFMEB report stressed the need for policy to promote 'cohesion', and a clear thread of continuity around both language and concern can be found between the pre-riots CFMEB and the later community cohesion reports (Cantle, 2001; Ritchie, 2001):

> Cohesion...derives from widespread commitment to certain core values, both between communities and within them: equality and fairness; dialogue and consultation; toleration, compromise and

accommodation; recognition of and respect for diversity; and by no means least – determination to confront and eliminate racism and xenophobia.

(CFMEB, 2000: 56)

The CFMEB report suggested British citizenship ceremonies for new citizens (p. 55) and a much closer relationship between 'human rights' and 'race equality' policy processes (p. 99), both later enacted by the Labour government in the name of community cohesion (Cantle, 2001; Home Office, 2005), and which were portrayed by critics as evidence of a post-2001, negative turn in the government's commitment to race equality, and as contradictory to the CFMEB proposals (Alexander, 2007; Back et al., 2002). Therefore, whilst some aspects of the CFMEB's recommendations, particularly their focus on Britain as a 'community of communities', with these 'communities' appearing to be implicitly fixed and essentialised ethnic entities, seemed to be a continuation of unreconstructed multiculturalism, other aspects of the report called for greater action to promote common values and cohesion: 'Britain needs common values to hold it together and give it a sense of cohesion' (CFMEB, 2000: 53). This suggests that the 2001 disturbances provided the moment for those calls for a re-balancing of race relations policies towards cohesion and forms of national unity and identity to be actioned more decisively by government:

Our central recommendation is the need to make community cohesion a central aim of government, and to ensure that the design and delivery of all government policies reflects this.

(Denham, 2001: 2)

The other policy antecedent that should perhaps be acknowledged is the wider 'social exclusion' policy focus prioritised by the Labour government from 1997 onwards. This presaged considerable policy focus on, and budget allocations around, social inequalities and marginalisation, and led to significant reconfiguration of education and welfare services in order to address these issues (Mizen, 2004). Issues such as youth disengagement and unemployment, teenage pregnancy and school truancy and exclusion were all addressed under the banner of 'social exclusion', a concept arguably flexible and slippery enough to enable government to move seamlessly between redistributive narratives and perspectives that focused much more on the agency and negative social capital of some individuals and communities seen as contributing to their own 'exclusion'. Here, the suggestion was that some 'socially excluded' communities were spatially and culturally cut off from the 'mainstream', living lives different and separate to those regularly engaged in employment or education, with unhelpful attitudes and lifestyles growing and becoming a barrier in themselves as a result (Levitas, 2005), an echo of the key themes of community cohesion explored below. A clear 'third way' (Giddens, 1998) parallel can be seen here between the 'socially excluded' and ethnically segregated Asian and white communities in British towns and cities suffering ethnic segregation and tension, a parallel focused on the interplay between structural realities and individual and community-based cultural responses seen as part, arguably a large part, of the problem.

The CCRT Inquiry process led by Ted Cantle introduced and defined the new term of community cohesion, a development accepted by central government:

> Community cohesion requires that there is a shared sense of belonging based on common goals and core social values, respect for difference (ethnic, cultural and religious) and acceptance of the reciprocal rights and obligations of community members working together for the common good.
>
> (Denham, 2001: 18)

In advancing this term, the CCRT Inquiry process was deploying a concept with no real history or familiarity within 'race relations' policy circles. Discussion of the actual meaning of community cohesion is surprisingly limited within the reports (Cantle, 2001; Denham, 2001), suggesting that the term had rapidly been adapted from work on 'social' (economic) cohesion (Forrest and Kearns, 2000) and applied to ethnic segregation. The local reports on the Oldham (Ritchie, 2001) and Burnley (Clarke, 2001) disturbances did not use the term community cohesion, focusing instead on 'parallel lives', but the meaning and core analysis was largely the same. This was also true of the report on ethnic relations in Bradford (Ouseley, 2001) produced before, but published after the Bradford riot of July 2001, and which focused on ethnic 'segregation'. The solution proposed by both national and local community cohesion reports was cross-ethnic contact and dialogue, something that urgently needed to be prioritised, in their view:

The promotion of cross cultural contact between different communities at all levels, foster understanding and respect, and break down barriers. The opportunity should be taken to develop a programme of 'myth-busting'.

(Cantle, 2001: 11)

The concern here is clearly that such contact should help to promote shared identities and common norms and values, a conception of shared citizenship that is sensitive to difference, but which must override any separate loyalties:

Respect for cultural diversity must be balanced by acceptance that in key respects people must come together much more than has happened recently in Oldham, if necessary laying aside some of their cultural preferences.

(Ritche, 2001: 7)

Whilst the overarching narrative of segregation and parallel lives is shared across all the 2001 national and local community cohesion reports, actual definitions are limited, meaning therefore that greater clarity on the concerns and approaches of community cohesion has come with the implementation of policy approaches and funding regimes in its name (Home Office, 2003a, 2005; LGA, 2002) and, in particular, through the Commission on Integration and Cohesion (COIC) (DCLG, 2007a), established in the wake of the 7/7 London bombings of July 2005, and whose recommendations re-energised many of the original proposals made by Cantle.

Whilst the fact of another inquiry process on community cohesion within five years of the first might seem surprising, COIC can be seen as a product of a confluence of forces and events, with the 7/7 bombings, the failed attacks of two weeks later and parallel foiled Islamist plots all making explicit the concern arguably implicit in the 2001 community cohesion reports about dangerously separate and oppositional identities growing amongst young British Muslims, whilst at the same time popular concerns around large scale immigration were at their height following the accession of Eastern European countries to the European Union (EU) that led to significant inward migration to Britain in search of employment denied by many other EU states. The response of COIC focused very much on local realities and strategies, a reflection of the great spatial variations in recent immigration. In its focus on 'shared futures', and the rights and responsibilities of all communities in building that shared future, COIC took one of Cantle's key themes further, by recommending that government should in future presume against funding and support for community organisations representing or engaging with one ethnic or faith community only, whilst warning of the dangers of white alienation from policies of multiculturalism that seem to ignore them through a focus on each separate ethnic minority community (DCLG, 2007a). Alongside this COIC refined the working definition of community cohesion used by government, linking it with integration to reflect their focus on the issue of significant immigration and the urgent need to integrate new arrivals. This integration focus on new migrants can clearly be seen as distinct from the focus of the 2001 community cohesion reports, which were concerned with relations between settled ethnic minority and white communities. Nevertheless, the approach of COIC was consistent with the key themes of community cohesion set out here. COIC's definition of cohesion and integration was:

Our new definition of integration and cohesion is therefore that

An integrated and cohesive community is one where:

- There is a clearly defined and widely shared sense of the contribution of different individuals and different communities to a future vision for a neighbourhood, city, region or country
- There is a strong sense of an individual's rights and responsibilities when living in a particular place – people know what everyone expects of them, and what they can expect in turn
- Those from different backgrounds have similar life opportunities, access to services and treatment
- There is a strong sense of trust in institutions locally to act fairly in arbitrating between different interests and for their role and justifications to be subject to public scrutiny
- There is a strong recognition of the contribution of both those who have newly arrived and those who already have deep attachments to a particular place, with a focus on what they have in common
- There are strong and positive relationships between people from different backgrounds in the workplace, in schools and other institutions within neighbourhoods.

(DCLG, 2007a: 10)

Below, this chapter outlines the key themes and concerns evident from the community cohesion reports and the way they were articulated by government ministers.

The key themes of community cohesion

Segregation and 'parallel lives'

Despite this lack of clarity or pedigree as a term, it is clear that community cohesion is centrally concerned with what it sees as a reality of significant ethnic/racial segregation, and the resulting lack of integration or 'cohesion':

> The team was particularly struck by the depth of polarisation of our towns and cities. The extent to which these physical divisions were compounded by so many other aspects of our daily lives was very evident... many communities operate on the basis of a series of parallel lives. These lives often do not seem to touch at any point, let alone overlap and promote any meaningful interchanges.
>
> (Cantle, 2001: 9)

Both national and local reports discuss ethnic segregation, or 'parallel lives' and the apparently negative experiences stemming from it, with this meaning for Oldham:

> A system of separate development within the town in which people from different ethnic backgrounds live lives largely separated from one another.
>
> (Ritchie, 2001: 3)

Here, the term 'separate development' may sound like hyperbole and is more suited to Apartheid-era, South Africa, but in the aftermath of the Oldham disturbances there was a serious proposal to build a dividing wall between specific white and South Asian areas of the town to reduce the possibility of 'border' conflict (Sutcliffe, 2003). The implication here is that parts of British towns and cities were starting to resemble the rigid sectarian divides of Northern Ireland, and it is no coincidence that post-2001 efforts to build community cohesion in Britain have drawn on organisations such as Mediation Northern Ireland and the experience they have of trying to break down rigid barriers between Loyalist and Nationalist communities in Northern Ireland. Whilst not using the term community cohesion, the local Oldham report (Ritchie, 2001) focused heavily on the 'parallel lives' lived in

Oldham, and the lack of shared understanding, respect and common values apparently flowing from this segregation. The clear implication within the community cohesion discourse is that physical ethnic segregation has deepened and hardened the lack of common identity, and the tension and mutual fear that results from that lack of commonality, suggesting that this segregation was causal to the growing pre-riot tensions outlined above. Central here is how profound ethnic segregation breeds separate, monocultural identities, with lack of meaningful or positive contact with the 'other' encouraging the growth of oppositional, exclusive identities that are suspicious of and antagonistic to communities and individuals of a different ethnic background. This analysis would see the phenomenon of Islamist extremism (Hussain, 2007), or increased support for overtly racist political parties with neo-Nazi roots (Copsey, 2008), as an inevitable by-product of such a generalised situation of separate monocultural communities and identities.

Also implicit within the national and local community cohesion reports was the feeling that this physical and cultural ethnic segregation was actually getting worse in some areas, a highly contested suggestion that Chapter 3 examines in greater detail. The report by Sir Herman (now Lord) Ouseley (the former Chairman of the Commission for Racial Equality (CRE), the government agency charged with policing Britain's anti-discriminatory measures and now amalgamated within the Equality and Human Rights Commission), which was prepared before and published after the Bradford disturbances of July 2001, is blunt about the extent of the local ethnic segregation in Bradford: 'We have concentrated...on the very worrying drift towards *self* segregation' (emphasis added) (Ouseley, 2001: Introduction). Any suggestions that the use of the term 'self' in relation to segregation was simply a slip are dispelled later in the same report:

> Self-segregation is driven by fear of others, the need for safety from harassment and violent crime, and the belief that it is the only way to promote, retain and protect faith and cultural identity and affiliation.

> (Ouseley, 2001: 10)

This suggests that ethnic segregation is real, problematic and partially at least due to the choice or agency of communities, a theme echoed by the CRE (2001), who spoke of 'congregation', or self-segregation in their own post-riots report. Whilst acknowledging the continuing reality of racism locally and nationally, the CRE focused on the heavy geographical concentration of Asian communities in the areas witnessing disturbances, with the clear suggestion that this is a problem in itself. The existence and importance of ethnic 'segregation' in Britain, and its relationship to issues of racial tension or inequality, is highly contested (Finney and Simpson, 2009; Flint and Robinson, 2008; Kalra, 2002) in a situation of shared educational content and common cultural interests amongst Britain's diverse youth population, but others feel that Britain is 'sleepwalking towards segregation' (Phillips, 2005) and that community cohesion has provided a timely focus on this issue. The issue of 'self-segregation' highlights a controversial theme of community cohesion, the suggestion of considerable agency by individuals and communities in the creation and acceptance of the present segregated reality, which is explored below. The solution clearly proposed by community cohesion is to break segregation down through direct contact and dialogue, with calls for action towards more integrated schooling and housing, new schemes of contact, such as school-twinning, and the development of genuinely multi-ethnic community organisations and facilities, rather than separate ethnic-specific ones (Cantle, 2001; Ritchie, 2001).

Agency and responsibility

Within the community cohesion policy discourse at both national (Cantle, 2001; Home Office, 2005) and local level (Clarke, 2001; Ritchie, 2001), there is a clear concern with agency and individual/community responsibility in overcoming segregation. Arguably, these concerns are consistent with the broader direction of New Labour social policy after 1997 (Levitas, 2005; McGhee, 2006), and which is unlikely to disappear under the new government. Whilst individual and institutionalised racism, such as the reality of racial harassment (Modood et al., 1997) and Oldham local authority's past policy of allocating Asian and white tenants to different housing areas, clearly were central to the creation of ethnic segregation (Kundnani, 2001), the suggestion here is that the 'agency' (Greener, 2002) of individuals within all communities has played a role in accepting and so deepening this segregation, as shown by their housing and schooling decisions. This is highlighted by the focus on both 'white flight' (Cantle, 2001) and ethnic minority 'congregation' (CRE, 2001). In stressing the need for individuals, communities and the organisations that represent them and work with them, to take responsibility within day-to-day decisions over work, schooling and housing choices for breaking down 'parallel lives' (Ritchie, 2001) and making contact across ethnic divides, community cohesion is clearly echoing a communitarianist agenda (Etzioni, 1995; McGhee, 2003). This position is that an unintended consequence of the post-war welfare regimes in the USA and the UK has been a loss of the necessary balance between rights and responsibilities:

> Communities constantly need to be pulled toward the centre course where individual rights and social responsibilities are properly balanced.
>
> (Etzioni, 1995: x)

Communitarians extend this analysis to what they term 'one-sided' proponents of multiculturalism, who deny any common or shared values or positions, at the risk of creating ethnic tension. From this perspective, uncontrolled relativist pluralism (Watson, 2000) can lead to 'Balkanization', with the solution being an acceptance of, and adherence to, shared values, a position clearly anticipating community cohesion. Arguably, Britain's lack of a written constitution and a clearly agreed 'national story' (Winder, 2004) in a post-imperial, post-industrial era adds urgency to government efforts to debate shared national values and the meaning of 'Britishness' that have followed on from the emergence of community cohesion. The solution offered is a re-birth of the 'spirit of community', or the 'big society' as the Prime Minister David Cameron has described it, the acceptance of wider responsibilities and obligations, with this conception of community being about the making and acceptance of moral claims on each other. This position clearly assumes that individuals can and should influence structural realities, such as ethnic segregation, a suggestion questioned by many commentators. Following this perspective, Ouseley (2001) suggested a 'Bradfordian People Programme' to promote understanding of and support for diversity, which he saw young people learning about and changing their attitudes and behaviour as a result. Similarly, central government community cohesion initiatives (Home Office, 2003a; LGA, 2002), discussed in more detail in Chapter 3, have focused on capacity building around mediation, conflict resolution and community contact, in order to equip communities to help themselves (McGhee, 2005).

This communitarian agenda has strong parallels with the emergence of the 'third way' (Giddens, 1998), an analysis of implications stemming from the profound social and economic changes underway as part of globalization and the move to an increasingly post-industrial economy in Britain (Byrne, 1999). This analysis was central to post-1997 New

Labour social policy approaches, with a clear concern around welfare dependency and sole reliance on government to create social change. Giddens argues that individuals must learn to confront risks and to anticipate that their own lives will be less secure, seeing such a cultural transformation as necessary:

> We have to make our lives in a more active way than was true of previous generations, and we need more actively to accept responsibilities for the consequences of what we do and the lifestyle habits we adopt.
>
> (Giddens, 1998: 37)

This suggests that government cannot create 'cohesion' on its own, and that individuals and communities have to be active 'agents' of contact and cohesion. Hesse (2000) sees Giddens as arguing for a cosmopolitanism which recognises the importance of national solidarity, in contrast to the 'radical multiculturalism' of the left that is culturally relativist and committed to pluralism at any cost. Here policies, based on a 'rights and responsibilities' approach, can be viewed as either a necessary programme of behaviour modification in an uncertain and fast-changing world, or a shifting of responsibility from state to the individual (Byrne, 1999).

Given the prominence of 'third way' and communitarian thought for policy-makers, there is clearly a revival of interest in theories of human agency within social policy (Greener, 2002), including community cohesion. Bourdieu's key concept of 'habitus' is important here, with its focus on a set of dispositions that incline 'agents' to act and react in certain ways. For Bourdieu, habitus orients behaviour without determining it, and the 'fields' within which habitus operates for individuals depends very much on the 'capital' to which they have access (Greener, 2002: 691/2). Bourdieu discussed how the habitus of actors may enable reflexive behaviour, or agency, but that they may lack the right type of capital, or any capital at all, to make any impact. This clearly suggests the limits on individual agency outside of economic and social structures and forces, yet New Labour's supply side 'welfare to work' policies focused heavily on the development of agency and human capital (Hills et al., 2002; Levitas, 2005). The community cohesion focus on direct contact and individual/community responsibility for developing shared values (Cantle, 2001; Ritchie, 2001) arguably displays a similar naivety about the power of agency, in the absence of action around structural issues, such as housing and schools. Underpinning Gidden's position on approaches to modern social policy, including ethnic tension, is a belief:

> That individuals hold the power within them to 'escape' from their present circumstances should they choose to do so.
>
> (Greener, 2002: 693)

This highlights the 'Catch 22' nature of Gidden's positions, with such reflexive agency only possible in a state where equality and empowerment for all was already a reality. Arguably, the community cohesion reports' stress on the need for new migrants to learn English and mix more is a clear example of the 'third way' emphasis on self-government and the need to take individual and community responsibility (Back et al., 2002).

Problematic social capital

Alongside community cohesion's focus on agency and responsibility is a concern with 'social capital' (Putnam, 2000) or community. This helps to explain the concern with segregation and the need to overcome it within the community cohesion discourse (Cantle, 2001). A distinction must be made here between 'bonding' and 'bridging' social capital (Putnam, 2000). 'Bonding' signifies the institutions, networks and practices that bind existing communities together, whilst 'bridging' social capital signifies the mechanisms, structures and sites that enable cross-community dialogue, understanding and networks to grow. Community cohesion offers a critique of excessive and unhelpful bonding capital (McGhee, 2003) within segregated, monocultural white and Asian communities who have few or no 'bridging' links that allow meaningful contact and relationship building with the 'other'. Whilst strong communities with well-developed social capital can be very positive for both individuals and society, the dangers of excessive 'bonding capital' in the absence of balancing 'bridging capital' within individual communities have been highlighted in studies (Back, 1996; Hewitt, 2005) exposing the fierce, racist and reactionary cultures of some white (and, arguably, Asian/black) communities. In both studies, this antagonism to 'different' outsiders could not be explained by parental attitudes, and seemed to be growing in responses to perceptions of policy and socio-economic trends, suggesting that the nature of 'bonding' social capital within communities is not fixed or unchangeable.

Here, the belief is that the 2001 disturbances exposed a reality of 'bonded' monocultural communities who have little interest in other

ethnic communities in a situation of minimal contact. From this perspective, there is an urgent need to develop avenues for meaningful
bridging social capital which will enable dialogue and relationships
across ethnic divides, so facilitating the development of shared values
and priorities. In the case of the areas experiencing disturbances in
2001, the dominant textile industries (the reason why Asian communities were recruited to these locations) and the trade unions associated
with those industries partially provided forms of bridging social capital in the past (Kundnani, 2001). The disappearance of these industries,
and the failure as yet to develop viable, post-industrial economies
locally, is clearly relevant to the lack of bridging social capital, as
is the suggestion that within many of the white and Asian communities experiencing post-industrial social exclusion as 'losers' in a
rapidly globalising economy, inward-looking and defensive forms of
'neighbourhood nationalism' (Back, 1996) are developing. There is also
a clear belief within community cohesion (Cantle, 2001, 2005) that past
policy approaches have unintentionally bolstered bonding social capital, especially in ethnic minority communities, whilst neglecting the
need to develop bridging forms of social capital that would enable the
promotion of good relations between ethnic groups.

Blaming past policy approaches

Underpinning all these key themes of community cohesion discussed
above is the belief that government's multiculturalist policy approaches
to race relations over the past 30 years have, whilst achieving notable
progress in tackling racial inequality (Modood et al., 1997), had unintended and negative consequences. In particular, these policies have
deepened and solidified the divides between different ethnic communities. As a result, within this community cohesion analysis of
segregation and the importance of agency lies a critique of the impact
and unintended consequences of past race relations policy approaches,
particularly those prioritised since the last watershed moment of 1981
(Solomos, 2003). This analysis sees those policies which flowed from
the widespread urban disturbances of 1981, and popularly understood
as approaches of 'equal opportunities' or 'anti-racism', as having privileged essentialised, separate ethnic communities, and their 'community
leaders', through funding for ethnic-specific facilities and organisations. Such policy approaches have rightly been characterised as a
neo-colonialist approach to managing unrest within ethnic minority
communities (Kundnani, 2007), but the agency of some ethnic minority
community groups and their 'leaders' in agitating for such community

management roles and the funds to enable them cannot be overlooked (Sivanandan, 2004, 2005). Alongside this came an enhanced focus on equality for each separate ethnic group, and the importance of ethnic data with which to measure progress towards that equality. This encompassed the inclusion of an ethnicity question for the first time in the 1991 Census, and the use of such ethnic data to identify areas of the economy and society where non-white ethnic minorities were under-represented, or doing less well than average, with the clear implication that this 'ethnic penalty' was due to individual and institutional white racism (Modood et al., 1997; Solomos, 2003). Such data, and assumptions based on it, continues to be central to social policy questions, as shown by controversy over the role of ethnicity in educational underachievement (Gilborn, 2009).

Arguably, this approach meant that ensuring 'equality' in terms of educational and employment outcomes, and in community facilities, for each *separate* ethnic group took priority over common needs and identities, including over multiracial movements against racism (Sivanandan, 2005). Whilst this policy approach of political multiculturalism (or 'anti-racism' as it was popularly understood) became increasingly dominant after 1981 through action by left-wing Local Authorities and gradual adoption by central government, the seeds of this approach could be seen from the late 1960s, following the new direction set by Roy Jenkins. This saw the gradual development of pluralist political structures of consultation that accepted ethnic difference, and which attempted to accommodate diversity around religion, custom and dress within the public domain of schools, welfare services and the workplace. It was particularly recognised in the establishment of the CRE in 1976, alongside the passing of the 1976 Race Relations Act. Whilst representing a welcome strengthening of anti-discriminatory measures, these developments saw the downplaying of what had originally been a parallel policy track, the importance of 'promoting good relations' between different racial groups (Cantle, 2005). Although the post-1981 focus on equal opportunities and anti-racism overtly criticised what it characterised as weak and apolitical 'multiculturalism' (Chauhan, 1990), these policies actually represented a significant ramping up of a one-sided multiculturalist focus on difference and separate needs, an approach that represented continuity in that it continued to work with rather fixed and essentialised understanding of ethnic identity and experience (Bhavnani, 2001) at a time when the currency of social class identity was being increasingly downplayed.

Conclusion

This perspective suggests that the post-1981 phase of 'race relations' policy approaches (Solomos, 2003) involving the development of anti-racism and equal opportunities strategies, which whilst important and needed in many ways (Chauhan, 1990; Gilroy, 2002; Williams, 1988), contained serious drawbacks that have become more pronounced during the rapid economic and social changes of the past 20 years. Law (1996) portrays this phase of policy development as being one of 'strategic essentialism' hobbled by an increasingly dominant and divisive 'ethnic managerialism'. Here, community cohesion can be seen as a necessary and overdue correction to the successes and associated problems of past policy approaches, with a focus on commonality, rather than on difference (Cantle, 2001, 2005). The explicit criticism of 'multiculturalism' for perpetuating, or even partially *causing*, ethnic segregation suggests that it be sidelined as a policy approach. This explains the overt attacks on multiculturalism per se from equality campaigners (Phillips, 2005) as prolonging and even fuelling ethnic segregation and tension that have opened the door for a blaming of multiculturalism for a wider range of policy problems, including a growing domestic terrorism threat (Prins and Salisbury, 2008). This is arguably both wrong and misleading, with the book's position being that community cohesion represents a re-thinking specifically of the continued helpfulness and relevance of the post-1981 phase of multiculturalism popularly understood as anti-racism, rather than a rejection of multiculturalism itself, and it uses the empirical evidence presented in Chapter 4 to support that contention. Nevertheless, there are concerns that community cohesion does represent the 'death of multiculturalism' (Kundnani, 2002), with this perspective and associated debates on how we might understand what multiculturalism can or does mean for Britain discussed in Chapter 3. Firstly, however, this new British policy development of community cohesion, its concerns and assumptions, is contextualised by discussion in Chapter 2 of recent developments around identity and multiculturalism in two other multi-ethnic Western European states, France and the Netherlands.

2
Going with the Flow? International Comparisons

Introduction

Chapter 1 outlined the violent disturbances in northern England during the summer of 2001, and the significant change in the tone, priorities and focus of British race relations policies as a result. It went on to outline the key themes and concerns of this new British policy of community cohesion, all of which are highly contested and controversial, as Chapter 3 examines. Before engaging in detailed discussion of those critiques, it is helpful to step back and reflect on how this policy shift might be understood in relation to the approaches and debates in other Western European countries that are also grappling with the challenges of rapidly evolving multicultural and multifaith societies. Accordingly, this chapter examines the position in two contrasting, close neighbours of Britain, the Netherlands and France. These countries have been chosen both because of the distinct ways in which their respective policy approaches to ethnic diversity and identity have traditionally been understood, and because issues of multiculturalism and national values and loyalties have been prominent in their recent political discourses. The aim here is a modest one; not to offer new data on these countries but rather, in considering their differing policy approaches and conflicts, to shed further light on how we might understand the post-2001 British policy approach of community cohesion and examine the extent to which this policy shift is, or is not, out of line with trends in other European states.

The Netherlands: retreat of the multiculturalist standard bearer?

The Netherlands has long been portrayed as the most progressive and liberal state in Europe due to social policy approaches that have included significant progress on women's rights and gay and lesbian equality, and tolerant approaches to drug use. Alongside that have been policies that aimed to 'promote the most ambitious programme of multiculturalism in Western Europe' (Sniderman and Hagendoorn, 2009: 18). This multiculturalism programme was sanctioned and directed from the highest levels of the Dutch national government, an overt and well-funded commitment that can be seen in contrast to British approaches to multiculturalism that have tended to be more de-centred and locally varied (Joppke, 2004), often emerging as much from below as above through dialectical processes of debate and conflict (Solomos, 2003). Dutch policy approaches have included state-subsidised minority community TV and radio stations, state-funded Islamic primary schools sometimes operating in minority languages, relaxed approaches to dual citizenship and guaranteed processes of state consultation with minority community leaders. The commitment to multiculturalism represented by such policies has now apparently waned, with significant policy shifts towards requiring greater conformity and Dutch language use by ethnic minority citizens, and recent election results producing large gains for explicitly anti-Islamic and anti-immigration political parties (*Guardian*, 12 June 2010). This shift has been accompanied by a number of shocking and high-profile incidents that have kept the interrelated issues of multiculturalism, identity and Islam at the forefront of Dutch politics. These have included the assassination in 2002 of Pim Fortuyn, an overtly anti-Islamic political maverick, the high profile of Ayaan Hirsi Ali, a Dutch refugee of Somali origin who has campaigned against Islamic practices through her controversial film 'Submission', the assassination of the film-maker of 'Submission', Theo Van Gogh, by a young Dutch Islamist in 2004 (Buruma, 2006), and the continued rise of an overtly anti-Muslim politician, Geert Wilders. Such events have created a similar impression to the one that developed in Britain, namely that the 9/11 attacks on New York, combined with graphic evidence of the threat from Muslim separatist identities indulged by a naive multiculturalist state, have led to a post-2001 Dutch backlash against multiculturalism. Joppke (2004: 243) argues that the Netherlands, like Britain, has retreated from official support for multiculturalism towards 'centrist policies of civic integration', but it is suggested here that this impression is somewhat misleading and that the Netherlands has been undergoing a more nuanced and longer-term re-think that represents, like that of Britain, a re-calibration of multiculturalist policies rather than an outright and reactionary rejection of multiculturalism per se:

> The countries that have made the most ambitious commitment to multiculturalism, The Netherlands and Great Britain, made the commitment first, then debated the consequences only later.
>
> (Sniderman and Hagendoorn, 2009: 2)

Multiculturalism, Dutch-style

Although comprehensive by the standards of other European states, Dutch multiculturalism did not start to develop until the late 1970s, in response to significant immigration from countries like Turkey and Morocco that had no previous ties to the Netherlands. Previously, foreign migrants had come from Dutch colonies such as Surinam, the Dutch Antilles and Indonesia, and so were familiar with Dutch language and cultural norms, but a shortage of unskilled labour in the early 1970s led to the Turkish and Moroccan immigration. Whilst the latter initially involved only men, the gradual arrival of wives and families, continued marriage links with countries of origin, and an increase in Asylum seekers and refugees from a variety of countries have all combined to increase and further vary the ethnic diversity of the Netherlands. Now 17 per cent of Dutch residents are categorised as being of 'foreign descent' (Sniderman and Hagendoorn, 2009), and ethnic minority concentration in the country's largest urban areas means that Amsterdam is projected to become a majority non-white city within a few years (Buruma, 2006). These non-white migrants came to a country with apparently well-established approaches to dealing with cultural and religious divisions. Until the 1960s, the Netherlands was a conservative country with sharp social distinctions based on religion, and only limited cross-denominational marriage and friendship ties (Bagley, 1973) between different Christian traditions. In a country where the south was historically Catholic and the north Protestant, subdivided between official and non-conformist traditions, religious distinctions were institutionalised through a system known as 'pillarisation', whereby each tradition had its own 'pillar' that contributed to the stability and peace of the overall state. Pillarisation involved each Christian tradition, as well as secular liberals and socialists, having their own school and university systems, distinct newspapers and trade unions, and national politics conducted via elite-level deals and compromises to maintain agreed balances. Indeed, a British academic investigating race relations policy approaches in Britain and the Netherlands in the early 1970s saw pillarisation as crucial to the apparent success of Dutch society as a whole, so failing to detect a decline already underway: 'These pillars of society are separate from one another; yet without any one of them, the society which they support would be considerably weakened' (Bagley, 1973: 2).

In light of this, the Dutch political response to large-scale, non-Dutch speaking immigration that gradually broadened to official policies of multiculturalism might plausibly be seen as a continuation of a 'pillarisation' approach that left the Netherlands better prepared than other Western European former colonial powers for the challenge of greater ethnic and religious diversity. Initially, Dutch policies were based on the belief that Turkish and Moroccan migrants would return home, with them being titled '*gastarbeiders*', or guest workers, in an approach similar to that adopted by Germany towards its own Turkish economic migrants (Shavit, 2009). The Dutch belief was that Turkish and Moroccan migrants should therefore be helped to maintain their languages and traditions, but gradually policy evolved towards recognition of the permanency of the migrants' presence. Such multiculturalist policies involved the early granting of local voting rights for migrants who were not yet citizens and, at one point, toleration of dual citizenship once they were Dutch citizens. Strong anti-discriminatory measures were included in the Dutch constitution in 1983 and added to over the next decade, as the country accepted that it was assuming a 'permanent multicultural character' (Vink, 2007: 341). Official support for distinct ethnic minority structures and institutions was strong and overt, including a publicly subsidised Dutch Muslim broadcasting service in community languages, funding for around 40 Islamic primary schools where the medium of instruction was sometimes community languages rather than Dutch, dedicated ethnic minority housing schemes and formal processes of government consultation with ethnic minority 'community leaders'. Sniderman and Hagendoorn (2009) suggest that such an accommodating policy approach to ethnic difference can partly be explained by collective historical guilt in the Netherlands over their perceived failure to do more to prevent the Holocaust, given that a high portion of Dutch Jews were transported and murdered compared to other Western European countries occupied by Nazi Germany. In light of these policy responses to non-white migration, many commentators have characterised Dutch multiculturalism of the 1970s,

1980s and 1990s as a continuation and extension of pillarisation, crediting that approach for what appeared to be peaceful co-existence between different ethnic groups, but this historical interpretation is increasingly challenged (Joppke, 2004; Vink, 2007).

Firstly, 'pillarisation' was in sharp decline in Dutch society generally from the 1960s as a younger generation rebelled against the conservative conformity and religious dominance it entailed, prompting moves towards a much more secular and fluid society that included the squatter movement and the political agitation of young 'Provos' in Amsterdam in the 1960s and early 1970s (Buruma, 2006). Secondly, the evidence of an 'Islamic pillar' for the growing Moroccan and Turkish-origin Muslim communities is actually very limited, with none of the civic and social infrastructure that had characterised Protestant and Catholic pillars, such as hospitals, sporting clubs and large-scale education systems, appearing (Vink, 2007). In fact, 'pillarisation' had been rejected by Dutch political leaders as they devised multiculturalist responses, with those policies involving much more limited processes of consultation and distinct, funded activities and facilities.

This suggests that from the start Dutch multiculturalism was more limited and partial than is sometimes portrayed, with the new migrant communities not having the power or autonomy to develop a genuine and equal pillar. It also raises the issue of the extent to which muticulturalist approaches were actually dominant and publicly supported in the Netherlands. Indeed, it is suggested here that public support has only ever been partial and conditional, and was weakening as early as the start of the 1990s, leading to policy reformulations and retreats much earlier than the high-profile incidents outlined above that together were understood as the early twenty-first century Dutch 'crisis of multiculturalism'.

The failure of Dutch multiculturalism?

Joppke (2004) suggests that the Netherlands was moving away from full support for multiculturalism and towards an emphasis on civic integration from the early 1990s onwards, long before the political agitation and subsequent murders of Pim Fortuyn and Theo Van Gogh, for a number of reasons. These reasons centre on the failure of multiculturalism to command enough white Dutch support in the face of increasing ethnic diversity, associated popular perceptions of growing cultural and physical segregation, and the feeling that multiculturalist policies were not addressing the real economic and social causes of ethnic minority marginalisation and segregation. All of these themes continue to be central to Dutch political discourse, as shown by recent political events (Beaumont, 2010), and also have direct parallels in post-2001 policy shifts and debates in Britain.

In fact, the seeds of this reaction against multiculturalist policy approaches could be detected even as apparent Dutch success in integrating new migrants was being celebrated. Comparable survey data on white indigenous attitudes in Britain and the Netherlands to non-white migrants in the late 1960s and early 1970s found anti-black racist prejudices to be significantly higher in Britain. Data was collected in the era of Enoch Powell's reactionary campaigning and public demands in Britain for much greater restrictions on immigration, whilst in contrast, 'the Dutch express markedly less prejudice than their English counterparts and practise markedly less racial discrimination' (Bagley, 1973: 246). In comparison, Dutch attitudes were much more tolerant and appeared to give much greater optimism for a successful multiculturalist future, but were based on the clear and non-negotiable assumption that migrants would fully integrate into Dutch society through use of Dutch language and acceptance of Dutch customs, traditions and values. The historical Dutch approach to empire of fostering Dutch language and traditions within colonies meant that migrants from Surinam, the Dutch Antilles and Indonesia were comparatively well equipped to meet this integration challenge despite the racial prejudice they have consistently received from a minority of Dutch citizens. The position in relation to integration into Dutch society of migrants from Turkey and Morocco, the largest groups of non-white immigrants, with many of them coming from poor and rural backgrounds where very different values and traditions are held, has proved much more problematic.

Integration of these migrants from outside Dutch traditions has been hampered from early on by economic restrictions. Whilst a shortage of non-skilled labour in the Netherlands led to this migration, the 'oil shock' of the 1973 Arab/Israeli war and the subsequent global economic slowdown reduced both the demand for such unskilled labour and the government's ability to fund their ambitious multiculturalist policies. The Dutch economy may have seen subsequent upturns but, like other Western European countries such as Britain, it has progressively moved towards a post-industrial economic model whereby demand for unskilled labour has permanently declined. This new European economic reality privileges 'human capital', formal education qualifications and skills of effective interaction in an increasingly complex and diverse society (Byrne, 1999). As in Britain, certain Dutch migrant groups, such as Turks and Moroccans, have arrived with low human capital and limited Dutch language skills, and so have struggled to integrate and achieve equality on the economic level, hampered further by racial discrimination. This economic, and so social, marginalisation of Turkish and Moroccan communities, despite official policies of multiculturalism, was becoming obvious by the 1990s, and was highlighted by a liberal academic and commentator, Paul Scheffer. In a controversial and high-profile essay 'The multicultural drama', Scheffer (2000) suggested that policies of multiculturalism had failed to address the economic and social marginalisation of these migrant communities, and that their effective segregation from wider society and progress towards being an ethnic underclass was undermining the social cohesion of Dutch society and its comprehensive welfare systems (Buruma, 2006). This can be seen as a direct precedent of Goodhart's (2004) essay that suggested too much diversity was undermining the social solidarity essential to Britain's welfare state. The way forward for Scheffer was to reverse policies of multiculturalism that treated all migrants as part of undifferentiated, essentialised ethnic communities, rather than as individuals needing help, or even coercion, to achieve economic and social integration into Dutch society.

Whilst Scheffer faced significant vilification from across the political spectrum, the suggestion that until recently in the Netherlands there has been 'a cross-party consensus to keep the issue of multiculturalism off the agenda' (Sniderman and Hagendoorn, 2009: 118) is simply not true. As early as 1991, the right-of-centre VVD Liberal party challenged continuing immigration, much of it driven by continued Turkish and Moroccan marriage links with their countries of origin. VVD leader Frits Bolkestein suggested that such continued immigration of non-Dutch-speaking family members and the accompanying multiculturalist policies were facilitating the growth of separate, Islamic values within Dutch society and so hampering integration. Buruma (2006) identifies this as an early indicator of an ideological switch becoming increasingly prevalent across Western Europe, whereby right-of-centre parties that formerly argued for culturally specific values and traditions now argue for the importance of the universal, individual rights of the Enlightenment, whereas left-of-centre parties that formerly championed that universal humanism now defend the right of specific cultures and traditions to remain distinct within society. Whilst such critiques of Dutch multiculturalism were publicly rejected by the political establishment, they clearly prompted policy re-thinks in the Netherlands. For instance, in 1997 the Dutch parliament clamped down on dual/multiple citizenship held by migrants, and significantly limited benefit availability for new migrants (Vink, 2007). In 1998, a 'Law on Civic Integration for Newcomers' was passed that obliged all non-European newcomers to take approximately 600 hours of language and civics lessons, with financial support for such training. Legal penalties for not taking part in these lessons exist, but were initially only used sparingly (Joppke, 2004). This Dutch development on civic integration of migrants has subsequently been replicated across Western Europe and Scandinavia, including post-2001 Britain (Cantle, 2001). As in Britain, such a Dutch policy re-think might be portrayed as a reactionary step, but it can also be seen as acknowledgment that previous and rather passive policies of multiculturalism did little to aid effective integration of non-white minorities. What this does clearly illustrate is that a re-calibration of the content and focus of Dutch multiculturalism was underway long before 9/11 or the subsequent incidents understood as causing the 'crisis of Dutch multiculturalism' (Buruma, 2006).

The 'crisis' of Dutch multiculturalism

The previous section suggested that the Netherlands has actually been in the process of re-thinking its multiculturalist policies of special treatment for essentialised migrant communities for some considerable time, but the popular perception has been of a much more recent 'crisis', one centred around the post-9/11 murders of Pim Fortuyn and Theo Van Gogh, and the continued rise of far-right politician Geert Wilders. It is important therefore to not only discuss these events themselves but analyse the popular feelings and attitudes underpinning them. At the heart of these developments has been the perception first identified in the 1990s, as outlined above, that separate identities and lifestyles had been allowed to grow amongst migrant-origin communities in the Netherlands, and that Islamic identities amongst Turkish and Moroccan communities in particular now pose a direct challenge to the values and social cohesion of broader Dutch society. Within this is an inherent critique of the negative effects of overt multiculturalist policies, and

These concerns were most clearly expressed in the rise of maverick politician Pim Fortuyn before his murder in 2002, a man voted the 'greatest Dutchman of all time' in one poll in 2004 (Buruma, 2006). Fortuyn was an openly gay academic who rose to political prominence outside of the traditional political party structures through overt, populist attacks on what he perceived as the Islamic threat to Dutch values and lifestyles, and on multiculturalist policies he viewed as undermining Dutch identity through toleration of separate identities. Previously a social democrat, Fortuyn's political perspective began to shift when local migrant youth attacked and harassed gay and lesbian bars that he frequented in Rotterdam. Backed by sections of big business and the media, his flamboyant and outrageous persona and political style helped him to mount an assault on what he portrayed as a corrupt political establishment, so rapidly building a political base from scratch. Fortuyn's attacks on Muslim values and behaviour might suggest that he represented nostalgic, backward-looking racism of the type embodied by Britain's British National Party (Copsey, 2008), but that would be too simplistic. In fact, Fortuyn was 'a populist who played on the fears of Muslims while boasting of having sex with Moroccan boys' (Buruma, 2006: 46). Here, Fortuyn voiced concerns that the advances won for gay and lesbian rights and for gender equality during the rapid Dutch shift from being a conservative, confessional society to a liberal and largely secular one were threatened by Muslim migrants who appeared to be demanding the re-prioritisation of religious values in society under the cloak of multiculturalism: 'I have no desire to have to go through the emancipation of women and homosexuals all over again' (cited in Buruma, 2006: 57). Here, Fortuyn stood for free speech, happy for Muslims to express their views, but demanding the equal right to speak out about what he saw as an un-Dutch, unacceptable Muslim intolerance of the lifestyles and values of non-Muslims that was legitimised by multiculturalism: 'multiculturalism, he charged, legitimised repressive practices of Islam, indeed it propped them up financially' (Sniderman and Hagendoorn, 2009: 19). Therefore, Fortuyn 'asked for civic adjustments on the part of immigrants which had been dodged under the reign of official multiculturalism' (Joppke, 2004: 249).

In voicing such concerns over values, Fortuyn was clearly articulating a popular mood, as shown by his rapid rise to political prominence that culminated in his creation, 'Pim Fortuyn's List', coming a strong second in the 2002 general election just days after he was assassinated by a white Dutch animal rights activist. As has been identified above, such critiques of multiculturalism had already been voiced in the early 1990s, so Fortuyn's rise was based on timing, the fact that he was able to fill a political vacuum at a time when most mainstream politicians were not connecting with popular perceptions and fears around cohesion and diversity in the Netherlands. Despite those early criticisms, Sniderman and Hagendoorn (2009) identify elite conformity over multiculturalist policies leading to no conventional space for popular dissent around diversity and its perceived effects at a time of significant state budget cuts, with Fortuyn filling that vacuum. Arguably this political vacuum was about much more than Muslim identity, with the waning of pillarisation and religious influence, the decline of Dutch distinctness through processes of globalisation and European union, and a suffocating political consensus all combining to create significant popular disenchantment, both with conventional politicians and the direction of political travel.

Underpinning this rise of Fortuyn, and earlier critiques of multiculturalist policies were significant Dutch popular attitudes around diversity and integration. It is clear that these attitudes, whilst highly problematic for muticulturalist policy approaches, are long term, and have not altered or grown significantly in reaction to 9/11 or the murders of Fortuyn and Van Gogh (Schalk-Soekar et al., 2009). Here, the authors draw on field research from respondents in Hengelo, a city in the east of the Netherlands to suggest that that there are significant divergences within Dutch society over multiculturalism, and that these have not altered significantly in response to the events highlighted above. Their key finding is a major difference of approach between migrants and native Dutch communities towards integration, with migrants found to:

> prefer cultural maintenance in their private lives and integration in their public lives, while the majority group in The Netherlands prefers an adjustment to the larger society in both domains.
>
> (Schalk-Soekar et al., 2009: 271)

This stress on divergent values and attitudes to integration is supported by a much larger-scale research process that started in the late 1990s, well before the political events now seen as the crucial watershed for Dutch multiculturalism (Sniderman and Hagendoorn, 2009). These research findings support not only the notion of value conflicts between white and Muslim Dutch citizens, but also significant differences of attitude within white Dutch society. These values conflicts, the authors suggest, have been unhelpfully exacerbated by multiculturalist policies that have stressed differences between distinct identities, so having the unintended effects of making everyone less secure in their own identity and undermining support for the notion of societal diversity per se (Sniderman and Hagendoorn, 2009). Again, a direct parallel can be found here with the post-2001 community cohesion critique of past multiculturalist policy approaches in Britain and their unhelpful focus on ethnic difference (Cantle, 2001, 2005). In particular,

Sniderman and Hagendoorn (2009) identify a value conflict between white Dutch (who they generalise as 'Western Europeans') and Muslims around the role of women, and authoritarian family relations, especially the treatment of children. Whilst such conflicts have strengthened since 9/11 and the Dutch murders, they were already there, and are mutual. Here, a substantial majority of white Dutch feel that Muslims restrict women within their communities, whilst a substantial majority of Dutch Muslims believe that Western women have too many freedoms. This suggests that multiculturalism has a problem of 'parallel barriers of prejudice: a desire of many western Europeans to hold Muslims at a distance combined with a desire of Muslims to keep their distance' (Sniderman and Hagendoorn, 2009: 26). The data suggests that the de facto ruling out within Dutch politics of critical discussion of such multicultural problems has made the majority of white Dutch citizens hostile to further immigration.

Such white Dutch attitudes might simply be understood as representing the societal racism that is a residual effect of colonialism in all major Western European countries, especially as a substantial minority of white respondents from a variety of social and political backgrounds expressed negative and stereotyped views about all non-white migrants, including the Christian, Dutch-speaking migrants from Surinam. However, Sniderman and Hagendoorn (2009) insist that their data shows a substantial group of white Dutch respondents who dislike Muslim cultural practices but not Muslims per se – they support cultural pluralism and different lives as a right, but see current Muslim approaches to living in Dutch society as highly problematic: 'The clash of Dutch and Muslim values does not lead the Dutch to reject Muslims precisely because the values of Dutch society are liberal values' (Sniderman and Hagendoorn, 2009: 40). Whilst half of all Dutch respondents express no negative views around migrants at all, it is clear that a substantial and important part of white Dutch opinion finds Muslim lives and values problematic, over and above feelings about immigration in general: 'The distinctive characteristic of Turkish and Moroccan migrants is that they are Muslims and distance themselves from the strong secular trends in Dutch society' (Sniderman and Hagendoorn, 2009: 46). Such a negative focus on particular non-white ethnic minority communities might be seen as evidence of what Hall (1992) identifies as the modern phenomena of differentiated 'racisms', and is certainly a parallel of the situation in Britain, where white unease at multiculturalist encouragement of diversity has particularly focused on the most culturally distinct Muslim communities, as Chapter 6 explores further.

Here, it is clear that there has been a Dutch popular backlash against policies of multiculturalism on the basis of values, whereby separate values and lifestyles seen to be in conflict with key Dutch values are perceived to have been tolerated or even encouraged in the name of multiculturalism, with this value clash at the root of perceptions that ethnic minorities have 'too many rights'. This leads Sniderman and Hagendoorn (2009) to suggest that the nature of and official backing for Dutch multiculturalist policies is directly responsible for this negative reaction. Here, in stressing difference to avoid racial clashes at the onset of non-white immigration, multiculturalist policies have gradually provoked racial clashes through counterproductively allowing, and even stressing, those ethnic differences. Sniderman and Hagendoorn (2009) discuss understandings of social identity theory and realistic conflict theory to explain the significant hostility to Muslim values and lifestyles found in their survey and conclude that 'threats to cultural identity, our analyses show, have a far larger impact on hostility to minorities than any other threat' (Sniderman and Hagendoorn, 2009: 91). A significant number of Dutch people, even those generally tolerant, *perceive* their cultural identity to be under threat from the values and lifestyles of Muslim migrants, a perception arguably encouraged by the content and manner of multiculturalist policies. This suggests that by stressing difference and the right to be different, and by supporting visible symbols of that difference that have included the more reactionary elements of Islamic culture, such policies provoke exclusionary, negative reactions from large sections of the white majority. The research summarised here does use 'Dutch' as an undifferentiated norm, and Sniderman and Hagendoorn (2009) acknowledge that political discussions around Dutch multiculturalism have given little focus on class difference within the white majority, or on who wins and who loses from unskilled immigration, a debate also sorely needed in Britain, as Chapter 7 explores. Nevertheless, this perspective suggests that encouraging commonality and integration, and focusing on a more limited tolerance rather than a sharply differentiated and high-profile multiculturalist 'difference' would help to address these substantial Dutch 'value conflicts'.

Conclusion: an overblown Dutch 'crisis'?

Such a longer-term analysis of the problematic impact of Dutch multiculturalist policies would suggest that the political furore around political murders and the rise of anti-Islam politicians in the first decade of this century are actually symbolic of long-term popular unease, as much as causal to it. Here, the reaction to the murders of Pim Fortuyn and Theo Van Gogh, and the continued rise of far-right political figure Geert Wilders can be seen not as a sudden, post-9/11 spasm, but as resonant of a much older, steadily growing public concern about the balance, content and effects of Dutch multiculturalism. Nevertheless, media and political responses to these events have clearly 'amplified' (Cohen, 1972) such popular feelings, providing particular hotspots, such as the aftermath of Theo Van Gogh's murder: 'There was something unhinged about The Netherlands in the winter of 2004' (Buruma, 2006: 10). Van Gogh, a controversial and iconoclastic film-maker, columnist and TV presenter, was at the heart of public soul-searching about multiculturalism in both life and death. He offered advice to Fortuyn, frequently talked publicly about Islam and made the film 'Submission' with Somalian-origin refugee, Ayaan Hirsi Ali. Ali had been subjected to female circumcision as a child, escaped from a forced marriage, and once in the Netherlands became an outspoken critic of Islamic culture and its treatment of women. 'Submission' was a provocative, 11-minute film that involved extracts from the Qur'an being projected on the naked bodies of women. It was broadcast only once and, like the later Danish cartoon controversy, became controversial for what it symbolised rather than in response to actual viewings. Van Gogh laughed off Islamic death threats but was subsequently murdered in execution-like style by a 26-year-old Dutchman of Moroccan origin, Mohammed Bouyeri, who had hoped to die a martyr's death but was captured, convicted and imprisoned. The killer had pinned a threatening letter to Ayaan Hirsi Ali to Van Gogh's body that also fulminated against 'Jewish cabals'. Bouyeri was highly educated and a fluent Dutch speaker, but his own social marginalisation and inadequacies had taken him down a road towards Islamic websites and Jihadist networks (Buruma, 2006).

Arguably, Van Gogh's murder had a similar social impact on Dutch society as the 7/7 London bombings of July 2005 had on British society – the shock that Islamist ideology could lead a seemingly 'integrated' young man to carry out cold-blooded murder and seek his own death at the same time. After living with round-the-clock police protection, Ali is now largely based in the USA. Whilst Van Gogh had often made provocative comments about Muslims, this was consistent with his approach to other groups in society, and his abuse of friends and colleagues, with his professional track record showed him to be no racist. Rather, he was part of Dutch literary tradition that saw open abuse as a legitimate part of expression and did not expect a violent response. The fact that some Dutch Islamists saw public abuse of Islam, such as 'Submission', as completely unacceptable in a mirroring of the earlier 'Satanic Verses' controversy highlighted the deep-rooted 'value clash' identified by Sniderman and Hagendoorn (2009), and echoed the secular, libertarian and free speech themes deployed by Fortuyn. His mantle has since been taken up by Geert Wilders, formerly an MP for the liberal VVD but subsequently the leader of the right-wing PVV 'Freedom Party', which came third and doubled its vote to 15 per cent in the 2010 general election. Wilders's stance is explicitly anti-Islamic, saying, 'Not all Muslims are terrorist, but almost all terrorists are Muslims....Islam is something we can't afford any more in The Netherlands. I want the fascist Qur'an banned' (Traynor, 2009). His programme includes a total stop to Muslim immigration, a ban on Mosque building and a tax on hijabs, the Muslim headscarf. Wilders has also made a provocative anti-Islamic film, 'Fitna', and was initially banned in 2009 from entering Britain to show it, something reversed in 2010 when his presence at the House of Commons inspired a supportive rally from the far-right English Defence League. The Freedom Party has made progress at the local level in some Dutch towns, including The Hague and Almere. Almere has a large ethnic minority population, and Wilders has successfully exploited racialised fears around street crime, even though it is a fairly typical Dutch city (Beaumont, 2010). This sort of racialised 'moral panic' (Cohen, 1972) is resonant of the campaigning in Britain by the British National Party explored in Chapter 7.

Whilst the recent progress of Wilders and the PVV suggests Dutch society is rapidly lurching to the right in an anti-Muslim backlash, such an impression would be misleading. Even the PVV's 2010 election advance was a smaller share of the vote than that achieved by Fortuyn in 2002, and is consistent with votes achieved by right-wing parties in other Western European countries, such as Belgium, France and Denmark, who also have proportional representation electoral systems (*Guardian*, 12 June 2010). In fact, it is arguably consistent with the history of the Netherlands itself, where the myth of liberal Holland 'has long kept a stranglehold over the well established and not always tolerant tradition of smaller parties, extremist or moderate, left or right, which rise up suddenly, gain power and occasionally disappear into obscurity as fast as they came' (Rendeiro, 2010). Such a tradition might be seen as a partial product of the pillarisation tradition, and certainly saw the rise and subsequent disappearance of the extreme-right Centrum Party in the 1980s.

What this Dutch support for explicitly right-wing, anti-Islamic parties and political figures over the past decade does illustrate is the continued relevance of the analysis (Schalk-Soekar et al., 2009; Sniderman and Hagendoorn, 2009) that Dutch approaches to multiculturalism have fuelled deep 'value clashes' that policy needs to resolve. Although the role of Fortuyn and the current rise of Wilders and the Freedom Party should not be exaggerated, they have prompted mainstream parties to harden their position on multiculturalism, including an increased focus on the responsibility, or 'duty' of migrants to integrate and more pressure for new arrivals, such spouses and family members to undergo the language and citizenship lessons. Such approaches are explicitly connected to a focus on the continued economic and social marginalisation of Moroccan and Turkish-origin communities: 'there is widespread acceptance in The Netherlands of the idea that without somehow restricting family reunification, underachieving in education and employment of the largest immigrant groups – Turks, Moroccans, and increasingly also Antilleans, will continue' (Vink, 2007: 547). A direct parallel can be found here with the frank examination of continued marriage and family holiday links between Asian-origin British communities and the Indian sub-continent in the post-2001 riots community cohesion reports (Cantle, 2001; Ritchie, 2001). Such a focus might be portrayed as reactionary, both in Britain and the Netherlands, but it can also be seen as the honest posing of difficult choices which need to be made if greater progress towards social and economic integration and equality is to be achieved for migrant-origin communities. Whilst Dutch policies of multiculturalism were never universally accepted, there was a large consensus in support of them amongst the Dutch political elite that has now been disrupted. Former Amsterdam Mayor and now Labour Party leader, Job Cohen, has suggested that Islamic identity has the potential to be a progressive force for progress and integration, a perspective explored further in Chapter 6 in relation to Britain, but this seems to be counter-intuitive to the current reality in the Netherlands.

Instead, it seems that there are significant similarities between the Netherlands and post-2001 Britain, whereby policies of multiculturalism seem to now be counterproductive in that they have unhelpfully stressed difference and allowed the growth of separate identities. In particular, the focus on difference has threatened the identity and cultural security of the white majority, a perception similar to the 'white backlash' (Hewitt, 2005) in Britain explored in Chapter 7, and which needs to urgently be engaged with at a time when the meaning and relevance of social class inequality in society has been politically sidelined. The way forward suggested by writers who have studied the Netherlands in depth (Sniderman and Hagendoorn, 2009) is to downplay multiculturalism's focus on difference in favour of more limited approaches of tolerance that 'cool' feelings about and commitments to separate ethnic identities, whilst enabling space for an enhanced policy focus on Dutch common-ality and shared needs to a much greater extent than has been true in the past. Joppke (2004) suggests that encouraging more a limited and priva-tised tolerance of diversity is a positive and pragmatic solution for states such as Britain and the Netherlands currently experiencing the problem-atic consequences of stressing difference through more overt policies of multiculturalism. In fact, Joppke (2004) even poses the question of where actually the evidence is of the supposed failure of colour-blind citizenship, but such evidence is arguably found in France, as the next section explores.

France: right all along?

The significant British post-2001 re-thinking of multiculturalist poli-cies represented by community cohesion and analysed in Chapter 1, and the Dutch crisis of multiculturalism outlined above, together could be seen to 'prove' that these countries have got it wrong and France has got it right in relation to multiculturalism, diversity and identity. It is clear that both Britain and the Netherlands have significantly re-thought their previously favoured multiculturalist policies of consid-erable recognition of, and autonomy for, distinct ethnic groups and their separate identities, and have moved to place greater stress on commonality and shared national identity and values, concrete poli-cies of integration that have included citizenship and language tests for all new migrants. In emphasising shared national identity, and the rights and responsibilities of all citizens to contribute and adhere to that identity, integration rather than diversity, these previous champions of multiculturalism might be seen as moving much closer to the historic position of France. The French model is popularly understood as one of colour-blind citizenship, whereby all French citizens, regardless of their ethnicity or faith, are seen as equal, a position informed by the princi-ples of the 1789 French Revolution, liberty, equality and fraternity. Such an approach recognises people as equal individual citizens, rather than members of 'communities' or groups, with distinct faith and ethnic cul-tural identities seen as something for the private sphere of home only and not for the public sphere (Watson, 2000). This seemingly historical position can therefore be seen as explaining recent developments in French politics, with moves to ban the wearing of the Muslim niqab (face covering) or burqa (full-length covering garment) (Silvestri, 2010) building on the previous 2004 ban on the wearing of religious symbols in French state schools (Bertossi, 2007). The logical consistency of this policy implementation and the parallel policy difficulties of Britain and the Netherlands might suggest that France has got its policy position right, that this position has been consistent, and that the approach to ethnicity within French society is therefore successful and stable. In fact, it is argued here that nothing could be further from the truth. Instead, this French approach of republican citizenship to ethnic diversity is actually a very modern creation (Flavell, 2001), it contains very significant contradictions and tensions (Bertossi, 2007), and France is arguably in the midst of a more profound 'crisis of multiculturalism' than either Britain or the Netherlands (Fekete et al., 2010). To explore this assertion, the chapter first explores the key elements of the French 'model', including how it has reacted to significant immigration and the resulting ethnic diversity in society. It then goes on to explore a number of ways in which the French approach, or rather the lack of an effective one, to that diversity can be seen to be crisis over the last few years, as illustrated by the very significant 2005 French urban riots (Waddington et al., 2009) and the highly racialised political reactions that continue to unfold.

The French model

What is often portrayed as an unchanging French position in relation to national citizenship and personal identity should actually be seen as a much more recent creation of specific political developments and events in the 1980s and 1990s: 'the underlying rationale of politics and practices towards the treatment of ethnic minorities was clearly different before the mid 1980s' (Flavell, 2001: 46). It is true that as far back as the nineteenth century French citizenship has been officially about the uniqueness of the individual and that 'ethnic, regional and religious categorisations have been ignored' (Bertossi, 2007: 3). Based on the revolutionary principles, this ideology was developed during the Third Republic's period of national building between 1871 and the First World War in 1914, when distinct regional identities and a large number of European immigrants were incorporated into 'French' citizenry (although French women did not gain the vote until 1945!). This approach included a strict separation of church and state, something formalised after the 1905 Dreyfus affair, when a Jewish army officer was falsely accused of treason. In reality, during the colonial period, French nationality and citizenship were *not* the same thing, with specific statuses such as 'French colonial national' and a specific electoral body in Algeria for the Muslim majority (Bertossi, 2007). Such a differentiated reality of approach can also be seen within France itself in the post-war period. In common with other Western European states facing unskilled labour shortages during the post-war boom, France experienced considerable immigration from the 1950s to 1970s. As those other ex-colonial powers of Britain and the Netherlands did, France drew that migrant labour from current or ex-colonies, in its case North Africa, sub-Saharan Africa and the Caribbean, with language proficiency therefore not being the problem it has proven for some British and Dutch immigrants. The common initial expectation that those migrants were 'guest workers' who would return home led to French policies of 'insertion', whereby the economic and social needs of migrant communities were addressed in specific local settings, an approach that continued as their presence was accepted as permanent and which was generally viewed as reasonably successful. Such localised policies were, and arguably still are, 'multiculturalism' in practice, even though France has long derided the communalist multiculturalism of the 'Anglo-Saxon' countries (a bizarre amalgam of the USA and Britain). This approach continued after the first immigration restrictions of the 1974 economic downturn, and it always involved state consultation and involvement with Muslim community religious organisations, contrary to the myth of the French model (Flavell, 2001). This flexible policy response altered significantly in the 1980s for a number of reasons.

The resulting policy shift might be seen as a response to the reality of a more diverse society, but should also be seen in the context of European integration, the very profound economic restructuring associated with globalisation and of a significant economic downturn, all of which impacted on perceptions of identity across increasingly individualistic Western European societies. What is beyond dispute is that the interrelated issues of integration and identity became the most heated political issue in France for the decade from the early 1980s onwards, with practical issues of diversity turning into highly charged, philosophical questions (Flavell, 2001). This was focused on the reform of the French Nationality Code initiated by the Chirac government between 1986 and 1988, a high-profile commission process that included evidence sessions broadcast daily live on national TV and resulting in a major report, 'Being French today and tomorrow', which emphasised that ethnic and religious difference must be relegated to the private sphere, and that loyalty and allegiance to France were essential to citizenship: 'consequently, French citizenship was reinvented while strict republican features were strengthened and legitimised' (Bertossi, 2007: 5). This included a formal end to differential treatment for ethnic minorities, a stricter interpretation of the principle of official secularism or '*laicite*', and taking away automatic citizenship from French-born children of foreign migrants, with young people having to actively choose French citizenship between the ages of 16 and 21.

This new approach of non-negotiable integration through citizenship directly led to the first headscarf controversy of 1989 (ironically the bicentenary of the French Revolution), '*l'affaire du foulard*', where three young Muslim schoolgirls were expelled (and sent back to the private sphere!) for their refusal to remove their hijabs at school. Left-wing commentators such as veteran socialist Regis Debray took an even harder anti-hijab line than the far-right Front Nationale (FN) party of Le Pen, with the majority of French society worrying about 'the high danger of political pluralism that the competing community-based allegiance of Islam seemed to pose' (Flavell, 2001: 154). Three key explanatory factors can be identified for this significant political development around ethnic identity in France. Firstly, there had been a very significant growth in the FN by the mid-1980s, arguably fuelled by continuing anti-Muslim bitterness in the aftermath of France's defeat in the Algerian war of independence in the early 1960s. Anti-immigrant feeling generally grew in some white working-class areas from the late 1970s onwards as the economy stalled, including amongst those previously supporting the Communist Party. The 1985 switch to a proportional representation electoral system by President Mitterrand was designed to split the mainstream centre-right parties, but had the unintended consequence of putting the FN in parliament for the first time. The FN's growth was partially also based on exploitation of stories around the previous 'insertion' policies of multiculturalism, including Muslim children being given lessons in community languages and support for Muslim organisations, approaches defended uncritically by some left-leaning politicians as the 'right to be different'. More recent and similar exploitation of muticulturalist policy 'facts' by the far right in Britain is explored in Chapter 7. Underpinning this French debate was the racist accusation that ethnic minorities were 'paper' citizens only, in France solely for welfare benefits. Secondly, alongside this was a reality of more assertive ethnic minority communities, particularly the first generation of French-born children of migrants who were no longer prepared to tolerate racial discrimination and marginalisation. This included increasing industrial militancy and was symbolised by the 1983 'march for equality and against racism', known popularly as the 'march of the beurs' (slang for Arabs), that involved ethnic minority campaigners marching from Marseille to Paris. This march became a major political event, with the march's arrival in Paris greeted by over 100,000 people and President Mitterrand, and spawning the powerful anti-racist movement 'SOS Racisme' (Hamidi, 2009). These two political developments, combined with significant economic re-structuring and recession, forced a political response from the French government, with the lurch towards coercive republican citizenship described above seen as an effective middle way forwards (Flavell, 2001). Its impact, however, in making (secular) republican citizenship a much more loaded concept than in Britain, was to set the French state on a continuing collision course with a perceived Islamic threat (Silvestri, 2010).

The headscarf controversy of 1989, coming hot on the heels of the Rushdie affair analysed in greater detail in Chapter 6, further fuelled the French citizenship debate. Left-wing Prime Minister Rocard launched the 'High Council on Integration' in 1990 whilst maintaining the previous political direction, leaving no space for opposition, and enabling the right-wing government elected in 1993 to cement this policy position. The French National Code was reformed in 1993 and assumed that there was no such thing in France as 'ethnic minorities', and that the legal equality for all French citizens is the same as full and actual equality, despite blatant, visible evidence to the contrary. More importantly, this coercive approach to citizenship that demands that allegiance to French citizenship must be *chosen* and visibly demonstrated at all times in public has put the French state in tension with French Muslims, whose religiously informed values and lifestyles are seen as an open challenge to this French model of citizenship. Both of these issues are discussed in the following section, which suggests that, as a result, France is currently in significant crisis over its attitudes to ethnicity, identity and multiculturalism. However, it would be wrong to suggest that there has been no positive progress since the early 1990s, with Bertossi (2007) highlighting how the impact assessment of the European Union has had a helpful impact on France's approach. Here, the 1997 Amsterdam Treaty, with Article 13 explicitly addressing discrimination on a variety of grounds, has prompted France to move under pressure. In 1998, automatic citizenship for French-born ethnic minorities was reinstated, and significant action was taken against racial discrimination for the first time. This included a 114 free phone number for anyone suffering racial discrimination in employment, an extension of legal liability for racial discrimination and stronger anti-discrimination measures in the area of housing. This culminated in 2004 in the establishment of HALDE, the government's 'Anti-Discriminatory and Pro-Equality Authority', a body further strengthened in 2006 (Bertossi, 2007). Despite this progress, it is clear that France's policy approach to diversity and identity is currently in crisis, and has been for the last decade or so.

The French model in crisis?

It is argued here that, rather than being a stable and successful policy model, French approaches to ethnicity and identity have been unstable ever since the policy developments of the 1980s and early 1990s outlined above, and that these tensions are currently worsening (Ramdani, 2010). This instability and tension exists for a number of reasons, each of which is discussed below, and this enables the chapter to draw conclusions, not only about the current state of French policy approaches to multiculturalism, but also to how this compares with the situations in Britain and the Netherlands.

The first problematic feature is the denial of ethnic identity inherent in the French policy approach fixed in the 1980s, and how this relates to current realities. The constitutional refusal to accept the reality of 'ethnic minorities' has meant a French impasse on even considering the possibility of collecting census data on the basis of ethnicity. Chapters 1 and 3 detail the vital role that the inclusion of an ethnicity question in the 1991 Census, and the accompanying, ongoing collection of ethnic data has played in British progress in acknowledging and combating ethnic inequalities across society. Despite French academic attempts in the 1990s to challenge their government's position, France continues to see such a policy approach as unconstitutional and remains limited to data about those born outside France only. Such data 'fails to represent the vast majority of North Africans in France who are full citizens, often of the second or third generation' (Flavell, 2001: 161). This approach is symptomatic of wider attitudes, with the continued use of the term '*etrangers*', or strangers, for long-term, non-white French residents within political dialogue, a high level of immigration spot checks on non-white French people on public transport and a police force dedicated purely to policing immigration. Alongside this, 'there seems to be very little action around racial violence in France and the Police have been accused of not taking racial violence seriously' (Fekete et al., 2010:

18). It is not suggested here that France as a country is more racist than Britain or the Netherlands; indeed, there is often positive evidence of non-racial French popular attitudes (Flavell, 2001: 191) but rather it is suggested that the refusal of French policy to accept the reality of ethnic difference and of unequal ethnic experiences inevitably translates into policy operations that can often tip over in uncontrolled, discriminatory practice, with none of the cultural journey towards non-racial operation that ethnic data evidence has forced upon British public bodies. This also means that French policy is not equipped to engage with the reality of non-white economic and social marginalisation, including an increasing spatial marginalisation of many ethnic minorities to the '*banlieues*', or suburbs, on the edge of prosperous, largely white French cities.

This was graphically shown in 2005 by widespread rioting in banlieue areas, and by the political responses to that rioting, both of which could be seen as evidence of French policy inadequacy (Waddington et al., 2009). The 2005 riots were sparked by an incident in Clichy-sous-bois on the edge of Paris, when on 27 October two African-origin teenagers, Zyed Benna and Bouna Traore, were electrocuted and died in an electricity sub-station whilst fleeing a police spot check. The immediate youth response was fuelled when, two days later, riot police fired tear gas at the entrance of a mosque in another Paris suburb. This led to three weeks of rioting that spread across Paris and then to virtually every significant town and city in France in an echo of the British riots of 1981. In total, over 3000 people were arrested, one-third of whom were under 18, with around 9000 cars burnt out. Arguably, the rioting had been intensified and prolonged by the political response of then Interior Minister and now President, Nicolas Sarkozy, who called the rioters 'scum' and suggested that they should be pressure-hosed off the streets: 'it was to his direct and macho-like challenge to their sense of dignity and self-respect that the youths from banlieues responded with such desire for confrontation' (Kokeroff, 2009: 148). For Bertossi (2007: 1), 'these images symbolised the limits of French republican integration and citizenship.' The wider political response was to blame ¦¦¦¦¦ ¦¦¦¦¦¦¦¦¦¦¦¦¦¦, ¦¦¦¦¦-¦¦¦¦¦¦ ¦¦¦¦¦¦¦¦ ¦¦¦¦¦¦¦ ¦¦¦¦ ¦¦¦¦¦¦¦¦¦, ¦¦¦¦¦¦¦¦ ¦ parallel with many responses to the 2001 British riots (Amin, 2003). However, the police, in a report quickly suppressed, suggested that the cause of the rioting was not a denial of French citizenship, but a reality of discrimination and marginalisation (Bertossi, 2007). What is clear is that the French riots originated from and spread across the public housing estates known in French policy as 'ZUSs', or 'sensitive urban zones'. The shared characteristics of these areas are that they have high unemployment, low incomes and a very high proportion of under 20-year-olds, all of which factors were also found in the predominantly Asian areas experiencing rioting in northern England in 2001. An exacerbating factor was that the French government had recently decided to respond to the poor state of the housing on such estates by large-scale demolitions and dispersals, the destruction of communities, rather than improvement (Lagrange, 2009).

Despite the crude and limited data, it was clear also that these areas particularly housed sub-Saharan African communities, more recently arrived and poorer than longer-established North African-origin communities, and that they were significantly spatially segregated from wider, white French society. These realities led Lagrange (2009: 121) to suggest that 'the incapacity of these youths to access social positions was combined with the new effects of ethnic segregation in poor neighbourhoods in France', a striking parallel of the reality for many Muslim (and, arguably, white) young people in the north of England, as explored in Chapters 6 and 7. In the aftermath, Sarkozy promised an action plan to improve the banlieues, but didn't have the money, with the result that the main change was simply greatly increased local policing of these areas. Meanwhile, in the absence of ethnic data and resulting action plans to address profound ethnic inequalities, France's ethic minority communities have little faith in the anti-discrimination efforts of HALDE (Fekete et al., 2010).

Instead, the last few years of French policy development have focused on a further hardening of republican citizenship, and an accompanying increase in conflict with French Muslims. In 2004, following a further Commission report, the government reversed the traditional approach to 'laicite' and instead of actual bans on public use of religious symbols being an exception, they became the everyday rule. Following the 1989 headscarf conflict, the heat had been taken out by allowing local schools to make their own decision, but this new move made religious dress a national political issue once again. Conflict has focused on Islam because of its supposed lack of distinction between religion and public life, something perceived as a direct challenge to French conceptions of citizenship. This quickly became caught up with analysis of the 2005 riots, despite clear evidence that rioters were *not* motivated by, or mobilised on the basis of, religion or ethnicity (Bertossi, 2007). The result was a move by Sarkozy's government to ban the wearing of the niqab or burqa in all public places, although available evidence suggested that this might affect as few as 2000 Muslim women nationally out of the approximately 5–6 million Muslims in France (Ramdani, 2010). The ban on public wearing of face veils was passed by the lower house of the French parliament in July 2010 by 336 votes to 1, although it was still to be approved by the French constitutional watchdog. This overwhelming support closely followed a unanimous similar ban in Belgium, a country which for some years hadn't been able to gain consensus on virtually any other political issue (Silvestri, 2010). At first, Sarkozy's government wanted to also ban the wearing of face veils in private also, and French feminists largely supported the public ban, agreeing with male politicians that such Islamic clothing represents the subjugation of women by fathers and husbands. This perspective of male dominance flies in the face of academic evidence around young British Muslim women who wear the hijab, as discussed in Chapter 6, and ignores 'what I would contend is a significant number of women who in fact define themselves by their veils, choosing to wear them despite what anyone else thinks or says' (Ramdani, 2010). It is arguably no coincidence that this political controversy was played out at the same time as very significant austerity measures by a struggling right-of-centre government and, 'the burqa debate is a convenient way to distract the public from unwanted economic cuts' (Silvestri, 2010).

This arguably represents another facet of the crisis of French policy, the highly racialised political climate created by such policy directions. The political distraction that the burqa question seemed to represent was augmented by the 'debate on national identity' launched in November 2009. This involved public debates and a website where over 58,000 people offered comments. The first results included requiring new immigrants to sign a charter outlining their rights and responsibilities, with lessons for new immigrant parents in French language and other issues to be rolled out nationally from September 2010, and all children to receive a 'citizen's handbook' (Willsher, 2010). For Guene (2010), 'hidden behind this debate on national identity is the recognition that being French and a practising Muslim are incompatible.' Arguably, the key aspect of this national debate was the timing, with the government worried about what the far-right FN would achieve in regional elections in March 2010. Such concern has arguably been central to the hardening of French citizenship policy approaches in the first decade of the twenty-first century, stemming from the profound shock of Le Pen making it through to the final run-off Presidential election in 2002 at the expense of the Socialist Party. Ever since then, mainstream parties have been concerned not to be outflanked on their right by voters frustrated by political elites. In fact, such political opportunism has simply played into the hands of the FN, just as Mitterrand's tinkering with the electoral system in the 1980s did, with the FN campaigning on a 'No to Islamism' platform that concentrated on the burqa, and which succeeded in gaining them 12 per cent nationally in the first round of voting and as much as 20 per cent in some areas in March 2010 (Fekete et al., 2010).

France: policy in a cul-de-sac?

At first sight, France's policy approach to multiculturalism, identity and diversity has been significantly different to that of the Netherlands and Britain, but it is also clear that there are some similarities. All three countries are ex-colonial powers that responded to post-war labour shortages by drawing in non-European migrant labour, often from current or former colonies. A common and naive assumption was that migrant labourers would return home and that policy should simply support their identity maintenance for the short time of their stay. Coming to terms with the reality of migrants putting down roots and forming significant communities through being joined by families was a significant challenge for the host societies, arguably one that they are still grappling with. The myth is that while the Netherlands and Britain responded through policies of multiculturalism that are now in crisis because of their indulgence towards separate ethnic identities that pose real risks to national identity and cohesion, France stuck with its historical policies of colour-blind republican citizenship that represents the direction the Netherlands and Britain are now travelling in. It is argued here that the reality is significantly different. In fact, prior to the early 1980s, France had policy approaches that were very akin to multiculturalism, with the approach of 'insertion' allowing local authorities and public bodies to develop differentiated services and facilities for specific ethnic communities, an approach that included open processes of consultation with religious bodies. Whilst not the official, national policy adoption of multiculturalism seen in the Netherlands (Sniderman and Hagendoorn, 2009), such an organic and localised approach was very similar to many aspects of the British multiculturalism that was developed as much from below through tensions and practice as much as by official dictat from above (Joppke, 2004; Solomos, 2003).

In the 1980s, as the Netherlands formally embraced multiculturalism and British multiculturalist approaches developed substantially at the local level, France went the other way for a number of reasons outlined above. Highly significant here was the emergence of the far-right FN of Le Pen as a political force, something given further momentum by changes to the electoral system which opened parliament's door to the FN. Arguably, that political challenge, as much as France's historic approach to citizenship, led to the policy response of a hardened and unresponsive republican citizenship in the face of a more visible and assertive ethnic minority presence, rather than the multiculturalist accommodation that resulted from a similar challenge in other states. The result has been that ever since the late 1980s France has seemed on a collision course with its Muslim community, the largest in Western Europe, through its '*moral orientalism*' (Flavell, 2001: 178), and its fixation on the supposed threat to national identity from any sort of distinct religious or ethnic symbol, whilst being ideologically incapable of devising effective policy responses to the visible economic and social marginalisation of many ethnic minority French citizens. Here, French approaches to integration are only capable of addressing new migrants, not the issues of diversity and equality for non-white French citizens. It can be argued that the widespread 2005 French riots, which had nothing to do with religion and everything to do with spatial and economic exclusion (Lagrange, 2009), and the highly divisive political discourse that accompanied them (Waddington et al., 2009), were the inevitable result of this retreat into a policy cul-de-sac, with the more recent moves to legislate against clothing items like the burqa and the niqab, worn only by a tiny minority of French Muslim women, evidence of a destructive downward spiral unlikely to be arrested by a 'national debate' on identity (Willsher, 2010).

As this chapter and Chapter 1 have highlighted, France is not the only country in significant difficulties over its policy approach to identity and diversity, or in experiencing divisive political discourse around these issues. It is clear that common challenges exist around the profound insecurities created by a globalised, neo-liberal economic model (Byrne, 1999), the impact on national identity from European integration and its free movement of European labour (Bertossi, 2007), and new perceived meanings that brand the multiplicities of competing identities for migrants (Shavit, 2009). Such developments have had a significant impact on the white majority population in each state considered, and on how they view policy approaches to diversity. The perception that multiculturalist policy has unhelpfully allowed separate identities and values to grow, arguably with disastrous consequences (Thomas, 2010), has prompted a significant change of emphasis in both the Netherlands and Britain. These British changes are controversial, as the following chapter discusses, but it is argued here that adjustments to an existing approach of multiculturalism give Britain and the Netherlands a more stable and progressive basis for addressing challenges of diversity and national unity in an increasingly uncertain future than the impasse and tensions resulting from the French policy position.

3
Community Cohesion: The Death of the British Model of Multiculturalism?

Introduction

Chapter 1 detailed the 2001 riots in the north of England and the subsequent emergence of community cohesion as a new British governmental policy priority. In outlining the key themes and concerns of community cohesion, the chapter underlined the significant re-think of past policy assumptions and approaches that community cohesion arguably represents. The meaning and implications of this shift are the focus for this chapter, which examines academic and political critiques of community cohesion in order to aid understanding. Much of these critiques have been overtly critical, or even hostile, suggesting that cohesion represents a retreat to failed policies of coercive assimilation (Back et al., 2002), a racialisation of structural economic and social problems and a resulting blaming of Asian communities (Alexander, 2004), a factually wrong, misplaced obsession with 'segregation' (Finney and Simpson, 2009; Kalra, 2002), and the 'death of multiculturalism' (Kundnani, 2002) in Britain, which has previously been seen by neighbouring European states as having a successful political approach to ethnic diversity. A common concern linking all these critiques focuses on the undoubted post-2001 shift from official prioritisation of respect for diversity towards a concern with commonality, cohesion and integration, with government apparently:

> Intent on replacing the emphasis on the respect for diversity as an end point of political tolerance and political unity in a multicultural, multi-racial and multi-faith context with a new 'integration' project

that insists on forging a new level of meta allegiance through establishing shared values.

(McGhee, 2008: 84)

The chapter examines these critiques in relation to the four key themes and concerns of community cohesion identified in Chapter 1: ethnic segregation and 'parallel lives'; the role of agency, individual and community responsibility, in maintaining that segregation; problematic 'bonding' social capital in the absence of forms of 'bridging' social capital; and the unintended, negative effects of past policies that have privileged the needs and identities of each separate ethnic community rather than common needs and identities. It uses these debates to pose questions about how we can then understand community cohesion that is subsequently addressed by empirical evidence analysed from Chapter 4 onwards, but also to start developing the book's position that much of this criticism of community cohesion is misplaced, with community cohesion actually representing positive continuity with past policies to a much greater extent than is first apparent.

A reality of ethnic segregation?

Chapter 1 highlighted the pivotal importance of problematic ethnic segregation in Britain's towns and cities to the emergence and prioritisation of community cohesion (Cantle, 2001), a focus re-emphasised by claims that Britain is 'sleepwalking to segregation' (Phillips, 2005), a process taking the country towards the abyss of American-style 'ghettos' whereby large sections of major American inner cities are almost entirely populated by non-white ethnic minority communities. Two distinct but interrelated arguments about segregation can thus be detected within the community cohesion discourse. Firstly, the overt suggestion in the wake of the 2001 disturbances that ethnic segregation is very significant in many towns and cities, and hence plays a substantial role in racial tensions and the lack of shared identities in these areas (Cantle, 2001; Ouseley, 2001; Ritchie, 2001). Secondly, the implicit suggestion that ethnic segregation is actively getting worse and thus represents an urgent challenge that must be addressed (Phillips, 2005). Both these assertions are highly contested, with the latter fuelling an already contentious debate around the trajectory of ethnic segregation in Britain (Carling, 2008; Finney and Simpson, 2009). The relevance of any notion of 'ethnic segregation' in a society of increasingly shared youth educational and cultural experiences is questionable for some (Kalra, 2002). Here, the actual rioters in 2001 were largely young men who had been through the British educational system, who spoke English, shared cultural reference points with non-Asian young people that include the recreational use by some of alcohol and illegal drugs, and simply wanted to be treated equally as young citizens (Amin, 2003), suggesting that the rioters' issue was inequality, not 'segregation': 'the debate about segregation in the UK has emerged with a contentious set of academic evidence primarily concerned with inter-group interaction rather than inequality' (Kalra and Kapoor, 2009: 1400).

However, the local and national community cohesion reports did highlight the very real physical and, arguably, day-to-day cultural, ethnic segregation that does exist in the riot areas, and similar towns and cities. The stress on cultural as well as physical segregation is important here, with claims that nationally, friendships and peer groups are becoming increasingly monocultural for all ethnic backgrounds (Phillips, 2005).

One immediate problem becomes apparent when discussing the reality of ethnic segregation; that is, there are statistical measures of segregation, using the Index of Dissimilarity, which measures the unevenness of the residential distribution of ethnic groups in an area, and the Index of Isolation, which measures the likelihood of residential contact with a different ethnic group (Burgess et al., 2005), but that is not necessarily the same as having friendships across ethnic groups, or as the *perceptions* people hold regarding segregation and racialised 'territory' in their area (Back, 1996; Thomas, 2003, Webster, 1995). To a significant degree, the community cohesion reports (Cantle, 2001; Ouseley, 2001; Ritchie, 2001) draw on qualitative evidence, perceptions and feelings regarding segregation, as well as any quantitative data around actual residential patterns, with Cantle (2005) subsequently talking about 'layers of separation'. Such an approach focused on perceptions and feelings has arguably inadvertently enabled factually questionable, implicit assumptions around the trajectory of ethnic segregation and any 'self-segregation' within the community cohesion discourse to grow, as explored below.

Concerns around ethnic 'segregation' are not new in the UK, with the 'bussing' of ethnic minority school pupils used in cities such as Leicester and Bradford in the 1960s and 1970s to try to ensure ethnically mixed schools, a policy approach eventually outlawed under Britain's race discrimination legislation (Kalra and Kapoor, 2009). The concern then for policy-makers was that ethnic minority 'congregation' (CRE, 2001), especially for Asian communities with distinct languages and religious faiths, would hamper integration into the wider society.

Here, community cohesion arguably represents a new focus on an issue that never went away. In discussing the reality and importance of ethnic segregation to social problems and tensions in Britain, two facts need to be borne in mind. One is that by far the greatest, and growing further in the past two decades, social 'segregation' divide in Britain is along economic class lines, a reality spanning all ethnic groups (Dorling, 2009). Secondly, the most ethnically segregated areas of the country are the very many geographical locations that are entirely or overwhelmingly populated by white people, given that Britain's 8–9 per cent of non-white people is not evenly distributed and is largely focused on large towns and cities in the south-east, midlands and Pennine areas of England (Finney and Simpson, 2009; Modood et al., 1997). Therefore, the segregation debate is, in reality, about those genuinely multi-ethnic towns and cities, its current dynamic and community perceptions of it.

A study that carefully assembles the available factual data to challenge key 'myths' around immigration and integration (Finney and Simpson, 2009) has challenged community cohesion's concern with ethnic segregation. This work makes a number of important points, including the fact that there are no non-white 'ghettos' in Britain, that the government's own evidence (ODPM, 2006) shows that ethnic segregation has not increased in recent years and that the 'spread of the population of each ethnic minority group has become more even and less clustered over time' (Finney and Simpson, 2009: 187). A significant part of this debate has focused on Bradford, partially because of its significant Asian population, but mainly because of the conclusions of the Bradford review (Ouseley, 2001) and the 2001 riots. Finney and Simpson (2009: 122–124) use census data to suggest that Bradford is *not* becoming more segregated, with the number of 'mixed' electoral wards growing, and net white inwards migration to the wards with the highest ethnic minority concentrations. This leads to the suggestion that the ideas of increasing ethnic segregation, and of 'self-segregation' in Bradford is a 'myth', something challenged as not proven by a Bradford-based academic (Carling, 2008). The allegation here is that Finney and Simpson (2009), drawing on earlier work by Simpson (2004), conflate self-segregation, residential segregation and increasing residential segregation as one 'myth' without differentiating or necessarily 'proving' each one (Carling, 2008). The fact that Bradford's schools are more ethnically segregated than the residential areas they serve (Burgess et al., 2005) is relevant here. A key point also is that the suggestion that Bradford's residential ethnic segregation is not getting worse on the available statistical evidence (Finney and Simpson, 2009) does not necessarily address the issue that ethnic segregation there remains very substantial, or that it is increasingly *perceived* to be worse. Similarly, a lack of growth in segregation since 2001 does *not* mean that there was not a substantial increase in segregation in the 1990s, with much of this debate focusing on changes to the small-scale enumeration areas, rather than larger electoral wards. Here, it can be seen that there are indeed more 'mixed' areas in Bradford, but that this masks a great increase in the number predominantly made up of Asian residents (Carling, 2008).

This heated debate over ethnic segregation in Bradford symbolises national conflicts over the stress on ethnic segregation within community cohesion. Whilst the meaning of the census data is contentious in itself, as shown above, in relation to segregation, it does highlight some broader realities which challenge the more pessimistic and racialised understandings of residential trends (Phillips, 2005). Firstly, a certain amount of 'segregation' is not necessarily a bad thing, especially for new migrant communities, as it provides a focus for community facilities, meeting points and places of worship that sustain them and aid integration (Finney and Simpson, 2009). For minority communities, this perspective continues to have some relevance, but academic theory, largely stemming from the 'Chicago School' of urban studies, has always assumed that gradual dispersal of minority communities is the mark of integrative success for societies. The community cohesion reports imply that no such progress is visible, but Finney and Simpson (2009) suggest that significant outward movement *is* happening from areas of ethnic minority areas of concentration in cities like Bradford. This is largely by more prosperous families, mirroring the moves towards suburban or even semi-rural areas that more affluent and ageing people of all ethnic backgrounds tend to make. In this same way, caution should be exercised here about the persistent claims of 'white flight' from inner-city multicultural areas, with racialised interpretations (Dench et al., 2006) arguably misinterpreting mundane and long-standing economic and generational trends (Finney and Simpson, 2009). Demographic realities also explain why ethnic minority concentration appears to still be very high in some areas, despite this outwards movement. Asian communities in Britain are much 'younger' in their age profiles than white communities; in Oldham, the overall ethnic minority population of about 14 per cent becomes 24 per cent for under 18-year-olds, and is projected to rise to 40 per cent of the area's under 18s by 2018 (Oldham MBC, 2006). Of relevance here also though is the continued importance of trans-continental marriage ties, with the arrival of a significant number of non-English speaking spouses from abroad, arguably a cultural force in favour of continued community 'congregation' more than 40 years after the first Pakistani and Bangladeshi large-scale arrivals (Cantle, 2005).

It is thus far from clear that ethnic segregation is worsening in Britain; in fact, evidence indicates that it is slowly breaking down in the ways that lessons from history would suggest (Finney and Simpson, 2009). Nevertheless, ethnic segregation is clearly very significant in some areas (Carling, 2008), and empirical evidence presented later in this book will suggest that the perceptions and fears of it has significant and negatively limiting effects on young people's attitudes and behaviour. In stressing ethnic segregation, community cohesion may actually represent a growing impatience and frustration with its reality in some areas of the country, rather than a factual claim that it is actively worsening (Phillips, 2005). In some ways, this focus on separate space and its negative effect on attitude and identity formation is consistent with wider New Labour policy concerns, with the attention to the cause and effects of 'social exclusion' (Byrne, 1999) concentrating very much on the interplay between marginalised space, societal norms at odds with those of 'other' marginal communities, and the resultant re-enforcement of separate and oppositional identities in those marginalised communities that are resistant to policy interventions (Levitas, 2005). As with such wider policy discourses, the real question here is the extent to which community cohesion sees agency or choice as causing or, at least maintaining, the ethnic segregation that does exist. Alongside this is the question of whether insular, monocultural attitudes, values and lifestyles are a result of segregation and are now problematic in themselves. The way community cohesion appears to address these issues, and critical analysis of this, is discussed below.

Birds of a feather flock together?

Whilst community cohesion's stress on the reality and importance of ethnic segregation is in itself seen as highly contentious, as discussed above, particularly contested has been the notion that this agenda is actually about self-segregation, especially by Asian communities. Such a perspective would suggest that agency is indeed central to the problems of ethnic segregation and racial tension that the national community cohesion policy discourse apparently seeks to address, and that communitarian (Etzioni, 1995) and 'third way' (Giddens, 1998) understandings of individual and community responsibility, as well as rights, in overcoming these problems are relevant here. These are discussed here, alongside suggestions that 'community' is a euphemism for Asian communities (Worley, 2005) and that community cohesion is largely a racialised agenda (Alexander, 2004, 2007; Bagguley and Hussain, 2008) that blames the cultures, values and lifestyles of Asian communities for what are actually structural social and economic issues.

Whilst the reality of physical ethnic 'segregation' itself is contested, there is a clear suggestion that 'communities' are doing this to themselves. The 'self-segregation' strand of the community cohesion discourse, with its analysis of communities actively using their agency to deepen segregation, can be traced to the review of Bradford's ethnic relations conducted by Sir (now Lord) Herman Ouseley, written before and published shortly after the Bradford riot (Ouseley, 2001), and the CRE's subsequent stress on 'congregation', or voluntary clustering of ethnic minority communities (CRE, 2001) in their own post-2001 riots analysis. Together, these two publications helped to set a clear tone for national debates around the meaning of community cohesion, despite Cantle's subsequent denial (2007) that he had ever used the phrase 'self-segregation'. This dominant tone was unsurprising, given that political pronouncements, such as by then Home Secretary David Blunkett, that accompanied the launch of the new policy of community cohesion seemed to very partially focus on the agency of ethnic minority communities in creating segregation (Travis, 2001), rather than on individual or far-right organised white racism, both of which can be seen as causal to the 2001 disturbances, as discussed in Chapter 1. Blunkett's comments, made just a few months after the 9/11 Islamist terror attacks on New York of 2001, helped to set a tone for a long-running public debate that focused on the apparent 'refusal' of some ethnic minority communities to 'become British' (Goodhart, 2004), with the suggestion here clearly being that the 2001 disturbances represented a refusal by Muslim communities to integrate into wider society.

Whilst arguably one-sided, such perspectives could draw on evidence, such as that highlighted in the section above, that types of ethnic segregation might indeed be increasing (Phillips, 2005). Relevant here is the fact that school segregation seems to be greater than residential patterns within itself, perhaps reflecting this at locations, and perhaps linked to the size of particular communities:

> On average, school segregation is greater than the segregation of the same group in the surrounding neighbourhood .... One interpretation of this is that greater density allows greater choice of schools and that this in turn is associated with greater segregation.
>
> (Burgess et al., 2005: 1028)

Such evidence seems to indicate that parents of all ethnic backgrounds do actually segregate on ethnic lines when given a choice of schools, but it is also established that schools have become increasingly 'segregated' on social class lines, something exacerbated by the 'choice' policies of successive governments in the past three decades (Dorling, 2009). Given the highly differentiated economic experiences of different ethnic groups, including different ethnic minority groups (Modood et al., 1997), whether such school-based 'ethnic segregation' is actually about choices made on ethnic or 'race' lines is very hard to assess, and debates around ethnic self-segregation arguably obscure more profound social fissures and trends in society (Burgess et al., 2005; Finney and Simpson, 2009).

To critics, the very existence of the 'self-segregation' debate was a 'blaming the victims' approach that diverted attention from the continuing reality of racism, with Kundnani (2001) highlighting how ethnic minority residential concentration in Oldham was a direct result of historic racist practices by public and private sector housing providers, and of endemic racial harassment of those Asian families daring to move to 'white areas'. Such criticisms of the segregation strand of the cohesion discourse were accentuated by the significant focus within the various reports on the 'cultural practices' of Muslim communities, a phrase that only ever seems to be applied to non-white ethnic minority communities (Alexander, 2004), and a selective reading of which seems to support the allegation of racialisation:

> .... And for the minority, largely non-white community to develop a greater acceptance of, and engagement with, the principal national institutions.
>
> (Cantle, 2001: 19)

Cantle's accompanying call for 'a universal acceptance of the English language' (2001: 19), and the frank discussion in the local Oldham report of the contribution to Pakistani and Bangladeshi community educational underachievement of long sub-continental holiday breaks in term time, and the lack of English use in the home that was explicitly linked to continued trans-continental marriage (Ritchie, 2001, Secs 3:24 and 3:20), all served to fuel a sense that community cohesion was really a policy response to the British 'Muslim problem' (Masood, 2006). The apparent foregrounding of cultural factors rather than economic/structural forces (Kalra and Kapoor, 2009) in the community cohesion reports' discussion of the causes of segregation and racial conflict meant that much media and political focus has subsequently been on the 'problem' of Muslim communities:

> The official response to the riots evident in this and other reports lays much (but not all) of the responsibility for them on to Muslims.
>
> (Pilkington, 2008: 4)

For Alexander (2004), community cohesion, in its partial focus on the cultures and lives of Asian communities, and their roles in maintaining and overcoming segregation, is an inherently racialising agenda resonant of Islamophobia that locates the lack of cohesion in the cultures and attitudes of Muslims, rather than in structural realities of poverty and racism. Nevertheless, the focus in the community cohesion reports on the use of English by poor Asian communities, and the threat to it from sub-continental marriage links and long school breaks (Cantle, 2001; Ritchie, 2001) can also be seen as recognition of the reality that English language skills are increasingly vital in a post-industrial 'knowledge economy' (Mizen, 2004), and that the dialogical exchange vital to a successful and complex multicultural society cannot occur without shared understandings and use of English (McGhee, 2008). Here, focusing on the link between English use and educational attainment within Pakistani- and Bangladeshi-origin British communities is not 'othering' them but rather focusing openly and honestly on barriers to genuine and equal participation in society, and on access to economic progress.

Whilst such themes of problematic Muslim cultures are partially implicit in the community cohesion reports, concerns with the apparently separate cultures and values of Muslims are explicit in the subsequent 'Preventing Violent Extremism' strategy (DCLG, 2007b), with the large-scale, monocultural focus on the attitudes of young Muslims in general suggesting that separate Muslim lives and identities are the real threat to a cohesive and safe society (Thomas, 2009, 2010). This policy initiative and its implications for community cohesion are discussed more fully in Chapter 8.

Community cohesion: the death of multiculturalism in Britain?

Such selective reading of post-2001 riot material has led some to portray the new policy prioritisation of community cohesion as a lurch back towards the policy of coercive assimilationism officially abandoned in the 1960s, where ethnic minorities had to give up any distinctive culture and 'fit in' (Solomos, 2003). This accusation seems at one level to be supported by the striking historical parallels between the discourses and language of the community cohesion reports and governmental positions of the early 1960s, including the assumption (Cantle, 2001; Ouseley, 2001) that ethnically mixed schools are best for everyone, without any supporting educational evidence. In fact, the much-praised Leicester (Cantle, 2001) has even more stark residential ethnic segregation amongst Indian-origin pupils than there is amongst Pakistani- and Bangladeshi-origin pupils in Bradford, but has much better educational results (Kalra and Kapoor, 2009), suggesting that geographical location and pre-existing levels of 'human capital' within communities are greater determinants of economic and educational integration than any local residential patterns (Modood et al., 1997). Solomos (1988) quotes from the 1964 report of the Commonwealth Immigrants Advisory Council, which led to policies of compulsory English language training for ethnic minority pupils, and the dispersal, or 'bussing', of non-white pupils on the basis of colour rather than language need. The justification of such policies is arguably echoed by the themes of the current community cohesion debates:

> A national system of education must aim at producing citizens in a society properly equipped to exercise rights and perform duties that are the same as other citizens. If their parents were brought up in another culture or another tradition, children should be encouraged to respect it, but a national system cannot be expected to perpetuate the different values of immigrant groups.
>
> (Commonwealth Immigrants Advisory Council, 1964: 7, cited in Solomos, 1988: 162)

However, this suggestion that the post-2001 focus on cohesion and integration (DCLG, 2007a) was at odds with New Labour's earlier, pre-2001 acknowledgement of 'Institutional Racism' and proactive strengthening of race equality measures (Back et al., 2002) is countered by the community cohesion reports themselves:

> That also means an acceptance that we are never going to turn the clock back to what was perceived to be a dominant or monocultural view of nationality.
>
> (Cantle, 2001: 18)

Denham states in section 3.12 'We must tackle head on racism and Islamophobia' (2001: 20). Denham then goes on to emphasise the range of anti-racism measures which the then Labour government already had underway, including the watershed Race Relations (Amendment) Act 2000, the focus on raising the educational achievement levels of certain ethnic minority groups, the clear focus on ethnicity within the government's overarching focus on social exclusion (SEU, 1999), and their development of legislation outlawing discrimination on the basis of religion. Here, the frank comments in the community cohesion reports (Cantle, 2001; Ritchie, 2001) aimed at ethnic minority communities should be seen within the Labour government's wider communitarian framework, and as indicative of the need to move on from treating ethnic minority communities as recent arrivals in need of special, sensitive handling towards full citizens who need to be engaged with fully, robustly and honestly to aid genuine, two-way processes of citizenship (Blunkett, 2004). In fact, the then Home Secretary David Blunkett (2004), in a speech exploring the government's explicit linking of community cohesion with its wider race equality goals in their overarching policy agenda (Home Office, 2005), specifically repudiated the charge of assimilationism. On this basis, a fairer analysis of the post-2001 move towards community cohesion would be that it is a fundamental reconsideration of the meaning and implications of 'multiculturalism' in Britain, and, arguably, a repudiation of the particular *form* of multiculturalism dominant over the preceding two decades, 'political multiculturalism' or 'anti-racism' (Cantle, 2005; Solomos, 2003). That enhanced policy version of multiculturalism was first developed by left-wing local authorities, such as the Greater London Council, from the early 1980s onwards (Williams, 1988), reflecting a groundswell of demands for stronger and more meaningful action against racism and stark ethnic inequalities (Solomos, 2003). This reality emphasises the fact that, rather than being imposed from above by national government dictat, multiculturalism in Britain largely developed dialectically through struggle and practice at the local level (Bourne, 2007), so helping to explain the significant political reaction to the change of tone and emphasis represented by community cohesion. Such approaches of political multiculturalism were gradually taken up by successive national governments, under the prompting of bodies like the CRE, with the decision to include a question on ethnic identity in the 1991 national census generating data on ethnic difference in all aspects of life that inevitably sped further policy responses that continue today, such as the aim of reducing employment and educational achievement gaps between different ethnic groups. Despite the criticisms made here and elsewhere (Cantle, 2005; Malik, 2009) of some of the unintended impacts of these anti-racist policies, it should be acknowledged that such policies have made a significant impact to the reduction both of ethnic inequalities and racial tensions in Britain in the past 30 years, with such policies characterised as 'ethnic and racial minorities requiring state support and differential treatment to overcome distinctive barriers in their exercise of citizenship' (Meer and Modood, 2009: 479). This approach of anti-racism is discussed below, within consideration of the broader context of how multiculturalism has been understood and practised in Britain.

In Britain, despite claims (Bourne, 2007) that it is a comparatively recent policy approach, multiculturalism can be seen as a move towards pluralist integration from the late 1960s onwards, in the wake of acceptance that assimilationism had not succeeded in producing an integrated, harmonious society (Solomos, 1988). This move included the progressive strengthening of the national race discrimination legislation that culminated in the 1976 Race Relations Act that legally recognised and protected difference in service provision and in the workplace. Admittedly, these measures were also accompanied by increasing restrictions on non-white immigration to Britain, a necessary counterbalancing measure, according to political orthodoxy (Solomos, 2003). Despite that, the actual term 'multiculturalism' was rarely used outside of educational circles, with race relations (Solomos, 2003) a more common term for this pluralist social policy approach. Following the watershed 1981 urban disturbances (Scarman, 1981), anti-racism or equal opportunities became dominant terms, although they arguably represent the operationalisation of a particular type of multiculturalism (Cantle, 2005; Thomas, 2007b), and it is argued here that it is that particular phase of multiculturalism that is re-thought by community cohesion, rather than multiculturalism per se.

It is impossible to compare community cohesion and multiculturalism without a clearer focus on different understandings and possible meanings of multiculturalism (Modood, 2005; Parekh, 2006; Watson, 2000) in relation to Britain's multi-ethnic society. Whilst all supporters of multiculturalism believe that policy should acknowledge, support and ensure equality for different ethnicities, faiths and traditions in society, differences emerge between those who believe that such policies should revolve around the needs and claims of what they identify as strong, distinct and homogenous communities or groups (Parekh, 2006) and 'those who see such accounts as involving an overly essentialist analysis of identity' (Wetherell, 2008: 314). The former perspective was largely represented by the Commission on the Future of Multi-Ethnic Britain (CFMEB, 2000), which portrayed Britain as a 'community of communities', whilst accepting that 'there should be considerable inter-dependence and overlap within and between the various communities that constitute a society, and that these dynamic realities should be welcomed and protected' (2000: 43). Community cohesion (Cantle, 2001, 2005) arguably suggests that the policies of the two decades prior to 2001 had focused too much on these individual communities rather than the overlap between them, with this approach actually hardening those separate identities for some (Malik, 2009). Sen (2006) suggests that, in reality, Britain's pre-2001 multiculturalism was actually a system of 'plural monoculturalism', with each separate ethnic group encouraged to go its own way whilst not breaking the law. Here, there is real concern that the privileging of essentialised ethnic communities can fail to recognise the complexity and multiplicity of individual identity, and lead to the intra-community policing of individuals, especially women, who fail to obey the norms of such 'communities' (Cantle, 2005). Such social realities, and the increasingly 'hybrid' experiences of young Britons, led Gilroy (2004) to question whether 'groups' have any real role to play in further development towards what he terms 'convivial cosmopolitanism'. Modood (2005) identifies five positions on state responses to identity in society ranging from the individual republican citizenship of France to different multiculturalist-influenced approaches to diversity. The approach he favours as a constructive solution to these tensions between specific group loyalty, individual autonomy and integration to the larger community within multiculturalist approaches is what he terms the 'plural state', which is:

> able to offer an emotional identity with the whole to counterbalance the emotional loyalties to ethnic and religious communities, which should prevent the fragmentation of society into narrow, selfish communalisms, while the presence of these strong community identities will be an effective check against monocultural statism.
>
> (Modood, 2005: 149)

Proponents see multiculturalism as founded on an implicit egalitarianism, so exposing the essential naivety of the concept in relation to the reality of power structures for many radical critics (Chauhan, 1990). This traditional understanding of multiculturalism is a liberal concept that allows for and indeed celebrates the co-existence of several cultures within an identifiable greater society. The 'melting pot' analogy of many cultures boiling down to a new, distinctive culture provided a narrative for the development of the modern United States, with this gradually giving way to the 'salad bowl' concept that sees cultures retain their distinctiveness but produces a whole which is something unique and recognisable (Watson, 2000). This can be seen as a contrast to the 'coercive assimilation' of some European states, most notably France, discussed in Chapter 2. This position privileges personal autonomy over group identity, and assumes a neutral, non-ethnic state acting for the good of the greatest number. Inherent is an opposition to the notion of 'group rights' as culturally relativist, with all the dangers to collective cohesion and individual liberty that may come in the wake of such relativism (Watson, 2000). Clearly, this republican assimilationist perspective takes national homogeneity and culture as a given within individual states, so begging obvious questions around the arbitrary and often artificial creation of 'national' identity (Anderson, 1991; Winder, 2004), as well as making assumptions around the reality of 'equality' and 'fraternity' for all citizens, regardless of their ethnic background or skin colour.

The acceptance from the late 1960s onwards of the need to counter and outlaw racial discrimination was a decisive turning point within Britain, and a key stage in the move from assimilationism towards multiculturalism. It also led to attempts to 'promote good race relations' (Cantle, 2005), and 'multicultural education', sincere attempts to learn from each other's cultures and beliefs, and to encourage acceptance of diverse ways of living, whilst still holding on to shared laws and norms (Popple, 1997). However, anti-racist critics (Chauhan, 1990) saw this approach as hopelessly naive and individualist, based on the belief that racism is about individual prejudice and ignorance, which can be removed through education and direct contact with 'others'. Such critics are particularly scathing of the resulting approaches to education and young people (Chauhan, 1990), with multiculturalism understood here as a process of essentialising and reifying fixed and simplistic notions of separate ethnic 'cultures'. Arguably, this concept of multiculturalism comes close to the belief in irreconcilable cultural differences held by 'new right', arguably 'racist', thinkers (Gilroy, 2002; May, 2002). This approach of multiculturalist education failed both to address the racism experienced by ethnic minorities and to confront the racist prejudices and actions of individual white people and white-dominated power structures in society (Popple, 1997; Solomos, 2003). The individualist assumptions here within multiculturalism as then deployed took no account of historical patterns and power structures of racism, whilst the cultural sharing central to multiculturalism was often one-sided:

Culture came to mean Black cultures and implicit in learning about these cultures was the idea that they were different from the norm, that they were inferior in comparison to white British cultures.

(Bhavnani, 2001: 76)

Allied to this was a total failure to challenge normative understandings of 'whiteness' (Bhavnani, 2001; Bonnett, 2000). In light of such critiques, many of the community cohesion recommendations relating to education and communities, such as school-twinning and joint parental activities (Cantle, 2001, rec. 5.8.12), and the perceived need for ethnically mixed schools, might be seen as a new phase of hopeful, liberal multiculturalism which does not engage with the power realities of racism and poverty (Kalra and Kapoor, 2009). At the heart of the anti-racism which developed in the wake of 1981 urban disturbances was a critique of multiculturalism as having no understandings of these structural and historical realities (Gilroy, 2002; Sivanandan, 1981), with anti-racists seeing racism not as the aberration of prejudiced individuals, but as the product of, and justification for, white Western domination and exploitation of non-Western countries during the imperial age, the patterns and structures of which still dominate our world, and which shape any 'cultures'.

These debates highlight what has often been seen as a profound dichotomy between multiculturalism and anti-racism. However, the relationship between the two concepts, both in theory and practice, has been much messier and more complicated (Bhavnani, 2001; Bonnett, 2000). Arguably, anti-racism has accepted and utilised concepts of 'race' just as uncritically as multiculturalism, with ethnically essentialised and reified understandings of identity deployed to both provide a historical narrative and to explain modern power relationships within society (Bonnett, 2000; Gunaratnam, 2003; Winder, 2004). The starkness and simplicity of this social and political analysis was demonstrated during the operationalisation of anti-racist policies, which often portrayed 'racism' as the sole preserve of white people because they apparently all had power *and* prejudices, unlike any non-white people (Sivanandan, 2001). By offering such a simplistic analysis, anti-racism can deny any notion of agency, or of negotiation, in the creation of identity and experience, just as simplistic multiculturalism has, with both essentialising notions of ethnic identity (Bhavnani, 2001).

From this perspective, the post-1981 policy approach of anti-racism built on multiculturalism's acceptance of diversity, but lost interest in developing commonality through contact and dialogue at the expense of promoting equality for each separate, essentialised ethnic group

(Cantle, 2005). Despite the accusation (Chauhan, 1990; Solomos, 1988) that multiculturalism essentialised ethnic cultures, direct dialogue and contact, albeit on a liberal basis, was and is central to multiculturalism (Hesse, 2000), but this was lost under the new post-1981 phase of political multiculturalism or anti-racism. Competing critiques from anti-racists and from the right squeezed multiculturalism as a policy concept, but it did become part of the common sense of British life for many people (Gilroy, 2004; Hesse, 2000).

Arguably, since 2001 community cohesion has both provoked and enabled a renewed public debate around the meaning and practice of multiculturalism. Inevitably, this has been framed to a considerable degree by the wider political events of 9/11, the 7/7 bombings, the 'war on terror' and the invasion of Iraq, but this debate around the continued appropriacy and meaning of multiculturalism as a policy approach was clearly underway in Britain even before the 2001 disturbances (CFMEB, 2000). Much of this debate has characterised multiculturalism as a neg-ative, threatening collective identity and solidarity (Goodhart, 2004; Phillips, 2005). A highly influential essay juxtaposed solidarity/sharing with diversity, raising issues of what should be the acceptable limits to pluralist diversity within a society that has any pretence to cohesion, mutual obligation and social capital (Goodhart, 2004). This perspective draws on research suggesting too rapid a change in the ethnic make-up of areas can threaten cohesion, and the mutual solidarity that under-pins welfare systems (Putnam, 2000). This perspective echoes Gidden's (1998) view that multiculturalism depends much more on the major-ity's sense of 'fairness' than is commonly supposed, and that, in an age of profound transition, we have to find new ways of generating solidar-ity. In a more ethnically diverse Britain, it is inevitable that that the glue of ethnicity has been, and has to be replaced with the glue of 'values', common ways of thinking and behaving:

> If we can take for granted a limited set of common values and assumptions ... but as Britain becomes more diverse, that common culture is being eroded.
>
> (Goodhart, 2004: 2)

Relevant here is the relatively high level, and increasingly diverse nature of the inward migration to Britain from the late 1990s onwards. This has included high levels of 'white' immigration from the Eastern European countries joining the enlarged European Community, so arguably exposing the simplistic black/white assumptions of past anti-racist policy approaches (Solomos, 2003). Post-2001 attempts by senior New Labour government figures, such as Gordon Brown and David Blunkett, to debate and promote a new, forward-looking, notion of 'Britishness' (Perryman, 2008) can be seen in this light. Whilst clumsy and top-down, they arguably recognised the need to recast understandings of national and local community and solidarity, with community cohesion central to broader policy thinking here (McGhee, 2005, 2006). Inevitably, though, such public debate about what it means to be 'British' has strayed dangerously close to cliché, with the debate provoking further concern around 'assimilation' for some (Alexander, 2007), who see the very idea of one conception of 'British values' as profoundly out of step with Britain's tradition of *not* defining an 'official' national identity:

> Britishness is, to me, an overarching political and legal concept: it signifies allegiance to the laws, government and broad moral and political concepts – like tolerance and freedom of expression – that hold the United Kingdom together. But there is no overall British culture, only a sharing of cultures.
>
> (Bernard Crick, *Guardian*, 12 April 2004)

Whilst initially hostile to questioning of multiculturalism (Goodhart, 2004), CRE (now the Equality and Human Rights Commission (EHRC)) Chief Trevor Phillips subsequently claimed that 'separateness' is over, and that it is time to discover the nation's belief in 'core British values' (2004b: 24). This re-think was extended in the wake of the 7/7 bombings of July 2005, when Phillips claimed that Britain was 'sleep-walking to segregation', and urgently called for the promotion of a unifying Britishness: 'we need a kind of integration that binds us together without stifling us' (Phillips, 2005: 10). This segregation was squarely blamed on 'multiculturalism', although the policies and approaches negatively characterised as such were clearly what is popularly known as anti-racism and equal opportunities. This belief that the post-1981 phase of political multiculturalism known as anti-racism had focused too much on the separateness of essentialised ethnic groups rather than on common needs and identity was shared across a surprisingly wide political spectrum (Cantle, 2005; Goodhart, 2004; Phillips, 2005; Sivanandan, 2004), suggesting that even if the term community cohesion was viewed negatively, its analysis is significantly accepted.

Underpinning these debates is a concern over how national, local and ethnic identities can all be managed and accommodated within a rapidly changing society (DCLG, 2007a). Arguably, the debates outlined here are all part of the coming to terms with the post-colonial and increasingly 'racialised' reality of Britain (Hall, 2000). Here, the 'imagined community' (Anderson, 1991) signified by 'British' is in urgent need of debate and re-working following profound social and economic changes, and the contested nature of multiculturalism is its value (Hall, 2000). Inherent here is the need for more open dialogue between communities, and less uncritical acceptance of identity claims by each 'community'. The notion of 'community' for ethnic minorities in Britain actually covers a wide variety of practices; whilst some ethnic minorities are deeply committed to 'tradition', for others traditional identification has been transformed by being intensified (for instance, radical Islam in the face of global political events and domestic exclusion), and for others hybridisation is advanced, but not in an assimilationist sense (Hall, 2000). Here, multiple identities are increasingly part of the reality of British life, and from this perspective, the identity positions and choices within communities are more political than anthropological, with 'traditional' cultural practices operating alongside interaction with (hybridising) mainstream culture (Hall, 2000: 220).

For some post-modern commentators, 'hybridity' or 'convivial cosmopolitanism' (Gilroy, 2004) is an unstoppable and inevitable feature of British life (Hall, 2000), and community cohesion is concerned with enabling that, but, for others, this view of dynamic multicultural, metropolitan life seems a long way from the realities of life in Oldham, Burnley and Bradford (Kalra, 2002). Many post-modernists expect youth culture to become increasingly hybrid, diverse and, hence, non-racist and less contingent, but 'hybridity' theorists may be underestimating the persistence and value of 'rooted' identities. Instead, globalisation and de-industrialisation may actually be leading to a retreat into essentialist and singular identities, a reaction to the rapid social change and greatly increased economic uncertainty which necessarily provides the conditions for the 'cultural hybridity' of those lucky enough to be the 'winners' in the global economy (May, 1999b). Other commentators go further here:

> One consequence of the new industrial, urban and cultural transformation is a disembedding of traditions and a collapse of employment and other infrastructures, and feelings of rootlessness, generating anxieties which become exploited and mobilized around endless searches for 'roots' and projects of racialised nationalism.
>
> (Rattansi, 1999: 90)

From this perspective, it is no coincidence that pockets of the most virulent white nationalism and racism, and most defensive and insular ethnic minority communities that can produce religious-based extremism, can be found in towns like Oldham, Burnley and Bradford that have been de-industrialised and which have yet to see the development of viable, post-industrial economies (Byrne, 1999; Kundnani, 2001). Whilst not an assimilationist agenda (Solomos, 2003), there is a clear tension within the community cohesion discourse over the relationship between separate, ethnically specific experiences and lives, and overarching beliefs, behaviours and values. Can community cohesion allow, guarantee the right to, and even celebrate, genuine difference, while building stronger and more genuine cohesion and 'Britishness'? (Amin, 2003).

One critique of community cohesion is that it includes an 'uneasy trade-off' between diversity and shared values, with diversity managed rather than celebrated (Alexander, 2004). The idea that Britain pre-2001 was 'celebrating diversity' seems at odds with the reality of many 'multicultural' areas (Ouseley, 2001), while the 'diversity' and 'pluralism' concerning Alexander and Amin is that between distinct and, for this author, essentialised ethnic groups. It is suggested here that in promoting stronger shared identities, community cohesion hopes for, or even requires, separate ethnic and faith identities to weaken and loosen somewhat in greater recognition of diversity and complexity:

> For New Labour, shared values are to be found in the process of all groups undergoing transformation. In this dream of a new Britain, no one (or no group) is allowed to remain in place.
>
> (McGhee, 2005: 167)

Arguably, ethnic essentialism shows little regard for the complex, negotiated and contingent identities of the individuals and groups under discussion, even if ethnicity is overwhelmingly the creator of their conscious self-image:

> It may be growing with increasing unease if the passing away of what at one time seemed to be a necessary fiction. Namely, that ... all black people are *the same* (emphasis in original).
>
> (Hall, 1992: 254)

That position enabled Hall (2000) to recognise that the challenge for British multiculturalism now is the balancing of group rights and individual self-determination and identification. Here, the 'trade-off' (Alexander, 2004) is actually an overdue and open recognition of the complexity of experience within multicultural Britain, and government's attempts to create a citizenship based on more complex and fluid identities (McGhee, 2006) involve a fine but necessary balancing act (May, 2002).

However, in its emphasis in 'border crossing' (Modood and Werbner, 1997) and 'transruptions' (Hesse, 2000), even advocates of 'hybridity' assume distinct and established ethnicities as a precursor for such processes. Furthermore, it assumes that sites and channels for 'border crossing' are available, a prerequisite that arguably only partially applies to Oldham and other de-industrialised towns and cities (Cantle, 2001; Ritchie, 2001). This stark and tense racial segregation seems, and often is, a long way from 'convivial cosmopolitanism' (Gilroy, 2004), but, arguably, there is a necessity of such a cosmopolitan outlook becoming the norm if Britain is to face up peacefully and cohesively to future economic and social challenges, including the reduction of internal inequality and exclusion (Giddens, 1998).

Here, the concept of 'critical multiculturalism' (May, 1999a) may be helpful, and it certainly matches the changes in work with young people in Oldham and other racially segregated towns and cities, as described by respondents in the following chapters. 'Critical multiculturalism' attempts to address the tension between ethnicity and other identity factors in peoples' lives which underlie debates over community cohesion, anti-racism and multiculturalism, drawing on Bourdieu's concept of 'habitus'. This is arguably helpful, as it covers all the social and cultural experiences that shape us as a person, and suggests a 'critical multiculturalism' (May, 1999a) that directly addresses racism, but which also avoids reification of culture and the essentialising of ethnic difference. Particularly in relation to educational work with young people, this can be described as a critical pedagogy drawing on Freire and Giroux to create a radical, anti-racist conception of multiculturalism that avoids reductionism, and which takes account of profound economic changes:

> Critical multiculturalism, as it is broadly articulated here, incorporates post-modern conceptions and analyses of culture and identity, while holding on to the possibility of an emancipatory politics.
> (May, 1999a: 7–8)

Rattansi (1999) prefers 'reflexive multiculturalism', seeing 'critical' as unnecessarily polarising and binary, with the potential to reproduce the sterile multiculturalism/anti-racism debate. Arguably, Britain's community cohesion discourse has been edging in such a contingent and non-essentialising direction (McGhee, 2005). Underpinning this is a 'differentiated universalism', an other friendly citizenship grounded in difference. Within this, ethnic/cultural boundaries will remain in place, but they 'Must be flexible and, importantly, open to change' (McGhee, 2005: 163). Here, the community cohesion discourse represents the replacement of the old 'politics of identity' with the 'politics of difference'. The former took identities, including dominant white, male, heterosexual ones, as read, whereas the latter challenges them and questions them. In that way, community cohesion marks a significant change in policy direction from previous approaches of multiculturalism and anti-racism. Here, a 'cosmopolitan citizenship' is being privileged over other, defining characteristics:

> It is dialogue between diverse cultural groups that is at the very heart of cosmopolitan citizenship.

> (McGhee, 2005: 173)

This contains the clear suggestion that dialogue changes perceptions and understandings. Direct contact and dialogue is clearly at the heart of community cohesion activity (Home Office, 2003a), with advocates (Cantle, 2005) stressing such contact as the only way to overcome the 'parallel lives' of ethnic segregation that have been re-enforced by the post-1981 policy assumptions and priorities. This perspective suggests that direct contact and dialogue across ethnic divides can enable individuals and communities to develop 'bridging' social capital (Putnam, 2000), and to so use their agency to challenge existing divisions and limitations. For such approaches to direct contact to be successful, the lessons of 'contact theory' (Hewstone et al., 2007) need to be learnt. This social psychology-based understanding of prejudice reduction (Brown, 1995) suggests that for contact between distinct, antagonistic and fearful communities to be successful, it has to be engaged in voluntarily, it has to be over time, and it has to be conducted in groups, both to ensure safety and to avoid the trap of 'I'm all right but...'. Unsurprisingly, many of these 'contact theory' lessons for towns like Oldham come from Northern Ireland (Hewstone et al., 2007). Critics of community cohesion suggest that voluntary contact activities, through youth activities of the type discussed in Chapter 4, and parallel 'twinning' activities between schools with different ethnic populations (Cantle, 2001), have been encouraged because New Labour lacked the political will to tackle the fundamental ethnic segregation issues of housing and school allocation (Kalra, 2002), but the evidence from attempts to force the creation of 'socially (that is, class) mixed' housing areas is negative, with much more positive evidence from initiatives promoting voluntary contact and cooperation between social (rented, low income) and owner-occupied (middle income) housing areas (Robinson, 2005). Such an approach of voluntary, group-based contact work suggests what has been described as 'transversal politics' (Yuval-Davis, 1997), safe situations where people can come together and which allow a 'rooting and shifting' of identities, a re-thinking of prejudices and assumptions towards others because one's own identity is not being threatened or demeaned.

Implicit in such processes is the suggestion that over time they would lead to 'cooler', more complex and cosmopolitan understandings of identity by all concerned (McGhee, 2005, 2006). Here, an overarching 'human rights' framework is being developed that recognises diversity of *all* kinds, but which also insists on universal adherence to 'core' values whereby religious/ethnic 'identity' cannot be allowed to supersede fundamental individual rights. In an increasingly complex and 'hybrid' (Hall, 2000) Britain, community cohesion is part of attempts to create 'cooler', de-centred and intersectional forms of identity, rather than (inevitably conflictual) 'hot' forms of identity (McGhee, 2006). The concept of intersectionality suggests that the reality of, and the interplay between, different forms of identity for individuals must be considered, with implicit conclusion being that no one of those identities can or should be seen as dominant or as simplistically determining the experiences or lived realities of individuals. Here, progress towards genuine multiculturalism can only be made if *all* forms of identity are given weight and respect by policy and its implementation, with the rights and access to equality of gay and lesbian people, or women of all ethnic backgrounds being just as valid and important as the rights and equality of ethnicity, faith or class-based 'communities'. This suggests that *all* backgrounds and identities need to be willing to adapt their assumptions and behaviour to accept the legitimacy and diversity of individual preference and of the resulting complexity of identity within local and national society, and that the Labour government was quite consistent in amalgamating the separate equality bodies like the CRE, the Disability Rights Commission and the gender-focused Equal Rights Commission into the singular, overarching EHRC to reflect the reality of multiple identities and experiences and the complex interplay between different forms of identity and experience, an approach confirmed by later policy pronouncements (DCLG, 2009c).

Conclusion

Whilst community cohesion has been explicit in its criticism of the unintended impacts and effects of the post-1981 policy approaches of anti-racism or equal opportunities (Cantle, 2001, 2005), it is less clear whether this post-2001 emergence of community cohesion as a national policy priority represents a repudiation of multiculturalism itself. For critics, the clear rejection of the title and language of multiculturalism, and the emphasis on shared values and common identities, such as Britishness, rather than the previous stress on difference is proof in itself of the 'death of multiculturalism' (Kundnani, 2002). A partial reading of the sections of the community cohesion reports that overtly question the continuation of certain linguistic and cultural practices within Asian communities might be cited as supportive evidence here, with community cohesion's concern with agency, responsibility and problematic social capital possibly being a one-sided and racialised critique. Such a perspective has been apparently confirmed by overt attacks on multiculturalism itself (Goodhart, 2004), including from equality campaigners (Phillips, 2005). However, this chapter has argued that charges of community cohesion as a return to assimilationism are not supportable, and are not borne out by significant sections of the community cohesion reports, or by wider New Labour government policies aimed at tackling social and ethnic inequalities. Therefore, it is suggested here that community cohesion is more a critique of particular forms of multiculturalism policy formation and operation that have focused exclusively on the needs, identities and concerns of each separate ethnic group without consideration of relations, links and experiences shared between those groups. Here, community cohesion might be seen as a re-balancing of multiculturalist policy approaches to reflect both the need for a greater stress on commonality and integration, and the way individual agency is increasingly used to interpret and express 'identity' (Meer and Modood, 2009). This proposition is explored further in Chapter 4 by drawing on empirical evidence as to how community cohesion has actually been understood and implemented at the local level in work with young people.

4
Myths and Realities: Community Cohesion in Practice

Introduction

Chapter 1 outlined the emergence of community cohesion as a post-2001 British policy priority around the area of 'race relations', detailing the key themes and concerns of this new agenda. What community cohesion stands for and is trying to achieve is highly contested, as the debates analysed in Chapter 3 make clear. Most academic analysis of community cohesion has been negative, with its key themes and concerns understood by critics as representing a lurch backwards to the coercive assimilationism of the 1960s (Back et al., 2002), as a racialised blaming of the cultures and values of Asian communities for deeper structural economic and social issues (Alexander, 2004, 2007), and as an outright rejection both of the reality of ethnic difference in society and of the need to address the inequalities and conflicts associated with it (Kundnani, 2002, 2007). Some of this criticism is understandable, as it is clear that community cohesion has represented a profound shift in the language, tone and stated priorities of government's policy approach, with community cohesion itself being a term that has emerged from nowhere (Robinson, 2005). A selective reading of some parts of the national (Cantle, 2001; Denham, 2001) and local (Calrke, 2001; Ouseley, 2001; Ritchie, 2001) community cohesion reports, and some ministerial pronouncements upon their publication, could indeed support an analysis of a reactionary and racialised step backwards on a profoundly important policy issue, the stakes of which had been illustrated by the violent disturbances in Oldham, Burnley and Bradford during the summer of 2001.

However, these criticisms of the meaning and intent of community cohesion, even the most thoughtful and nuanced ones (McGhee, 2003,

2005, 2008), have been almost entirely evidence-free, with virtually no empirical data on how community cohesion has been understood, implemented and measured on the ground being produced since 2001, and the empirical data that has been produced (Thomas, 2006, 2007a) often ignored by critics. The intention of this chapter, and one of the key aims of this book, is to contribute to redressing this balance. It does this firstly by providing a focus on how national government has gone about operationalising community cohesion, and the directions it has hence indicated. It then goes on to examine in-depth, empirical evidence from Oldham as to how youth workers have understood and implemented community cohesion since 2001, supported by data from young people in Oldham and Rochdale on their actual experiences of ethnic division and cohesion in their lives. This enables the chapter to suggest some of the key theoretical concepts and approaches underlying this community cohesion practice in Oldham. In focusing on data from a geographical case study, the chapter is well aware that the challenges of cohesion and integration are often very specific to particular geographical areas (DCLG, 2007a), and that policy approaches to race relations and ethnic diversity have always been 'worked out' at the local level (Kalra and Kapoor, 2009). Therefore, in using this empirical data, the chapter makes no claims that this represents the uniform picture of community cohesion practice nationally. Rather, this data illustrates what some of the key themes and concerns outlined in Chapter 1 could and do look like when energetically pursued by local policy-makers and practitioners, and, so, what community cohesion nationally has the potential to represent and to be in relation to work with communities in general and young people in particular.

National responses

Consistent with their approaches to wider social policies, such as the social exclusion priorities (Levitas, 2005) of reducing levels of school truancy, teenage pregnancy and the number of young people Not in Education, Employment or Training (NEET) (SEU, 1999), New Labour's approach to community cohesion was to point directions and require measurement by targets set nationally, but to encourage local decision-making over methods and priorities, a classic 'third way' (Giddens, 1998) approach to policy development:

> Community cohesion lies at the heart of what makes a safe and strong community. It must be delivered locally through creating

strong community networks, based on principles of trust and respect for local diversity, and nurturing a sense of belonging and confidence in local people.

(LGA, 2004)

The inherent tension of community cohesion here around locally interpreted implementation of an imposed national agenda was subsequently replicated on a much larger scale in the PVE agenda (DCLG, 2007b), as Chapter 8 explores. The 'Pathfinder' process of pilot cohesion work (Home Office, 2003a, 2004) commenced in April 2003, involving 14 local authority areas, funded by the Home Office and the Neighbourhood Renewal Unit of the Office of the Deputy Prime Minister, with the latter representing a clear link to the government's wider social exclusion programme. Funded Pathfinders included the areas of Leicester and west London previously praised by Cantle (2001) for their good race relations, whilst the unfunded 'Shadow Pathfinder' areas, who were allowed to participate in national discussion events, included Bradford and Oldham, suggesting that government was keen to avoid the accusation made after the urban riots of the 1980s (Solomos, 2003) that rioting effectively brought government investment.

The fact that those funded included areas with comparatively small non-white populations, including Middlesbrough that faced high levels of social exclusion, and Peterborough that faced significant (white) immigration from abroad, hinted at broader understandings of the scope and remit of community cohesion, which are explored further below through the use of empirical evidence. Whilst clearly focused on 'race relations' issues primarily, something confirmed in the government's later foregrounding of it within their race equality strategy (DCLG, 2009a; Home Office, 2005, 2007), and including further development of inter-faith dialogue and combating racial harassment work that challenges notions of a retreat to assimilationism, the 'Pathfinder' work also included a focus on intergenerational dialogue (often within monocultural communities), or on tensions between settled and travelling communities: 'the programme outputs are similarly varied, tackling the gap between youth and age, interfaith and intergenerational tensions, and gender differences. What binds these apparently disparate programmes together is the common objective of breaking down barriers between and within communities' (Home Office, 2003a: 1).

Such a broad and varied understanding of community cohesion, allied to the newness of the term itself, has meant that local authorities and other strategic bodies have struggled for clarity over definitions and priorities. This has been addressed by government documents (DCLG, 2009a; Home Office, 2003a; LGA, 2002, 2004) that have offered guidance on devising strategies and measuring impact, with the latter focus becoming more integral over time through regular 'Best Value' and Citizenship surveys aiming to measure perceptions of how 'different sorts of people get on round here', and the resulting data guiding attempts to address local 'hotspots' of tension. Clearly, such survey data relies on public perceptions and the state of taken for granted assumptions within particular communities, something not necessarily the same as the factual realities around trends in ethnic residential patterns (Finney and Simpson, 2009), or the facts of which geographical areas and communities are actually benefitting the most from government spending, as Chapter 3 discussed. In 2006, community cohesion became a mandatory indicator for inclusion in the Local Area Agreements (LAA) that govern national funding for local authorities, whilst a duty to 'promote cohesion' was extended to schools and other publicly funded bodies from September 2007 (Home Office, 2007). A further progress report (DCLG, 2009a) highlighted how the responsibility on local authorities to pursue community cohesion strategies had been strengthened through Public Sector Agreement (PSA) 21: 'meaningful interaction is one of the three measures of Cohesion in the PSA' (DCLG, 2009a). Local authorities were incentivised to make progress on this area by community cohesion being included as one of the criteria for gaining the sought after 'Beacon' status for local authorities. Within this process, managing the 'integration' (DCLG, 2007a) of new migrants and so avoiding tensions with established communities became an increasingly important part of cohesion strategies, reflecting the rising immigration levels resulting from the expansion of the European Union to include countries of Eastern Europe.

Throughout this post-2001 definition and operationalisation of community cohesion, young people have been seen as key, based both on their centrality to racial tensions of the present and their pivotal role in a more peaceful and cohesive future. Cantle (2001) saw young people as central to the cross-community direct contact he advocated, with a focus on schooling and programmes of universal citizenship education (p. 30) through schools and youth projects that should be focused on real contact with other communities, whilst Denham (2001) devotes a whole section to youth services and the crucial role of youth work with the most marginalised young people to the reduction on inter-community tensions: 'Both Ouseley and Ritchie make direct links between the lack of youth facilities and involvement, particularly

of young men, in anti-social behaviour' (Denham, 2001: 15). On the local level, Ritchie (2001) saw not just the poor resourcing of youth work in Oldham pre-2001 as causal to the disturbances but the approach of the work that had been taking place, with more formal, project-based work being prioritised over traditional 'youth club' approaches that successfully diverted marginalised young people away from trouble on the streets in the past. Just as he called for a re-think about the catchment areas and ethnic make-up of schools, Ritchie therefore called for youth work with young people to be re-prioritised to reflect the themes and concerns of community cohesion. Guidance of how community cohesion can be implemented (LGA, 2002, 2004) took this perspective on, highlighting the pivotal role of work with young people in general and youth work in particular: 'The quality and quantity of youth service provision is an important component in building community cohesion' (LGA, 2002: 23). However, in the only other youth work-based empirical survey of work on community cohesion prior to the empirical data discussed below, and what remains one of the very few empirical studies of community cohesion practice in general, a small-scale investigation of how an unnamed local authority youth service and its partners in south-east England were implementing community cohesion (Green and Pinto, 2005) found little or no progress and much confusion over cohesion. The picture painted was of under-resourced youth agencies being asked to take on an extra responsibility which they did not really understand:

> The majority of youth service staff had heard of the term, but had only a vague understanding, and were unclear of its distinction from other concepts such as social inclusion, community development and equal opportunities.
>
> (Green and Pinto, 2005: 54)

That research questioned the government's approach to the implementation of community cohesion, based on the confused and limited practice they saw, but the authors also acknowledged that 'there is a crucial need to address the lack of empirical research within the practical application of community cohesion policies' (Green and Pinto, 2005: 58). The remainder of this chapter aims to address that continuing evidential deficit around the implementation of community cohesion policies by drawing on empirical evidence around how youth work agencies in Oldham have understood and operationalised community cohesion, alongside data on how young people in Oldham and Rochdale experience ethnic segregation and cohesion.

Community cohesion in practice

The research data discussed below comes primarily from an in-depth study of how youth workers and their agencies in Oldham have understood and operationalised community cohesion. The choice of Oldham as the focus for this research obviously reflected the town's experience of rioting in 2001 and its subsequent role in the emergence of the new policy priority of community cohesion. Having identified above that the issues and solutions within community cohesion are apparently very local and particular (DCLG, 2007a; McGhee, 2008), this evidence does not claim to be nationally representative, but it can be indicative of the content and issues of community cohesion implementation. Similarly, evidence from young people in Oldham and Rochdale on their experiences of segregation and cohesion can be seen as indicative of wider national issues and realities, whilst being fully aware of the dangers of over-generalising around 'race' issues on the basis of quite specific and localised conditions (Bagguley and Hussain, 2008). The sections below start by examining how youth workers have understood, and the extent to which they support, the meaning and concerns of community cohesion, and compares this to young peoples' self-reported experiences and perspectives. It then examines in detail the changes to the assumptions, priorities and content of youth work professional practice with young people in the name of community cohesion, discussing this around key themes of meaningful direct contact, informality, working across ethnic boundaries and agency. The chapter then goes on to explore how we might understand this data, identifying key theoretical concepts that help to explain what this localised practice represents and what it suggests about the possibilities of and for community cohesion practice nationally.

What community cohesion represents

A very clear consensus quickly emerged amongst respondents around the definition of 'community cohesion' as being about 'meaningful direct contact', a finding in stark counterpart to the findings of Green and Pinto (2005). The emphasis of Cantle (2001) and Ritchie (2001) on the need for contact and dialogue across ethnic divides as a means of developing mutual respect and shared values beyond the cul-de-sac of 'parallel lives' had clear resonance for all the youth workers surveyed. Practitioners of all ethnic backgrounds accepted the analysis of an ethnically segregated town, and that all communities needed to do more to bridge divides. Respondents tended to be critical of their 'own' ethnic community or backgrounds here, rather than of others. Iqbal, a Pakistani-origin voluntary sector worker, explicitly blamed what he categorised as the insularity of the 'first' generation of Asian settlers, seeing them as focused solely on employment and economic security:

> Young people are not at fault because our parents have never mixed. So, the relationship hasn't been passed on, interaction at such a young age hasn't been experienced by these young people.

David was one of a number of white-origin workers who saw the racism and 'white flight' (Cantle, 2005; Kundnani, 2001) of the white community as more of a problem:

> My feeling about Oldham would be that a section of the white community has ... you have the feeling of people who are resentful about life ... it's almost a sense of loss of purpose and values.

This acceptance of agency, and its currently negative use by some individuals and communities, may be seen as evidence of the liberal assumptions of 'welfarist' youth work (Jeffs and Smith, 1988), but it can also be seen as shedding light on the gap between reality and the evidence-free academic discourse around community cohesion.

For the youth workers surveyed, community cohesion means *meaningful* direct contact and work between young people of different ethnic backgrounds. Asad, a Bangladeshi-origin full-time Oldham Youth Service (OYS) Area Manager running youth work provision in a mainly Bangladeshi area, defined it as:

> Building relationships, friendships and knowing what other cultures, other religions are doing and why, and understanding each other.

Stacey, an African-Caribbean origin OYS part-time worker studying for her professional qualification, commented that: 'You've got to mix to learn – if you don't mix, you aren't learning anything.'

For Johnson, a full-time OYS Area Manager for a largely Asian area, this direct contact has a clear focus on commonality:

> For me, you're bringing young people together, you're highlighting that they've got a common interest, that they're young, they experience the same things as in poverty, crime, whatever ... highlighting that the things that happen to them do happen to other people.

Whether this community cohesion 'direct contact' should simply focus on ethnic/racial differences alone, or also on much wider social differences of territory, class and geography provoked much more debate amongst respondents. Deborah, the white-origin OYS Participation and Empowerment Officer, describes this wider social understanding of community cohesion well:

> To me community cohesion is more about young and old, different races, different areas, different parts of the town, it's about wealth, it's about class, it's about all kinds of things.

To some extent these differences support the focus of Worley (2005) on the 'slippages' between 'social' and 'community' cohesion in the national discourse, but suggest that these are due much more to governmental ambiguity around how much the 2001 riots and longer-term racial tensions are simply about ethnicity, or are actually also about deeper economic changes and inequalities. For respondents supporting a wider, social understanding, this was partly an assertion of the traditional youth work professional belief that, first and foremost, young people are young people, with shared experiences and interests, rather than an amalgam of differing ethnicities, classes and genders (Davies, 2005). It was also a recognition that, in Oldham, other forms of difference and division are equally fraught and problematic. For instance, many respondents commented on the violent 'territory' (Kintrea et al., 2008) based feuding between young people from different geographical neighbourhoods, but of the same ethnic origin. Jennifer, a white origin OYS Area Manager in a white working-class area, comments that:

> There is this perception that community cohesion is about Asians and white, and them getting on together, and I think, 'well, hang on a minute.... I've got young people in X, and the idea of them mixing with young people from Y!
>
> (Both white areas)

Other respondents highlighted the extent to which intergenerational tensions are a major source of complaints about anti-social behaviour Michael, a white-origin voluntary sector youth worker, comments:

> In Branton especially, we've got a crown green bowling team where the older people are working with the kids, teaching them so they

don't wreck the bowling green . . . but, I think if you mention that, no one would give it a thought as being community cohesion.

These wider understandings of the forces and structures shaping the experiences and identities of young people in areas like Oldham are explored in more depth in the following chapter. However, there was a collective recognition that, given the events of 2001 and the current situation in the town, direct contact across ethnic and racial lines has to take precedence within community cohesion work in Oldham. This common understanding of community cohesion as meaningful direct contact between young people of different ethnic backgrounds con- tained the simultaneous recognition that the term has no meaning or recognition factor for young people. Habib, a male qualified full-time OYS worker, described a young person defining community cohesion as: 'Something you lot go on about!'. This lack of understanding of the term itself should not be seen as problematic, providing that young peo- ple understand, and agree, the purpose of direct contact work. Smith (1982) sees a key function of youth workers as breaking down complex events into parts that can be worked on, translating into meaningful, everyday language as they do so, and youth workers clearly understood that a challenge around community cohesion programmes of work was to explain its aims and content to young people and their communities in understandable, straightforward ways.

Young peoples' experiences

Contrary to the most pessimistic interpretations of 'parallel lives' and supposedly widening ethnic segregation (Phillips, 2005), the minority of young people who attended ethnically mixed high schools or col- leges across Oldham and Rochdale *did* have 'friends' of a different ethnic background, but these relationships only existed within the educational setting. The vast majority had no contact with each other outside of school, blaming the attitudes/prejudices of families and peers, fears about having to enter 'unsafe territory', and the lack of places, activi- ties and spaces that would enable young people to safely come together from a variety of ethnic and geographical backgrounds. These 'parallel lives' are leading to a significant number of young people from all eth- nic backgrounds being ignorant about each other, and having highly negative, prejudiced views about 'other' communities and individuals, as Chapters 6 and 7 explore. Clear majorities of young people from all backgrounds thought that ethnic segregation and tension are wrong and damaging, but young people were worried and pessimistic about ethnic relations and community cohesion in the future. Young peoples' evidence supported the view of the community cohesion reports (Cantle, 2001; Ritchie, 2001) produced in the wake of the 2001 disturbances that 'parallel lives' had become the norm in towns like Oldham and Rochdale:

> Because I just like stay in the streets of Oldham, I don't meet like other people, it's only like Asian people that I meet.
>
> (Asian Youth Group, Oldham)

> Q Do you have friends of a different ethnic background to you?
> A No. [From more than one].
>
> (Asian Youth Group, Oldham)

> There's hardly any Asians around here and hardly any Asians are in our school. We've got like one Asian guy in our school. I don't have a problem with them, I mean I get on with them but you know, I just don't see them.
>
> (White young person (WYP), Rochdale)

> Segregation?: That's a bad thing because then like they don't know how like English people can be and English people don't know how Asians can be.
>
> (Asian young person (AYP), Rochdale)

The impact of this significant segregation is that some young people don't see the point of trying to enable contact across ethnic divides: 'Because you don't have much things in common with them that's why' (AYP, Oldham); 'if they spoke to me I would but I wouldn't go up to them and start talking to them' (WYP, Rochdale).

   In contrast to such pessimistic views, some young people of all ethnic backgrounds reported having friends and positive acquaintances of a different ethnic background within school or college: 'We mix all right in school but don't mix outside' (AYP, Rochdale). However, because almost all of them had little or no contact with these friends of different backgrounds outside of school/college, the depth and quality of cross-ethnic friendships are very limited. There were a number of reasons for this experience being so common amongst those surveyed, one of them being the reality of physically ethnically segregated housing areas: 'They all live far away anyway, they don't live in the community that I'm from' (AYP, Oldham); 'they live kind of faraway' (AYP, Rochdale).

Another, more depressing, reason is that young people are already ruling out such possibilities, either on the grounds that differences are so great, or because of (often fully justified) security fears: 'they've never invited me and I've never thought of going myself' (AYP, Rochdale). Some of these reasons relate to fears about how family, friends and local community would react to friends of a different background visiting them. Here, peer pressure and expectations of friends is playing a crucial role: 'you talk to them [white young people] in lessons and if you see them in college hanging round you say hello. But I don't think they would like ... if they were with all of their mates you wouldn't approach them' (AYP, Rochdale).

Cultural differences and divides that have been emphasised and re-enforced by ethnic segregation are clearly part of the challenge here: 'I'm uncomfortable [about going to their houses] cos they pray' (WYP, Rochdale); 'the way they [white people] live is different to the way Asians live' (AYP, Rochdale); 'I'm not allowed out of the house, so if I want to see friends, I have to see them in school' (AYP, Rochdale).

Even this limited impact of mixed schooling is beyond the experience of some young people: 'My school, it's always been like just Asian people so never like mixed in with white people' (AYP, Oldham).

Underpinning young peoples' self-censorship over the possibilities of friends of a different background visiting them and their areas/families socially was a universal perception that 'space' in Oldham and Rochdale is racialised – that areas are 'safe' for one ethnic background, but not for another, and this issue of racialised 'territory' is explored further in Chapter 5. Clearly, this reflects the significant existing ethnic segregation within housing, and encompasses the wider reality of territory as an important factor in the lives of many young people (Kintrea et al., 2008). The next section explores how youth work practice has altered to meet the challenge of community cohesion.

Community cohesion: changed youth work professional practice

Youth work promoting 'direct contact'

The challenge for youth work in Oldham of creating this meaningful direct contact has been heightened by the reality that, prior to 2001, such contact had *not* taken place. Alex, the dual-heritage Principal Youth

Officer (PYO) of OYS, the local authority youth service, took over shortly after the 2001 disturbances, and comments that:

> They [youth workers] never even met each other, let alone worked with each other – some of them had never seen each other's areas or buildings.

Such parochialism might be seen as the downside of the community orientation of localised youth work provision. It can also partly be explained by the belief, following past professional guidelines associated with the development of anti-racist policy approaches, that ethnic minority communities needed separate, ethnic-specific provision, staffed by workers from their 'own' communities who, alone, were capable of meeting their needs, and that no good would come from attempting to bring young people of different backgrounds together. Whilst the historic case for such separate provision, in the face of stark racism and marginalisation of ethnic minorities (CRC, 1976; Davies, 1999) was strong, it had downsides, as Khan, a Pakistani-origin voluntary sector youth worker, comments:

> At one time, we didn't have a African-Caribbean centre, we didn't have a Pakistani centre, we didn't have a Bangladeshi centre, what we had was a Bankside Community and Youth Club, and that brought everyone together.

Youth work in Oldham developed direct contact community cohesion work post-2001, using a number of distinct vehicles: area-wide events, such as the annual 'Eid party' to celebrate the Muslim New Year, formalised working links between youth centres/units of different ethnic and geographical backgrounds, and the use of residential trips, joint programmes and activities to build these relationships and links. Young people who had experienced ethnic mixing and diversity through such work, or through education and training programmes, were positive about it: 'Once we started college it was completely different because we got to know so many different people from different areas and stuff, so you actually get on with them then' (AYP, Oldham). The majority of young people clearly wanted the opportunities to meet across divides and to be challenged to work at overcoming fears: 'You shouldn't just give them a lecture because they just sit there and think, you know, "shut up", instead you should stick 'em together and make 'em work together' (AYP, Oldham); 'If they get youth clubs where you can put them together and then get them to be all right with each other' (WYP, Rochdale).

> I'd love to have Indian friends, white, black friends and mixed race friends.
>
> (AYP, Oldham)

> I'd be worried about racism . . . but it would be really interesting and you'd learn lots of new stuff.
>
> (AYP, Rochdale)

Young people were also clear about the need generally for out of school activities and opportunities to engage young people and to facilitate them coming together: 'There's nothing to do for young people, there's nowhere for them to go so to keep themselves occupied they turn into gangs, groups of people, commit crimes and then they start a turf war over that . . . . You kick off because there's nothing else to do . . . . Nothing' (WYP, Rochdale). 'The way it's going now . . . communities are not getting together, things are not being done . . . there should be mixing and talking about religions and why they believe in things' (AYP, Rochdale). 'If they start putting people together at a young age I think it will help them to develop' (AYP, Oldham).

For such 'direct contact' between young people of different ethnic groups to work, certain principles need to be followed, as identified by the evidence from 'contact theory' (Hewstone et al., 2007) work to break down long-standing fears and prejudices between communities. These include ensuring that no participants feel that their backgrounds or cultures are being threatened or attacked, that contact is over time to allow genuine dialogue and understandings to develop, and that it is done in groups to avoid the danger of 'he is ok, but the rest of them . . .'. Developing cohesion work in groups also helps people to avoid feeling isolated and exposed, as a mainly Asian youth participation group from Rochdale reflected on the only white member involved in the session: 'Sometimes if you're the minority in a group you feel . . . . I don't know if this is how he feels, but sometimes he puts it across that he feels insecure around us because he's the minority isn't he?'

There was also positive support for the idea of more ethnically mixed housing areas, something already being successfully pursued in the Oldham and Rochdale areas though the Housing Market Renewal initiative, and supporting previous research amongst young adults (Phillips et al., 2008), as shown when young people were asked where they would like to live in the future: 'Build new houses and let people know that houses are being made and mixed environment…Whites and Asians' (AYP, Rochdale).

Informality

These approaches highlight a fundamental principle of the community cohesion youth work being developed in Oldham, that the direct contact has been based on association, fun and experiential activities, rather than more formal programmes of learning about diversity or 'anti-racism'. Contained within this is a stepping up of open access provision that young people can spontaneously opt in to, including purpose-built mobile units, in order to make contact with more marginalised young people out on the streets, and in direct response to the criticisms of Ritchie (2001). Asad comments about one of the regular linking events, bringing youth clubs from different areas together on the basis of fun activities:

> There was a break-dance competition. We invited Edgley [over-whelmingly white area] young people to come over, and we went to Edgley. The young people did a bit of dancing and we did see some links being made. What really impressed me was the Bangladeshi young people and the white young people took time out, not to come down to the centre, but to get the bus to Edgley and go down to the young person's house. So, that to me was a step towards community cohesion, some links made. I still see a young person from Edgley, and he says, 'how's X?, and how's Y?', and I say, 'come down', and he says, 'I will do, it's just dark, I will come down in the summer', so to me that's a step towards community cohesion.

Mark, an African-Caribbean origin OYS part-time worker, took a white group to a predominantly Asian youth club for the annual Eid party, at which every youth centre in Oldham was represented:

> Yes, it was hard getting them out of there. We had to come back for a certain time and they didn't want to leave!

These activities and events are deliberately experiential and fun, but the challenge involved for the young people taking part should not be underestimated, given the racialised reality of Oldham (Ritchie, 2001; Thomas, 2003). Johnson describes a joint residential weekend away from home and involving youth groups from the three ethnically and socially diverse youth projects linked up together on a regular basis:

> We went for an Indian meal on the first night we took them to Whitby...and one of the white lads said, 'God, if people on Thorndale knew what we were doing now, we'd get leathered', and that was just going to a restaurant...!

This story illustrates the dangers and pressures for the young people being brought together across ethnic lines in the name of community cohesion, when the communities that they come from are ethnically segregated and often have taken-for-granted prejudiced views about 'others'. The dangers of them bringing those community views in to the direct contact process means that such work could be disastrous without careful planning. The importance of planning is illustrated by the example of the annual 'Fusion' youth event. 'Fusion' involves young people from every high school in Oldham, including young people with physical and learning disabilities, taking part in a week-long programme planned and facilitated by Oldham Youth Service (now shared jointly with Rochdale Youth Service) at an out of town residential study centre. This event consists of experiential, fun activities that require young people to build relationships and to work positively together in teams, the members of whom have never met before. Alex comments of 'Fusion' that:

> Certainly, within the planning it's not up for grabs whether it's successful. It is planned with incredible detail to be successful, to make a difference with every single person in terms of their perceptions of young people from different cultural backgrounds, different genders and different geographical areas within the borough.

Mary, the white, Irish-origin Assistant Head of OYS in charge of planning 'Fusion', explains how preparation translates into the reality of the residential experience:

> It's how the staff managed the group, how the staff got young people interacting, how they bring issues in that young people would look at then or discuss. So, it's not so much the activity, it's the workers, the staff are the key for me.

This careful staff planning and preparation enables 'spontaneous', expe-riential learning around community cohesion, as Mary goes on to explain:

> We sort of set the scene, grow the seeds during the day and through the week, but once those young people start establishing relation-ships with each other, that's when a lot of the discussions were happening, and people were asking questions. For instance, one of the [Muslim] young women was praying at night, so the other girls watched her pray, and asked her really interesting questions about it. The fact was that it was done at one o' clock in the morning, and they should really have been in bed, but I didn't stop it because it was a really interesting piece of dialogue that was going on.

This creation of an environment during activities, events and residential programmes where learning that challenges previous assumptions can take place can be seen as illustrative of the hidden, informal education that is the core purpose of youth work historically (Davies, 2005; Smith, 1982). The fact that such approaches are being prioritised by youth work in Oldham in the name of community cohesion is noteworthy at a time when many perceive government agendas as having forced youth work down ever-more formal and compulsory modes of contact with young people (Mizen, 2004). A frequent accusation of informal education is that it can manipulate young people, bringing in issues without them realising, particularly around sensitive issues such as 'race'. Respon-dents refuted the charge that experiential community cohesion youth work activities are manipulating young people in this way. Rafiq, the co-originator of a voluntary sector youth work agency focused on cohe-sion issues, believes in being very clear with young people what their involvement in work programmes is all about:

> Up front, in terms of what they're going to get out of it, what are the challenges they'll face once they go back into their own communities
> ꟷꟷꟷꟷꟷꟷꟷꟷꟷꟷꟷꟷꟷꟷꟷꟷꟷꟷ

This perspective is based on previous, painful experiences of a backlash from young people and families who did not realise what 'anti-racist' youth work programmes actually involved, and found themselves in conflict with their wider communities as a result. Alex highlights how OYS believe in being entirely up front regarding the nature of community cohesion direct contact work:

> For us, quite deliberately, the Eid celebration is called 'Eid Celebration'; we don't just label it as a 'party'...Oh yes, they [young people from youth centres across the Service] knew what it was about, and that it was religious and culturally based. The organisers had taken the time to actually pick seven different quotes from the Qur'an and printed them, so that information was on each chair.

Working across ethnic boundaries: youth workers as models of 'community cohesion'

This new, post-2001, mode of community cohesion youth work practice in Oldham has been based around meaningful direct contact across ethnic lines, through traditional youth work mediums of experiential, association-based activity. It has been underpinned by the strategic use of staffing, a deliberate decision to create ethnically mixed staff teams that provide young people with adult role models of different ethnic backgrounds. This can be seen as directly challenging to the ethnic essentialism of 'anti-racism' (Bhavnani, 2001), which assumed that the needs of ethnic minority young people in particular can only be met by workers of the 'same' ethnic background. Instead, the new approach in Oldham has looked to use individual workers as role models, and as agents of community cohesion, through their relationships and interaction with young people. Qummar, an experienced Pakistani-origin worker, was asked to take over as OYS Area Manager for the notorious white estate of Oak Bank, targeted in the wake of the 2001 riots by the British National Party:

> It was a big challenge coming to a predominately white community as a black worker, but the experience from youth work training...enabled me to settle down quickly here. I've never had a problem here working as a black worker...yes, people have taken me very well.

Qummar went on to describe how he has expanded junior youth work provision through his community development work with a group of (white) young mothers. Such an approach has required workers to be prepared to use their own ethnic and cultural background and experiences as a resource. Habib has worked within a number of different

Youth Service clubs and units, including ones in all-white areas. His experience echoes young people's desire for information 'from the horse's mouth':

> One week, there were four or five of them [white young women] in the centre, at the coffee bar, we talked about teenage pregnancy and they were very, very open. They asked about the Asian culture, they asked about arranged marriages, they asked about a lot of different things.

For Habib, this encounter gave the young women involved the chance to air prejudices or myths without being censored, and to interrogate the experiences and views of a real person from a different background. Whilst space does not permit a fuller discussion here, this can be seen as a further, radical modal shift in youth work practice, breaking with (implicit) orthodoxies.

Agency

This post-2001 community cohesion approach within Oldham is underpinned by the autonomy and agency given to youth workers by the forms of delivery and the approach to them taken by managers, such as Alex:

> What I try and do here is create a culture that actually requires people to be creative and innovative by not providing them with the step-by-step 'how to do it' guidelines – and that is quite deliberate.

This focus on agency, the trusting of youth work staff to find ways of achieving agreed community cohesion goals without being told exactly how to go about it, is central to the approach taken to community cohesion, with the prominence of the concept encouraging greater responsibility within planning processes from youth workers, as Louise, a white-origin, qualified OYS Area Manager, highlights:

> If you've got it [community cohesion] there, then you're thinking about doing joint activities, you're getting people together ... we use the word loads now, and I think it does help.

This approach of agency, and the confidence and enthusiasm around community cohesion is in stark contrast to the approach and effects of anti-racism, as it has been understood by youth workers, and other welfare practitioners (CRE, 1999; Thomas, 2002). Michael reflects this:

> I think anti-racism is…automatically has quite a negative spin-off, because its anti-something, you're immediately challenging people's views.

Clearly there is a continuing need to identify and challenge racism, particularly in a tense and divided town like Oldham, but there also needs to be recognition that anti-racism as it has been understood by youth workers, did not lead to enthused and confident practitioners prepared to use their agency on this issue, supporting the findings of other research (CRE, 1999; Hewitt, 2005). Community cohesion, with its focus on direct contact and informality, has clearly engendered greater youth worker confidence and enthusiasm in the Oldham situation, no mean feat after the traumatic events of May 2001, and the resulting criticism of youth work's contribution (Ritchie, 2001). The unresolved challenge now for educational professionals in the town is how to ensure a clear focus on the continued reality of distinct ethnic communities, and on the continued challenge of racism, by youth workers at all levels, within the broad concept of community cohesion. Deborah uses the example of a successful piece of youth work with white and Asian young women to illustrate the need to integrate both anti-racist and community cohesion approaches:

> It had to be both. It had to be work within their own community, and the opportunity to integrate and mix with others, like the young women who did the drama project with me who spent three hours talking to the young women from Pakistani and Bangladeshi backgrounds, talking about the same things, but from a different perspective, saying, 'I didn't know you thought that'…really daft things and finding out there was more in common and that even the differences they thought were there, weren't, they were different differences!

Even with the major focus on community cohesion within youth work in Oldham, there is recognition of the need to integrate the challenge of anti-racism with the positive direct contact of community cohesion. Mary, Assistant Head of Service for OYS, comments of community cohesion that:

It has worked, so I'm ok with it, but maybe, yes, it is a little bit too twee, too comfortable. But it has worked for us, so I don't know.

Conclusion: the meaning of community cohesion youth work

Chapter 3 detailed the very considerable criticisms that have been made of the assumptions, aims and content of the new community cohesion policy strategy since its emergence in the wake of the 2001 riots. The bulk of this criticism has portrayed community cohesion as a retrograde step, and has focused on assimilationist approaches that aim to greatly reduce the space and respect for distinct ethnic and religious cultures, values and traditions in favour of adherence to the non-negotiable national identities and values of the British 'imagined community' (Anderson, 1991). The suggestion there is that community cohesion is a racialised agenda that mirrors the reactionary developments in the Netherlands outlined in Chapter 2, whereby the distinct cultures of ethnic minority communities are not only blamed for their own marginalisation and segregation, but for undermining the viability of the nation itself. However, such critiques have been almost entirely free of empirical evidence, relying on the assumption that community cohesion strategies and practice on the ground mirrors the shortcomings they detect in their, arguably partial, reading of the national and local community cohesion reports (Cantle, 2001; Ritchie, 2001) appearing after the 2001 riots, and elements of the accompanying political discourse (Travis, 2001). What this chapter has attempted to do is draw on empirical evidence from professionals implementing community cohesion approaches within their work with young people, and from young people themselves, to provide a more nuanced picture of what community cohesion actually looks like in practice in this case study area, and what it has the potential to be as an actively pursued national policy. What this final section aims to do is make sense of the empirical data presented above, so identifying its relevance for wider debates around what community cohesion does and could represent.

A clear conclusion from this empirical data is that the key community cohesion themes of problematic ethnic segregation and the role of agency in maintaining it (Cantle, 2001, 2005) are supported by both professional adult respondents and by young people. Both groups were clear that in areas like Oldham and Rochdale, ethnic segregation and the associated perception of white and Asian 'territory' was very much a lived reality, shaping and severely limiting the possibilities of cross-ethnic movement and friendships for young people, as the data presented in the following chapter illustrates. Associated with this is problematic 'bonding' social capital within largely monocultural communities, and the resulting impact of hardened separate and often oppositional identities, something amplified further by the data presented in Chapters 6 and 7. Whilst fully aware of the dangers of national generalisations on the basis of evidence from specific geographical circumstances (Bagguley and Hussain, 2008), this data does suggest that commentators need to perhaps be more cautious in dismissing community cohesion perceptions of problematic ethnic segregation (Cantle, 2005), racial tension and separate identities that are bolstered by public policy as alarmist or factually wrong (Finney and Simpson, 2009). Whilst ethnic residential patterns in other areas of the country are not as starkly segregated as in areas like Oldham, Burnley or Bradford that witnessed rioting in 2001, that does not *prove* that these issues or the response of a greater focus on community cohesion are not relevant there, as the violent disturbances between African-Caribbean and Asian communities in a multicultural area of Birmingham in 2005 (King, 2009) suggests.

The response by youth work agencies in Oldham to this analysis and challenge of community cohesion has been to radically alter the priorities, content and shape of their professional practice with young people. This shift has contained a clear critique of past policy approaches of anti-racism, as it was understood and implemented within youth work and education locally and nationally (CRE, 1999; Hewitt, 2005), whereby all work with young people had been in geographically and ethnically separate units; with no contact between them and the units staffed by professionals from the 'same' ethnic background as the young people; and the educational approach taken, especially with white young people, being one of disciplining 'racist' behaviour and attitudes and closing down any contentious discussions for fear of causing offence and so contravening rules. The new post-2001 youth work practice in Oldham has prioritised direct contact between young people of different ethnic (and social) backgrounds, mainstreaming it by making this a basic condition of all youth work activity through regular linking arrangements between projects and clubs, area-wide events that bring young people together from different backgrounds, and residential trips and events that provide safe, neutral territory to enable contact and dialogue. Cantle (2005: 130) suggests that community cohesion activity is about 'approaching the issue through everyday activities, which bring different cultures together and learning through experiences'. The nature of this direct contact work has been crucial, with the approach being one of informality, fun and association-based group work that has aimed to allow dialogue and understanding to grow naturally and organically during the process, rather be forced by overt discussion around social and political issues. This approach may not only be seen as contrary to wider recent trends in British education policy (Mizen, 2004) and as a return to traditional forms of informal education-based youth work (Davies, 2005), but, more importantly, as a repudiation of the more formal educational style of anti-racism that arguably attempted to 'teach' young people to respect difference, rather than enable them to experience it and embrace it for themselves.

This community cohesion approach to youth work in Oldham fulfils the key principles of 'contact theory' (Brown, 1995; Hewstone et al., 2007), which is a social psychology-based understanding of how prejudices and tensions can be reduced and overcome in situations where different and distinct communities have significant barriers and conflicts between them. Unsurprisingly, much of the recent learning about such approaches has come from Northern Ireland, where the history of starkly divided Catholic and Protestant communities with separate housing areas and schooling systems has meant little cross-community interaction even years after the peace process has made real progress. The key elements of progress in such situations, as identified by contact theory, are that neither community involved should feel that its identity or traditions are under attack or threat within the process, that it should be conducted over time to enable genuine movement in attitudes, that it should be conducted in groups to bolster confidence and avoid tokenistic contact, and that often neutral space has to be utilised to reduce tensions (Hewstone et al., 2007). All of these principles can be identified within the new community cohesion-based youth work practice in Oldham, with regular relationships between different youth clubs and projects, an informal focus on commonality and fun rather than difference, and residential events that allow young people to meet and form relationships in neutral territory all being central to this new, post-2001 practice approach. In not overtly threatening or questioning existing community attitudes and identities, and by operating through informal and fun methods, such a community cohesion-based approach can enable 'transversal politics', a 'rooting and shifting' of individual and group attitudes (Yuval-Davis, 1997) whereby people are willing to re-think their attitudes and values towards 'others', so subtly altering and moderating their own identity, because the 'rootedness' of that own identity is not under threat and they are not being pressurised to demonstrate specific attitudes as anti-racism has sometimes mistakenly done in the past (Hewitt, 2005).

What this data also shows is that community cohesion in practice is not an assimilationist approach, or indeed the 'death of multiculturalism' (Kundnani, 2007). Rather than denying different and distinct ethnic, religious and social identities and attempting to impose a non-negotiable, common identity, this community cohesion practice accepts and works with distinct communities and identities, seeking to augment them with common experiences and identities through a negotiated process, rather than replacing them. Respondents identified the importance of working with distinct identities and communities, often in their monocultural, geographically based settings, as a vital, preparatory stage of work processes that then bring young people together across ethnic lines in work processes that young people feel they have been informed about and given the chance to opt out of. This vital role for existing monocultural settings shows how badly wrong the Commission on Integration and Cohesion (DCLG, 2007a) got it when recommending a presumption against continued funding of 'single' community organisation and facilities (an approach later rejected by the Labour government), as this data suggests that such organisations and settings are a vital building block in processes of community cohesion. Here, future support should rest on what organisations do, whether they participate sincerely in cross-ethnic contact processes or not, rather than what their name, base or membership profile is.

As well as accepting and working positively with different, existing ethnic backgrounds, this community cohesion practice with young people has also engaged with a variety of other forms of experience and identity, suggesting that 'intersectional' (McGhee, 2006) understandings of identity are an inherent part of this work. Linking arrangements between different youth projects and clubs have not only connected areas with different ethnic backgrounds, but rural/suburban projects with inner-city ones, and areas of the same ethnic background that have a history of 'territory' based tension and violence. Similarly, initiatives such as the 'Fusion' residential project described above have deliberately included young people with physical and learning disabilities in an echo of wider educational integration strategies, whilst other work programmes have facilitated discussion of identity issues around sexuality and gender. Such an approach recognises the dangers of essentialising and reifying ethnic and religious identities in a situation where multiple identities and hybridisation of experience are a growing reality (Hall, 2000), suggesting that community cohesion practice must recognise the interplay between different forms of identity and the agency of individual young people in negotiating this dialectical interplay. Such an approach makes possible the concept of 'critical multiculturalism' (May, 1999a) discussed in Chapter 1, a practice approach that recognises the realities of ethnic difference and racial inequalities, but which also accepts and works with complexities of identities and social forces. Such understandings could be detected in the discussion around the proper focus for community cohesion reported earlier in the chapter, whether it should solely be concerned with ethnic differences and tensions, or also with wider issues and experiences that also shape and limit identity for young people. These wider issues, including 'territory' disputes, economic and employment experiences, and gender dynamics, are explored in the following chapter.

5
Community Cohesion: More than Ethnicity?

Introduction

A key issue already raised in earlier chapters is the focus and scope of community cohesion policy and practice. Arguably, this policy agenda is self-evidently about 'race' and ethnicity, having emerged directly in the wake of the 2001 disturbances (Cantle, 2001; Denham, 2001), having conceptual antecedents in an independent commission process that was directly focused on the future of multi-ethnic Britain (CFMEB, 2000), and an accompanying political discourse that has been overwhelmingly concerned with tensions between separate ethnic and religious affiliations in relation to common values and identities (Goodhart, 2004; Ouseley, 2001; Phillips, 2005; Travis, 2001). However, it is far from clear that this community cohesion agenda, both in stated policy and actual practice terms, is solely about ethnic identity and tensions. Such an ambiguity over focus can be detected in a number of ways that the 2001 disturbances and the subsequent emergence of community cohesion has been analysed, discussed and responded to. These include the immediate response by a range of elected local politicians, especially in Bradford and Burnley, that the 2001 riots were as much about drug-related criminality and associated territory-based feuding as they were about racial tension (Clarke, 2001; Vasagar and Dodd, 2001). Whilst summarily dismissed by government (Denham, 2001) as not fitting their overall analysis or the policy agenda they intended to operationalise in response, such concerns cannot simply be brushed under the carpet, and are not necessarily in conflict with an analysis of ethnic segregation and racialised tension. Indeed, the local reports produced in Oldham (Ritchie, 2001) and especially in Burnley (Bagguley and Hussain, 2008; Clarke, 2001) focused on deeper economic and social causes generally, and the profound de-industrialisation that their towns had suffered in particular, as much as the analysis of ethnic segregation and tension foregrounded nationally (Cantle, 2001).

In giving the government's official response to the CCRT (Cantle, 2001) process nationally, Denham (2001: Chapter 3) highlighted wider government policy priorities on employment, regeneration and housing, as much as those on community leadership, activities of extremist groups and tackling crime and disorder, as part of the government's holistic approach. This suggested that the associated change of language away from multiculturalism and anti-racism towards community cohesion was not just about a critique of past race relations policies and their unintended consequences for conceptions of commonality, but also marked an increased caution over the extent to which the violent disturbances and the longer-term ethnic tensions that they arguably symbolised could truly be understood only through understandings of ethnicity and 'race'. Chapter 2 highlighted how French policy limitations prevent them from considering ethnicity as a factor in the economic and social marginalisation of many non-white citizens, but Britain has arguably been reassessing whether policy has in the past overemphasised 'race' in relation to similar issues. This suggestion of a wider and more complex 'social' conception of community cohesion, rather than simply a 'narrow' one focused only on ethnic relations, was apparently confirmed by the 'Pathfinder' pilot community cohesion activity through local authorities (Home Office, 2003a, 2003b, 2004) and the associated national guidance to local authorities and other public bodies (DCLG, 2007a; LGA, 2002, 2004) discussed in Chapter 4, and which involved engagement with intergenerational and 'territory' tensions within monocultural communities, as well as tensions between settled and travelling communities, arguably also of the same ethnic background.

This raises important issues around the focus and meaning of community cohesion at two levels. Firstly, it suggests questions around the relationship between community cohesion and wider agendas of equality and diversity, and social inequality gaps which need greater future investigation elsewhere to explore initial indications of both overlap and tension (Monro et al., 2010). Secondly, and the key focus of this book, is what this suggests and raises for the understanding and implementation of community cohesion policies at ground level, especially around work with young people and their communities. This chapter uses empirical and academic evidence to explore these further, focusing in particular on how issues of 'territory' and associated issues of 'safe' and 'unsafe' space, economic changes and experiences, and gender affect and interact with the undisputedly core issue of ethnic identity and relations within conceptions and implementation of community cohesion.

The importance of territory for young people

In discussing the importance of 'territory' for young people, territoriality can be defined as 'a social system through which control is claimed by one group over a defined geographical area and defended against others' (Kintrea et al., 2008: 4). The local reports produced after the riots in Oldham and Burnley (Clarke, 2001; Ritchie, 2001) and that written before, but published after the Bradford riot (Ouseley, 2001), identified a strong sense of localised identity in specific geographical areas of those towns and cities, something confirmed by empirical research in Oldham (Thomas, 2003, 2006). This echoes the 'neighbourhood nationalism' (Back, 1996) or 'super place attachment' (Kintrea et al., 2008) reported in many studies of working-class young people, where defence of imagined local boundaries and territory is part of male youth culture and often has deep historical roots (Cohen, 1988). Such attitudes are not just representative of a strong, positive identification with neighbourhood, but can sometimes show a negative lack of identification with the larger town or city identity. There are clearly positive, and even necessary, aspects to this localised level of identity, especially for young people as they grow up. Imran, a Pakistani-origin voluntary sector youth worker, comments:

> I think young people in general are always very territorial, whether it's the school that you go to, the area you live in, the football team you support, they'll always have that territorialism about it. Yes, we do have a level of tension that exists between different areas and that would happen anyway irrelevant of the colour of your skin.

Other respondents reported this local identity as a feeling of 'ownership', and this strong local identity, and the perceived need to defend it, can be seen as a historic reality within settled working-class communities (Cohen, 1988). For some, the profound economic changes brought about in the last 25 years by de-industrialisation and neo-liberal globalisation (Byrne, 1999) have actually strengthened this 'neighbourhood nationalism', rather than weakened it in line with theories of hybridisation (Modood and Werbner, 1997), as unemployment and economic insecurity has limited the horizons and opportunities available for socially excluded young people, and turned their socially and economically marginalised communities 'inwards' (May, 1999a). Lisa, a white-origin youth worker who grew up in Oldham at a time of greater economic prosperity, agrees that the nature of working-class communities has altered in Oldham:

> If I go back to when I was younger, there were always certain areas that didn't get on, but it's just part of growing up. I do think it's a lot more vicious now what's happening with communities because a lot of older people are fighting the cause more than young people as well.

Ironically, whilst economic change and insecurity may well be fuelling this, current political agendas, such as the 'Big Society' conception of re-energising voluntarism, and the de-centralisation agenda of localism with its drive to make services more responsive and rejuvenate public involvement in political processes, have also contributed to this heightened awareness of the local. The clear consensus from respondents was that local territory, and perceptions of this territory, is a strong and real issue for young people of all ethnic backgrounds in Oldham. This concern with territory overlays, and often supersedes, ethnic conflicts, with many of the territory conflicts in Oldham being between young people of the same ethnic background. Deborah previously worked in Branton, a white working-class area of Oldham, and comments that:

> The biggest conflict wasn't between Newton [Pakistani area] and Branton, the two neighbouring parts of Oldham, It was between Branton and Moston, which is a neighbourhood in Manchester that borders with Oldham ... it was between white young people who live in different towns that hated each other.

Michelle, a white voluntary sector youth worker, is based in Newton, a Pakistani-dominated area, and similarly reports territory conflicts between Pakistani and Bangladeshi young people, viewed homogeneously by white outsiders as 'Asians'. Michelle takes this further, by identifying territory barriers within the 'Pakistani community' itself:

> Even here, and Woodthorpe [viewed as one area], because they seem more affluent in Woodthorpe than Newton (there is conflict). We had to work to get the Newton lads, we've had to actively work to

get them to go (to the Youth Centre in the Woodthorpe area), even though it's classed as being their area ....

This was confirmed during a later research visit made by the author to the Woodthorpe Youth Centre. As soon as the Newton young people arrived, the (younger) Woodthorpe young people immediately left, so highlighting the complexities of territory and social standing within mono-ethnic settings and in what is often a quite small geographical area. In this case, a slight age difference between the two groups seemed to suggest an important issue of deference to older young men within this Asian community, as well as that of different 'turf' within the geographical area (Alexander, 2000). Turf and territory for young people is often geographically identified by boundaries that may not appear significant to older people: 'conflict occurred on boundaries between residential areas, which were typically defined by roads, railways, vacant land or other physical features' (Kintrea et al., 2008: 5). This study of six case study areas of Britain found a strong interrelationship between territoriality and disadvantaged areas, suggesting that territorial behaviour could be understood as an attractive option of 'recreational violence' and as a coping mechanism, especially for young men, in a situation of limited leisure options and low aspirations (Kintrea et al., 2008), both of which factors fit parts of towns like Oldham and Rochdale.

The mono-ethnic nature of many of Oldham's housing areas (Ritchie, 2001) makes territory conflicts between different areas also conflicts between different ethnic groups in many instances (Thomas, 2003), with territory conflicts 'heavily overlain or paralleled' (Kintrea et al., 2008: 31) by ethnic conflicts. This ethnic physical/housing segregation therefore makes it very obvious when one group of young people are moving into the territory of 'others', raising the issue of whether ethnic difference is the cause of youth conflict or simply a 'marker' (Back, 1996). This echoes the findings of an important earlier study focused on the relationship between ethnic segregation and territory-based violence in Keighley, West Yorkshire (Webster, 1995). Keighley is a once prosperous and now poor and ethnically segregated ex-textile town with great similarities to Oldham and Rochdale. Webster (1995) found a complex interplay between high levels of racist violence, historically initiated by white young people, and significant, territory-based violence between young people of different ethnic backgrounds, with the justification of defence against racial attack sometime used to excuse gang-based violence, so making it often hard to determine the extent of the 'racial' component of such violence. However, more recent evidence from Bradford of rival 'gangs' of the same ethnicity sometimes teaming up for racial conflict does seem to confirm Webster's (1995) core concern with racism, 'suggesting an ascendancy of ethnic conflict over territoriality' (Kintrea et al., 2008: 32).

Asad runs a youth centre in a Bangladeshi area that is used by an all-white 'life skills' training for employment group during the day. At first, getting the group in and out of the area was not easy:

> Due to the fighting that took place in the bus shelter a couple of years ago, because a [white] group from here beat up a young person from the community with a snooker cue. The Asian young people wanted to retaliate and they gathered outside.

Whilst now resolved, this example illustrates the difficulties for young people of negotiating other people's 'territory'. For young people, moving on their own in the territory of 'others' leaves them exposed, but moving in a group makes them prominent, apparently issuing a 'challenge' (Kintrea et al., 2008) and so a target, in the perceptions of that community. This is illustrated by the experience of a mainly Asian youth group who were violently attacked whilst visiting a youth centre in an overwhelmingly white housing area as part of an ongoing project, and who acknowledged that this experience had provoked feelings of territory-based aggression in themselves as a result:

> We made so many friends and stuff and then out of the blue just wham bang off you go . . . . It's like if you were with loads of boys, and I have, we had about five six cars, we went down that road and we saw a group of boys there we'd want to get out of the car and just hammer them because it's happened to us in that same spot. We just want to like hammer them.
>
> (AYP, Oldham)

This section has highlighted the extent to which territory and [illegible] to young people of all ethnic groups, something mirrored nationally, and which can be seen as being at the root of more serious, gang-based violence and criminality (Kintrea et al., 2008). Such realities can particularly be seen as indicative of the historical as well as contemporary importance of local neighbourhoods to socially marginalised, working-class young people. The significant ethnic physical/housing segregation in areas like Oldham (Ritchie, 2001) means that ethnic difference is clearly a 'marker' of this area/neighbourhood difference, but respondents also clearly report territory distinctions and actual tension/violence within apparently mono-ethnic areas, so questioning the extent to which 'race' and ethnicity are the causal factors in local youth conflicts. This complex reality relates to discussions of what is regarded as 'safe' and 'unsafe' space for young people in situations of significant ethnic segregation and racialised perceptions of territory.

'Safe' and 'unsafe' space for young people

Young people were often very clear about which geographical areas they felt safe or unsafe in, with much of these perceptions focused on their own ethnicity in relation to the dominant ethnicity of particular geographical/housing areas: 'Especially "Moorside".... I know it's a white area and if I was seen there with a headscarf...' (AYP, Rochdale). 'Moorside...I got chased there' (AYP, Rochdale). This logic also works in mainly Asian areas, with local young people clear about why few white young people come into the area: 'Because people around this area they threaten people that they come down our area, they jump 'em' (AYP, Rochdale). An Asian youth group in Oldham discussed why they wouldn't go to the overwhelmingly white area of 'Thorndale': 'it's just known as that kind of place where, it's just a racist area, just like white people wouldn't want to walk into "Bankside" because of the Bankside reputation, there's a lot of racist Pakistanis there.' Clearly such characterisations of whole areas as 'racist' or 'dodgy' are unfair, but they do indicate that many young people have 'maps' in their heads (Kintrea et al., 2008; Webster, 1995) of what areas are safe or unsafe. Often, these understandings were ethnic-dependent, with space being 'safe' for some groups and 'unsafe' for others, depending on their (visible) ethnicity (Back, 1996). The vast majority of young people surveyed in Oldham and Rochdale had such mental maps, and this clearly limits their ability and willingness to travel around their wider areas for education, employment or social reasons. As much of these beliefs were actually stereotypes based on little or no direct personal experience, there is clearly both a challenge and 'myth busting' (Cantle, 2001) opportunity for enhanced community cohesion activity programmes.

Much of these discussions focused on the issue of the perceived safety of public spaces for people 'like them', on who was seen as 'owning' such space. For that reason, the post-2001 suggestion that new youth facilities should be built on the borders of ethnically segregated housing areas in Oldham to encourage mixed usage (Ritchie, 2001) was seen as naive, on the basis that one group would claim ownership:

> The first group into it would take ownership of it ... it would become a meeting place for violence, a symbol of conflict. Oldham has been segregated for too long; it's got to be small steps, maybe through small scale projects.
>
> (White female youth worker quoted in Thomas, 2003: 39)

A number of respondents focused on the very limited public spaces available to young people in towns like Oldham, so severely limiting the range of spaces for the most basic sorts of peaceful co-existence, the seeds of 'bridging social capital' (Putnam, 2000) to develop. Deborah highlights:

> In Oldham there is bugger all for young people to do beyond go to the youth club. We haven't got a bowling alley or big cinema complex that all these other towns have, just a tatty old cinema on the edge of town. There is no generic meeting place with café areas and pizzas where young people can chill out.

Other youth workers agreed with the urgent need to create 'safe' and fun shared spaces where young people could get used to being around others of a different ethnic background. Here, Oldham's 'space' problem is less about segregated housing and more about this lack of a shared recreational space where safe cultural negotiation, 'rooting and shifting' (Yuval-Davis, 1997) can take place. This suggests that for ethnic mixing to be positive, it has to feel like a choice people can make, and opportunities and spaces for this to happen need to be available for young people to opt into. For Habib, helping to create this situation will require the:

> Town centre becoming a hub where people come at the weekend, in the evenings, have a bit of fun and go home, is well lit and is well-policed ... at the end of the day, you've got a whole generation of 13–19 year olds that can't access that town centre because there's nothing of interest.

The one quasi-public space really open to young people in Oldham town centre is the Spindles shopping centre, a modern arcade built on several levels in the centre of town. The Spindles is limited, closing at 6 p.m., and having very few spaces for eating or drinking, but does attract many groups of young people. This in itself is a source of tension and conflict, as Johnson identifies:

> There's a fear . . . . I would say more than two or three times a week when I go out, [white] people will bring up in conversation about groups of young Asian people in the Spindles.

Here, Johnson is articulating the racialised awareness/concern (Ritchie, 2001) that seems to pervade life in many towns and cities – many white people see groups of Asian young people in the Spindles, but never talk to them or get to know them, so fuelling the 'moral panic' (Cohen, 1972) around 'Asian gangs' (Alexander, 2000). Sandy is a white-origin, experienced community worker and co-ordinator of a racial equality agency. He sees the use, and perceptions of use, of space within the Spindles as central to Oldham's current reality:

> You've got groups of clearly unemployed young people literally doing a tour, a walking tour, in a group around the Spindles; not causing anybody any trouble, saying hello to other groups who they see, and these are totally mono-racial groups . . . they're clearly at a very, very loose end and they are racially segregated.

This racialised, and often apparently aimless, use of space within the Spindles was very evident to the author during frequent field research visits to Oldham. This suggests that simply sharing space is not enough in itself to develop 'bridging social capital' (McGhee, 2003) or even to reduce prejudice. Many of these young people hanging around the Spindles are (at least nominally) at local colleges, or waiting to meet friends who are, and their presence there is symptomatic of youth social exclusion (Hills et al., 2002). For some people, town centre college sites are one of the few places where young people of different ethnic backgrounds can actually get to know each other, given the ethnic physical segregation in Oldham, and its knock-on effects on school rolls (Ritchie, 2001). This pivotal role of further and higher education institutions as potential sites for community cohesion is becoming increasingly important, given the trends in ethnic segregation in schooling in many areas nationally (Burgess et al., 2005) and the large-scale contraction in the youth labour market (Mizen, 2004). For Abdul, a Bangladeshi-origin, young community activist training to be a youth worker, attending Oldham College was a positive experience:

> It's only when I went to College where my class was a lot more diverse, and that's where my initial interaction with people from different faiths and communities, that's where it started. The life experiences you get are a lot more beneficial.

Abdul went on to discuss how this journey has continued to the point where he works on inter-faith activities that bring young people of different faiths and ethnicities together to explore common concerns. Asad can see the benefits of attending Oldham College for some of the young people attending his youth centre:

> They always talk about college and meeting new friends, because a lot of them have just gone into college and I think from that change they've matured, they've met more young people, different young people from different areas.

Oldham College can be seen as an example of a safe, mixed space for young people of all backgrounds, and has been positively built on by the subsequent opening of a university campus in Oldham town centre, attached to the nearby University of Huddersfield. A more common reality, as viewed by the majority of respondents, in Oldham is that some spaces are viewed as out of bounds for certain young people. Indeed, the allegation that there were genuine 'no go' areas in Oldham, and the sensationalist reporting of that claim, can be seen as a key cause of the 2001 disturbances, as discussed in Chapter 1 (Kalra, 2002; Ray and Smith, 2002; Ritchie, 2001). The distinction between the questionable reality of 'no go' areas and young people's *perception* of the situation was one that a number of respondents made, including Deborah:

> I never felt that I couldn't go somewhere because of my ethnicity but people believed there were 'no go' areas, it was a perception, rather than a reality, so I suppose there were 'no go' areas but they were in people's minds.

Other workers offered evidence of young people having ideas of 'no go' areas without any personal experience or knowledge of the area(s) in question. Clearly, concerns around the media's role in 'amplifying' (Cohen, 1972) claims and concerns about (racialised) crime and 'unsafe' areas in the build-up to the 2001 disturbances are relevant here (Kundnani, 2001). Habib clearly blames Oldham Police's public statements and their handling of racial incidents statistics, for fuelling the perception of 'no go' areas within the town:

> I've worked in Oak Bank which was meant to be 'no go' for Asians, I worked in Thorndale, which is meant to be 'no go' for Asians. I've seen Asians on the street here and vice versa with whites here [in Newton], so when the Chief Superintendent said Newton was a 'no go' area for whites, I was really, really shocked....

Iqbal described taking a group of young people from Newton to Belfast, Northern Ireland, in the aftermath of the 2001 disturbances to experience what rigid residential segregation and genuinely 'no go' areas are actually like:

> The actual expression on the young people's faces when they saw the walls actually dividing streets.... Well, they felt like they didn't want to be there. They don't want Oldham to become what's happened in Northern Ireland.

Nevertheless, Jane, a white-origin, experienced youth worker, who is a co-ordinator for Oldham's provision aimed at young people disengaged from employment and education, sees young people's belief in 'no go' areas as often based on personal experience:

> Some young people...have had experiences of actual violence, sort of racial violence and stuff, both white young people and Asian...they've understood it as racial but when I've broken that down even further actually they've not been random attacks, they've been people known through college or training who they might not necessarily get on with.

This illustrates the complex interplay of territory, gender, space and ethnicity within the urban environment (Back, 1996; Cohen, 1988), but also provides further proof that in Oldham's highly racialised and ethnically segregated climate, conflicts will be perceived as 'racial' in nature. Respondents clearly see space and perceptions of it as central to the problematic current reality of Oldham. The lack of 'safe' public spaces in Oldham town centre that can genuinely be used and enjoyed by young people of all ethnic backgrounds is a real issue, with community

cohesion-based mixed youth activities and further and higher educational institutions showing the potential when 'safe' space can be
positively mediated to create 'bridging social capital' (Putnam, 2000).
Meanwhile, there is a widespread belief amongst young people that 'no
go' areas exist in towns like Oldham and Rochdale, fuelled by 'amplified' media coverage (Cohen, 1972), but also by personal experience in
a segregated, racialised climate where individual incidents are usually
understood as 'racial'.

Boys will be boys?

For some respondents, territory-based violence, and the more hard-
edged, racialised form it can take in areas like Oldham and Keighley
(Webster, 1995), is actually underpinned by gender and the gendered
performance of roles (Alexander, 2000). Virtually all those charged following the 2001 disturbances in Oldham, Burnley, Bradford and Leeds
(Farrar, 2002) were men, largely younger men under the age of 35 years.
Whilst there needs to be caution over any construction of the 'typical
rioter' (Bagguley and Hussain, 2008), the 2001 disturbances and other
modern riots in the UK (Campbell, 1993) have largely featured men as
the active participants. Campbell's analysis of the 1991 riots on white
working-class social housing estates on the periphery of towns and cities
like Oxford, Cardiff and Newcastle-upon-Tyne focused on how gendered
the response was to structural economic and spatial social exclusion,
with many young adult men reverting to adolescent teenage lifestyles
and petty criminality that included confrontations with the police,
whilst young women struggled to maintain family life and to navi-
gate paths towards post-industrial employment. Similarly, the anecdotes
offered by respondents concerning territory or town centre-based conflict and violence in Oldham always involved young men, as confirmed
by national statistics around recorded racial crimes (Sibbit, 1997). Are
the conflicts in areas like Oldham rooted in maleness and testosterone
(Cohen, 1988), or are young men simply acting out wider community
prejudices and fears? Alex sees the former perspective as highly relevant:

It is very much gender-based and gender-related – that's borne out
in terms of the response from a lot of women in the community.
Certainly there was quite a strong move and a big event following the
riots which was labelled something like 'wives and mothers coming
together'.

This feminist perspective sees much of the conflicts and violence in Oldham as driven by patriarchy and male aggression (Macey, 1999, 2007), and was shared, at least partially, by a number of respondents. Salma, a Bangladeshi-origin, trainee youth worker, sees young women as much more willing to take risks, and to contemplate direct contact across ethnic and territory boundaries:

> Girls, they do overcome the territorial barrier a lot faster than boys.... I think just women to women they're able to ask more questions, they are not afraid to ask questions in that sense.

Ian, a white-origin, experienced youth worker, has direct experience of such 'race'-related male aggression within a town centre youth support facility that he is responsible for:

> It kicked off in the Centre, a very serious affair with people throwing chairs and so on. At the start, it was not racially motivated, but it was a gang of Asian youths who felt people were after them, because there was an incident three days before when two white youths were abusing the Asian lads.

This has led the agency to be much more directive and assertive in their management of the open access centre, proactively employing youth work intervention skills to shape young peoples' approach to use of the space. This perspective also suggests that racial prejudices are both stronger amongst young men, and that they are more willing to interpret incidents as 'racial' due to their greater natural aggression. However, Ian's colleague, Jane, disputes the implicit suggestion from many of these experiences and anecdotes that young women are less racist or prejudiced:

> No, I wouldn't really agree with that. I think maybe young men voice that opinion or are more visibly demonstrating those opinions and attitudes but I work with quite a lot of white young women who are extremely racist and who have extremely prejudiced attitudes.

For Michael, young women may *appear* more tolerant and less confrontational because they don't carry the same pressures and expectations regarding roles as young men:

I think they [young women] do find it easier to mix but I don't think they have the same pressure as young men to uphold their ego and their reputation.

This opinion supports the view that working-class young men of all ethnic backgrounds understand defending 'their' territory from 'others' as a key responsibility (Cohen, 1988). It also suggests that in a highly ethnically segregated environment like Oldham, racism will be the symptom as much as the cause of male, territory-based violence. Whether young men in Oldham are really more hostile to 'others' than young women is a moot point, but a small-scale research project carried out in Oldham soon after the 2001 disturbances found that youth workers were concentrating on young women because of the more overt racism and resistance to 'others' demonstrated by young men (Thomas, 2003).

It's the economy, stupid!

The perspectives discussed above suggest that responses to the reality of physical ethnic segregation and tension in Oldham are gendered, even if underlying fears and prejudices are shared by all sections of the community. However, such racialised territorial conflicts, and gendered responses to difference, amongst young people, are not unique to towns like Oldham (Back, 1996; Webster, 1995). The deeper question may be why the 2001 disturbances occurred in Oldham, Burnley and Bradford, rather than other parts of Britain. Cantle's own conclusion to this question when posed within his report (2001) was that other towns and cities, such as Leicester and Southall, had managed their diversity better. However, for many of the respondents, the explanation for these differences lies in the economy, in the economic changes Oldham and northern industrial towns like it have experienced over the past 30 years. This perspective suggests that ethnic and racial tensions contributing to and symbolised by the 2001 riots are, at least partially, a symptom of deeper economic insecurities and changes that have had a profound impact on wider British society, but which have not been evenly spread (Byrne, 1999; Modood et al., 1997). Here, the difference between Oldham and Leicester is *not* their management of ethnic diversity, but the relative success of Leicester in developing a viable, post-industrial economy and the relatively well-rewarded jobs that go with it. Rafiq believes that issues of poverty and social exclusion

(Hills et al., 2002) must underpin any understanding of the situation in Oldham:

> I didn't see any middle class people from any community rioting on the streets, they were the poorest of our people who were out there regardless of what [ethnic] background they come from. You'd be setting yourself up to fail if you didn't understand that, whilst not necessarily joined together, what you've got is a direct correlation between poverty and racism.

This suggests that experiences of poverty and social exclusion are a crucial influence on young people's perceptions of their own situations and that of 'others'. A historical perspective on the nature of economic change and its impact is vital here in understanding Oldham's situation. David, an ex-local councillor, stresses the historical changes to Oldham's economy that have taken place:

> When I was a councillor in 1994, I went to an Education Committee meeting, and the Careers Officer was giving us a survey of the past 25 years. In 1969, *one* male school leaver in Oldham failed to get a job at the age of 15. In 1994 it was something like 12% he was quoting.

That profound economic change involved the disappearance of the textile industry and associated engineering industries in Oldham, with the loss of many full-time, semi-skilled and unskilled jobs. The results have included long-term unemployment for a minority (Ritchie, 2001) and less-secure (and often lower-paid) jobs for a significant part of the workforce (Bagguley and Hussain, 2008; Kalra, 2000). This structural economic change has also meant much more uncertain paths to employment generally for young people, and associated delays in work, housing and family 'transitions' to adulthood (Hills et al., 2002; Mizen, 2004; SEU, 1999). For Khan, the changed nature of employment for many people in Oldham has had a profound impact on the extent and nature of cross-community contact and understanding within the town:

> It was only [Asian] males who came to this country at first, there were no women, so the only communication they had was through employment and working in the cotton industry, in the labour market. They did create the bond with one another and people working there created friendships. Then the cotton industry completely collapsed and that created a further gap because then communication

and community cohesion collapsed.... When they were in employment they were sharing their rights, they were all working in one
industry and they all had something in common.

Here, Khan identifies the industrial employment that dominated
Oldham until the 1980s as naturally producing (albeit, racist and imper-
fect, as shifts were often racially segregated within textile mills) forms
of 'bridging social capital' and cross-community contact now identified as lacking (Kundnani, 2001; McGhee, 2003). For Khan, necessity
has led many Asian people to work or establish businesses within their
own community, and so only have superficial economic contact with
other communities through low-paid service sector jobs, such as restau-
rants, fast-food takeaways and taxi work (Kalra, 2000). The nature of this
contact often undermines, rather than strengthens, inter-ethnic respect
and understanding. Habib believes that this economic experience of the
past 30 years has had a negative impact not only on the aspirations of
young people of all backgrounds, but on their more general interest in
anything outside of their immediate environment:

> It's happening in Newton [predominantly Asian area], I've worked
> in Oak Bank [predominantly white area] and it's a similar situation,
> where young people are not inspired enough to say, 'the opportuni-
> ties are out there for us', because they've seen Oldham, and they've
> seen failure, quite a lot of it, so they expect failure.

Conclusion

This suggests that the profound economic changes experienced by
towns like Oldham over the past 30 years have had a huge impact
on young people's sense of self, community and aspirations, as well
as upon their attitudes to 'others'. For some of the most socially
excluded sections of youth, this has led to the growth of a defensive
and inward-looking 'neighbourhood nationalism' amongst the 'losers'
in an increasingly insecure and transient globalised economy (May,
1999a), suggesting that any solutions must focus on the poverty and economic social exclusion (Byrne, 1999). Such a heightened focus on their
local area for marginalised young people of all ethnic backgrounds,
who have not been able to access the wider experiences afforded by
employment of full-time further and higher education, has exacerbated historic youth concerns with defending local territory (Cohen,
1988). This explains an increase in territory-based violence and youth

perceptions of safe and unsafe space amongst the most socially and economically marginalised young people nationally (Kintrea et al., 2008).
When such territoriality is combined with significant ethnic segregation, ethnic difference becomes the key 'marker' of the 'other', so
fuelling conflict that is perceived by young people and their communities to be all about 'race' (Webster, 1995). The acting out of such tensions
is significantly gendered, as shown in previous riots (Campbell, 1993),
but it is far from clear whether young women in such areas hold significantly different attitudes to 'others', even if they don't act them out
in the same way. This chapter has focused on the key issues of territory, space, the economy and gender to caution against understanding
riots and longer-term tensions in multicultural towns and cities like
Oldham purely in 'racial' terms, without considering space, poverty and
social exclusion as factors. This suggests that local community cohesion strategies need to understand and work with such complexities,
whilst accepting the centrality of ethnicity and 'race', a balancing act
that respondents agreed with and were trying to operationalise in their
community cohesion-influenced practice with young people.

6
Unwilling Citizens? Muslim Young People and Identity

Introduction

The empirical data explored in Chapter 4 around how community cohesion is actually being understood and practised in work with young people suggested that the characterisation of community cohesion as a retreat to previous policy approaches of coercive assimilationism (Back et al., 2002) is misplaced. Instead, the community cohesion youth work practice in Oldham has accepted and worked positively with distinct ethnic, religious and geographical identities, and its aim has been to augment those identities with overarching, common identities and experiences through work that follows the principles of 'contact theory' (Hewstone et al., 2007). However, this does suggest the need for greater understanding of what these separate identities held by young people are and how they impact on their receptiveness towards cohesion-based efforts to promote shared identities and values. Furthermore, this empirical evidence does not necessarily contradict the implicit thesis of community cohesion (Cantle, 2001; Ouseley, 2001) that ethnic segregation and policy approaches that have re-enforced it (Malik, 2009) have encouraged separate ethnic identities that are inherently problematic in their antagonism to the 'other' and their lack of interest in and commitment to commonality.

This chapter and the one that follows aims to address this through presentation and analysis of empirical research around how young people of different ethnic backgrounds in Oldham and Rochdale understand and prioritise their 'identity', including how they view 'others'.

In doing so, and in discussing how we might understand the resulting data, the chapters focus on issues that have arguably been inherent in the policy developments of the past decade, and which have been directly concerned with the 'identities' of young people in a context of ethnic segregation and racial tension. Much of this focus has been on Muslim young people, suggesting that Britain has a 'Muslim problem' (Masood, 2006), and fuelling fears that community cohesion is part of a larger, racialised agenda (Alexander, 2004), made more explicit by the 'Prevent' anti-terrorism strategy (as discussed in Chapter 8), that blames the cultures and values of Muslim communities for wider social problems, as explored in Chapter 3. These interrelated concerns over Muslim youth 'identity' are, firstly, that many Muslims lack loyalty to Britain and are antagonistic to British national identity (Mirza et al., 2007), so threatening national security (Prins and Salisbury, 2008) through attraction to Islamist ideologies that are implacably anti-Western, a critique that echoes the 'clash of civilisations' thesis (Burke, 2007) that sees the 'West' and Islam as irreconcilable opposites. That underpins the second claim that Muslims have a strong and separate religious identity, a problematic prioritisation of faith identity at odds with the approach of other sections of society. Thirdly, this Muslim faith identity is therefore inherently oppositional to other lifestyles and identities, an assertively reactionary religious ideology that is increasingly threatening to the future of multicultural societies, such as Britain and the Netherlands, as discussed in Chapter 2. Whilst these issues focus on Pakistani- and Bangladeshi-origin British communities described as 'Muslim', with this characterisation itself a key focus for this chapter, the community cohesion thesis also suggests that antagonistic, oppositional identities have increasingly developed in predominantly white communities, as evidenced by the growth of white support for far-right political groups (Eatwell and Goodwin, 2010), and the reality and meaning of such white youth identities are discussed in the following chapter.

Research data

As discussed in the Introduction, the empirical data drawn on here is from the Oldham and Rochdale Youth Identity Project (Thomas and Sanderson, 2009), which surveyed young people of all ethnic backgrounds, using a variety of qualitative research techniques. For the purposes of this chapter, and the following one that focuses on white young people, the material drawn on is from the 'Identity Ranking' exercise, plus sections of the questionnaire that asked respondents to agree or disagree on questions such as 'I am proud to be British', 'Britain is a stronger country because of difference' and, conversely, 'Britain is stronger if groups live separately'. This was supported by word association and sentence completion exercises that invited young people to express what they associated with different forms of identity, both their 'own' and that of 'others'. The Identity Ranking exercise asked respondents to rank eight different forms of identity encompassing ethnic, religious, national and local identity. Other academic work around the identity of ethnic minority young people (Hutnik and Coran-Street, 2010) has seen both 'country of origin' (e.g. Pakistani- or Bangladeshi-origin) and religious affiliation as an undifferentiated 'ethnicity' when exploring the identities that are important to young people, but the intention of the research reported here was precisely to investigate any distinctions made by young people between 'ethnicity' and 'religion', as well as between different forms of 'national identity', such as 'British' and 'English'. The data produced through this research process are presented below and relates only to the identity prioritised by the Pakistani- and Bangladeshi-origin young people surveyed, and the ways that this identity was deployed during the research process, with the data from white young people analysed in the following chapter. The abbreviation AYP is used here to represent 'Asian young person'.

The majority of Muslim young people surveyed were positive about 'British' identity: 'British: Me' (AYP, Rochdale). Sixty-three per cent of those self-identifying as 'Muslim' definitely agreed with the statement 'I am proud to say that I am British', and only 10 per cent definitely disagreed. Whilst this was less than the 80 per cent of the non-Muslim young people who agreed with the same statement, the difference is arguably surprisingly limited, given the significant criticisms of and misgivings about British foreign policy of recent years, such as the interventions in Afghanistan and Iraq, frequently expressed by Muslim young people during the research process:

British means attacking other countries

Muslim people are targeted, victimised

English people are to blame for the war in Iraq.

(Asian young people, Rochdale)

This suggests that recent British foreign policy has *not* had a significantly alienating effect on the national identity of the majority of Muslim young people:

> British means live with different people
>
> British means loving your country
>
> British means being loyal to England and not being a terrorist and blowing it up
>
> British means you can be multi-cultured yet keep your identity.
>> (Asian young people, Rochdale)

For these Asian-origin young people, Britishness is more positive than Englishness: 'I suppose because British is more inclusive, that's how people can relate to that more than just the St George flag' (AYP, Rochdale). This could be a function of Britishness being associated with ideas about inclusive citizenship, as expressed in this word association from Oldham:

> British means you live in Britain, abiding laws, treating each other respectfully, a citizen of Britain, having rights in Britain.

By contrast, Englishness appeared to be more associated with socio-cultural traits: the last respondent identified English people as 'sometimes racist, to blame for the war on Iraq, good at football, good cricketers, to blame for street crime', and in the following example Englishness is seen more negatively, as it is viewed as being about 'being white'.

> English people are the opposite of us
>
> English people are white people.
>> (Asian Young People, Rochdale)

This is clearly problematic, as most white young people see English as a more important identity than British, as is indicated in the table below, and discussed in Chapter 7. This table summarises how young people of different ethnic backgrounds viewed the relevant importance of ethnic, national and religious forms of identity. One of the clearest distinctions between the different identified ethnic groups was the significance of religion as a source of identity. Self-ascribed ethnic categories were grouped together to facilitate meaningful comparison, and responses ranking identity factors 1 or 2 were also aggregated to allow for those with a shared religious/national identity to emerge. This table clearly highlights the primary importance that virtually all Pakistani- and Bangladeshi-origin young people placed on religion/Islamic faith as a form of identity. This finding represents a qualification to the positive responses given to the finding that the Muslim sample were proud to be British, in that it is clear that for this group, unlike their counterparts, religious identity trumps national identity.

Self-ascribed ethnicity	Rank religion 1 or 2 (%)	Rank English 1 or 2 (%)	Rank British 1 or 2 (%)
White British, English, White, White English, White Christian, British (N = 57)	7	75	56
Asian Pakistani, British Muslim, Pakistani Kashmiri, Pakistani, British Asian, Bangladeshi/Bengali, British Bengali, British Asian (N = 54)	93	3	20
Black African, Black British, mixed race, other (N = 16)	44	56	44

Islam/faith was clearly seen as the most important form of identity for virtually all Pakistani/Bangladeshi-origin young people surveyed, consistent with other research nationally (CRE/Ethnos, 2005; Mirza et al., 2007), and in strong contrast to all other ethnic/faith backgrounds. This clearly gave a lot of Muslim young people a strong and positive sense of identity: 'Pakistani Muslim...I'm a very strong believer in all religious rules' (AYP, Rochdale). 'British Muslim – I'm very religious' (AYP, Rochdale).

However, this strong Muslim identification also gave a minority of young people a basis in negatively judge the morals and lifestyles of non-Muslims. The extreme negativity and prejudices towards white people from some Muslim young people (arguably echoed in the racist statements of many white young people surveyed, and discussed in Chapter 7) was often expressed in moral or religious terms, suggesting that the religious identity seen by all Muslim young people was being used by a minority to judge and label others , with terms such as 'drunkenness' and'godless' being utilised, as this excerpt from the exercise completed by one youth group in Rochdale shows:

> White people: Shameless, not believing in God, no respect for other people.

This suggests that the strong faith affiliation of Muslim young people led some of them to make negative judgements on people not prioritising religious culture and tradition to the same extent:

> I don't understand their tradition – they haven't really got one, they haven't got a background.
>
> (AYP, Oldham)

Unwilling Britons?

This data suggests that claims of a profound dichotomy between 'Muslim' and positive national identity and affiliation are exaggerated, and that British national identity is relatively unproblematic for most young Muslims. The relationship between Muslim young people and the growing sense of English national identity (Ward and Carvel, 2007) is explored elsewhere (Thomas, forthcoming), but how can we understand this evidence suggesting strong Muslim youth support for British identity? The strength of the 'proud to be British?' response from Muslim (and even more so from white young people) contradicts suggestions that younger people are 'indifferent' to national identity (Fenton, 2007). That Bristol-based study indicated that young adults were 'suspicious of collective identities' (Fenton, 2007: 336) in general, and that this lukewarm support for national identity represented a desire to avoid being seen as 'nationalist', something seen as negative and akin to racism. The significantly positive responses to the 'proud to be British?' question in the survey data presented here suggest that substantial cultural change in ex-industrial towns, the community cohesion focus for the past decade on 'parallel lives' and the need to overcome them, and the intense media speculation over the affiliation and loyalties of Muslim communities have all combined to produce clear and positive positions on national identity from young people in areas like Oldham and Rochdale. The reality of ethnic segregation and the accelerant of the Iraq and Afghanistan wars might have been expected to lead to a 'Pakistani' or 'Bangladeshi' affiliation rather than a 'British' one. A previous survey of Pakistani-origin young people in Bradford found that:

Young people in this sample make clear that they consider themselves as 'British' as opposed to 'Pakistani' – 87% said they describe
themselves as 'British', 11% said they describe their identity as being
'Pakistani' and 2% as being English.

(Din, 2006: 76)

This new data on Muslims and national identity supports this, and
evidence from the 2003 Home Office Citizenship Survey found that
'Muslims as a group, are only slightly less likely to feel that they belong
to Britain than Whites and are, in fact, more likely to feel that they
belong to Britain than those in the African-Caribbean group' (DCLG,
2007d: 26). The large majority of Muslim young people surveyed
describe themselves as 'British Muslim' or 'British Asian', mirroring
data gathered from another Bradford survey of Pakistani-origin young
adults (Bagguley and Hussain, 2005) that detected a 'bi-cultural' affiliation. This type of national identity can be seen even more clearly
in Scotland, where the long pre-devolution process of discussing what
'Scottishness' means and the post-devolution process of building an
authentic national identity has had positive impacts on non-white ethnic minority willingness to associate positively with Scottishness, in
clear contrast to feelings about 'Englishness' in England (CRE/Ethnos,
2005). A survey of Pakistani-origin young people in Scotland as devolution became real (Saeed et al., 1999) found that almost 60 per cent used
a 'bi-cultural' term to identify themselves, with 'Scottish Pakistani' the
most popular. For that sample, there was no conflict between 'Scottish'
and 'Pakistani', leading to the observation that 'hyphenation is still a
much underused resource in the reconfiguration of plural identities in
Britain' (Saeed et al., 1999: 839).

Muslim citizens?

Whilst this data from Oldham and Rochdale addresses the suggestion
that Pakistani- and Bangladeshi-origin young people reject British identity, the strength of this Islamic faith identity preference shown in the
identity of many Muslims in comparison to national identity needs to
be explored further. For some critics, the privileging of such a distinct
faith identity is in itself problematic, suggesting a lack of a strong and
overarching shared national identity that might well be undermining
essential social solidarity (Goodhart, 2004) and making Britain inherently weak and unstable in the face of a very serious Islamist terror
threat. Indeed, it has been suggested that such a strong and distinct

Muslim identity is precisely the cause of this home-grown terror threat (Prins and Salisbury, 2008). How can we understand the strength of this 'Muslim' identity, and should we be concerned by it? Firstly, it needs to be acknowledged that the importance placed on faith identity by Muslims in this research process is in stark contrast to the lack of prioritisation of faith by non-Muslims, a gap replicated in other studies: '86% of respondents also believed that their religion was the most important thing in their life.... When asked the same question, only 11% of the wider British population felt the same way' (Mirza et al., 2007: 37). In light of this social reality, Tariq Modood (2005) has cautioned against what he sees as an increasingly assertive secularism in the public sphere, suggesting that such a process will make it harder for Muslims to 'integrate'. Clearly, this warning highlights the roots of the current tensions in France, as discussed in Chapter 2. Arguably, moves by the Labour government in Britain to extend aided-school funding status to Muslim schools and to strengthen legal safeguards against religious discrimination and incitement to religious hatred were designed to address such a problem.

The uniqueness of the strength of Muslim attachment to faith identity does pose the question of whether this identity is, and has been, an ahistoric constant that has increasingly been forced into open public conflict with wider society through aggressively secular and even Islamophobic political and media discourses (Geaves, 2005), or rather is one that continues to develop (and, arguably, further intensify) through dynamic political and social processes (Malik, 2009). From both perspectives, the 'Satanic Verses' controversy of 1989, following the publication of Salman Rushdie's controversial novel, has proved a watershed, as the meaning of 'Muslim' experiences, values and identities has come under increasing public scrutiny. That Satanic Verses campaign can certainly be seen as the point where overt political demands started to be made in Britain on behalf of 'Muslim' communities. Arguably, such demands, and the needs on which they were based, had been previously smothered by all-encompassing labels like 'Black' and 'Asian', all of which only had very limited meaning for communities of Pakistani and Bangladeshi origin (Modood, 2005). This narrative suggests that 'after the protests [against Rushdie], South Asian settlers would become more aware of their rights as citizens and no longer satisfied to be a silent and passive presence hidden within their own communities' (Geaves, 2005: 30). This seems to ignore previous and significant Muslim involvement in anti-racist and anti-fascist initiatives of the 1970s and early 1980s (Malik, 2009; Solomos,

2003), but it is true that overt 'Muslim' demands had not previously been made.

Analysis of race relations policy approaches adopted by the Conservative central government and left-wing local authorities following the violent urban disturbances of the early 1980s would suggest that such Muslim political campaigning was not inevitable, but instead was a product of deliberate policies of 'ethnicisim', of the public recognition and funding of each separate ethnic and religious group to the detriment of common concerns. This approach has been characterised as a deliberate, neo-colonial 'divide and rule' attempt to undermine the cross-ethnic solidarity underpinning the anti-racism movement (Kundnani, 2007), and certainly represented a concern with the 'needs' and position of separate groups at the expense of overarching identities and commonality (Cantle, 2005). Whilst such approaches initially focused on 'ethnic' identities such as Pakistani, Bangladeshi and African-Caribbean, it paved the way for the claiming of distinct needs and rights by faith identities, with *The Satanic Verses* providing a key turning point. At a local level, Bradford Council encouraged the establishment of the Bradford Council of Mosques in 1981; by 1989, this group was publicly burning Rushdie's book and gaining international media coverage. On the national level, both Conservative and Labour governments encouraged the formation of the Muslim Council of Britain (MCB), granting it favoured political status as the authentic voice of Britain's 'Muslim community' until contact was summarily cut off in 2006, due to the MCB's policy positions on the Middle East, yet it was clear from the start that such religious leadership came from a minority Islamist perspective that saw 'Muslim faith communities' in overtly political terms (McRoy, 2006). Not only did this multiculturalist policy approach of ethnicism from the 1980s onwards stress difference, it also increasingly saw Muslims as a distinct group that needed to be engaged with through the Mosque-based networks represented by the MCB. Whilst this faith analysis was questionable in itself, it failed to understand the significant changes happening within British Islam at the same time. The Iranian revolution of 1979 and the growth of socialism in parts of the Arab and Muslim world was seen as a threat by the conservative regime of Saudi Arabia, leading them to invest a significant portion of their oil wealth in propaganda material, designed to promote their traditional and literalist version of Islam (Lewis, 2007). At the same time, a new generation of young British Muslims, some of them disillusioned by the decline of anti-racist movements, was being attracted to Islamist groups that took an overtly political stand and operated in English, both of which made them seem much more interesting than the traditional Mosque leadership (Malik, 2009). The result was that 'Muslim' demands were actually led by overtly political and unrepresentative Islamists, with government attention to these demands simply encouraging further and more ambitious claims of separate Muslim needs and issues, so creating a vicious circle:

> Rather than appeal to Muslims as British citizens and attempt to draw them in to the mainstream political process, politicians and policymakers came to see them as people whose primary loyalty was to their faith and who could be politically engaged only by Muslim 'community leaders'.
>
> (Malik, 2009: 76)

This perspective suggests that the very strong Muslim faith identity expressed by the Pakistani- and Bangladeshi-origin young people in our survey needs to be understood as the results of dynamic political processes over the past 20 or 30 years, whereby policy has privileged ethnic difference and increasingly reified faith as the main form of experience (Malik, 2009) at the same time as the negative reality of post-industrial social exclusion (Levitas, 2005) has encouraged a retreat to essentialised identities. For some respondents of Muslim/Asian background, 7/7 showed the need for more openness around the support for, and extent of, extremist perspectives held by minorities within Muslim communities (Husain, 2007). Khan identifies the levels of denial, echoing similar conspiracy theories over the 'true' perpetrators of the 9/11 attacks on New York, around responsibility for these events:

> The number of people, particularly young people, that we talk to and their understanding is it's a conspiracy, 7/7 is a conspiracy, there is no evidence of what had happened. That followed up from the 9/11 issue, that's also a conspiracy, if you talk to them, they will not believe whoever did that were Muslims.

For Rafiq, the media exposure of the 'extreme' views of minorities within Muslim communities following 7/7 is not a surprise:

> I think any of us who've lived in those Muslim communities have known about this sort of stuff taking place for a long time, but haven't challenged it, or haven't felt skilled to challenge it, or got support to challenge it. It's not hidden in those communities.

We actually consulted with groups of young people right across the north-west [following 9/11] and what was coming across in all honesty a level of support for the likes of Bin Laden from Muslim communities, and these are mainstream Muslims....

Rafiq sees extremist Islamic groups as focusing on young Muslims socially excluded, although evidence from the 7/7 attacks and from 'extremist' Islamist groups generally (DCLG, 2007b; Husain, 2007) suggests that young people attracted to such causes are actually often successfully engaged in education and employment, but are disillusioned with the values of British society. Such Islamist groups are being highly selective, to Rafiq, in the way they focus on world affairs through a singular Islamist narrative (Burke, 2007), with no interest in situations not confirming to the 'Muslims as victims' perspective, such as Somalia, or Sunni/Shia conflicts in Iraq. Arguably, it is unsurprising that such ethnically/religiously focused political messages have found some support, just as the BNP has found some level of support in white communities, given social policy's privileging of ethnic/racial/faith identities over the past 30 years (Cantle, 2005; Malik, 2009). As a race equality activist, Sandy sees this growth of extremism as proof of failure of the, arguably neo-colonialist (Sivanandan, 2005), approach of the state working with, and controlling, ethnic minority communities through arrangements with so-called 'community leaders':

We've worked with young people who go to the Mosques and we're beginning to realise now that there's an awful lot of young people who do not feel, and aren't, accountable to the Imam, or the Mosque, or the Mosque Council, and they need to be worked with by other agencies.

Abdul is a youth worker heavily involved in faith-based work with Muslim young people, and in inter-faith youth work activity. He echoes many of the criticisms (Cantle, 2001) regarding how little relevance mosques and 'community leaders' have for many Muslim young people:

The local Mosques don't provide much for young people in terms of, number one, the language barrier [for many Imams] is a big problem and, number two, the upbringing of the generation above us was completely different to the upbringing we're having now, there's a big gap in that sense.

This suggests that policy and media concern with 'Muslim' identity and attitudes is as much a cause of it as a reflection, with young Pakistani and Bangladeshi people of the type surveyed in Oldham and Rochdale articulating a strong faith identity that has been projected onto them by normative political and media discourse. This would question how meaningful overt Muslim identity really is to the lived experience of communities, with clear evidence that the apparently increasing emotional attachment of young British Muslims to the key Islamic concept of the *Ummah*, one Muslim people of all backgrounds, united by their faith, 'does not transcend residential segregation or marriage within ethnically bounded groups' (Lewis, 2007: 22). Residential patterns, community organisation and marriage practices amongst communities with a Muslim background all suggest that ethnic/national background and family and kin (*Biraderi*) links are what determines choices and experiences of young Pakistani- and Bangladeshi-origin Britons, *not* their faith (Din, 2006).

The arguments made above suggest that the strong Muslim identity identified in our survey is a product of multiculturalist policies of ethnicism, and the successful exploitation by overtly political Islamist groups of the 'space' offered by such policies, both combining to essentialise and reify 'Muslim' identity. However, it can be argued that the clear evidence of a strong Muslim faith identity offered here and supported by other surveys (CRE/Ethnos, 2005; Mirza et al., 2007) is the inevitable reaction to the systematic racist vilification of Muslim communities over the past two decades. Here, it is suggested that the reality of changing 'racisms' (Hall, 2000) and political events focusing on Muslim states and communities has led to an increasingly overt 'Islamophobia' within British society, manifested in both media coverage and political approaches that have made Britain's Muslim communities the domestic focus of the 'war on terror':

> It is clear that the nation is under the grip of a kind of rampant Islamophobia . . . a media-driven phenomenon that is supported by a wider geo-political campaign to undermine, destabilise and effectively remove Islam's ever-growing presence.
>
> (Abbas, 2007b: 295)

This would suggest that the strong preference for Islamic identity within our data is an inevitable response, a 'defensive identity' that provides support and solidarity for young Muslims, and which enables them to express publicly defiance through this identity and its symbols, such as the wearing of the hijab, in the face of overt prejudices. 'Radical' versions of this Islamic identity that have been adopted by a minority of young Muslims might arguably be seen here as the product of 'cumulative extremism', whereby societal prejudice and the rise of far-right political organisations such as the BNP and the English Defence League produce a counter-reaction and a 'hardening' of identity from many young Muslims (Eatwell, 2006). The problem for such an analysis is that the evidence of 'Islamophobia', prejudices and discriminatory behaviour towards people solely and specifically because of their Islamic faith is complex. Racial prejudice and discrimination towards non-white citizens has been an ongoing reality throughout Britain's post-war movement towards a multicultural society (Solomos, 2003). It is beyond dispute that sections of the media have shown overt prejudices towards Muslim figures over the past few years, this being the latest focus for long-standing racist approaches to news coverage that previously pathologised African-Caribbean young men (Gilroy, 2002; Kalra and Kapoor, 2009), but even allowing for the operation of such differential 'racisms' (Hall, 2000), the claims for an Islamophobia that is clearly distinct to racism need to be questioned. The evidence that Pakistani and Bangladeshi young people achieve less well educationally than any other educational group is put forward as evidence of Islamophobia, but it is clear that those groups do less well than other ethnic groups because of the limited 'human capital', in terms of educational qualifications and confidence and English language skills of the first generation of migrants and their misfortune to settle in areas soon to face profound, structural de-industrialisation (Modood et al., 1997), rather than any inherent Muslim discrimination. Indeed, statistics of apparent Muslim disadvantage come from conflating this with Pakistani and Bangladeshi origin, as they make up approximately 75 per cent of Britain's Muslim population; the remainder is largely of Turkish and Arab origin and is significantly more successful educationally (Lewis, 2007). Whilst the concept of Islamophobia has been promoted by Islamist-dominated Muslim representation groups (Malik, 2009), the effect may well have been counterproductive: 'The exaggeration of Islamophobia does not make Muslims feel protected but rather encourages feelings of victimi-sation and alienation' (Mirza et al., 2007: 18).

Active citizens?

The preceding discussion around how this strong faith preference can be understood, and how Muslim identity has become so prominent in

Britain, could suggest that the young people surveyed in Oldham and Rochdale are simply passively reflecting an identity given to them by a mixture of Islamist activists within Muslim communities, the operation of government policy and Islamophobic media discourse, but that would ignore the agency of young people. Here, it is suggested that the strength of this Muslim faith identity, and the ways that it was expressed during the research process, gives insights into the way young British Muslims are actively constructing and exercising identity for themselves. Furthermore, there is an implicit assumption in much of the debates around increasing religiosity amongst young British Muslims that such a trend represents a reactionary step backwards (Ismail, 2008), a 'false consciousness' denial of the reality and attractions of modernity, but it is argued here that the strong faith identity and the manner of its expression revealed in the Oldham and Rochdale survey can be seen as something more complex, both symptomatic of modernist identity development by these Muslim young people, as well as possibly indicative of gendered understandings of power. A generational change in the use and importance of faith identity within Britain's Muslim communities might be important here (Din, 2006; Lewis, 2007; Malik, 2009), with other empirical data both supporting the strength of faith identification amongst young Muslims and highlighting a degree of change from older generations (Mirza et al., 2007). Whilst intergenerational tensions are a reality in all communities, the history and circumstances of Britain's Pakistani- and Bangladeshi-origin communities (Modood et al., 1997) have led to particular pressure, with young people's embracing of Islamic identity arguably a key and progressive part of their efforts to move forward positively. Din's (2006) study of Mirpuri Pakistani-origin young people in Bradford highlighted how they overwhelmingly felt constrained and controlled by the culture and expectations of the parental generation, with the 'biraderi', the clan network that had provided a vital source of support in the early days of migration, now a block to progress, as it was understood by young people. Central to this experience is the importance of hierarchies and barriers, with the maintenance of 'honour' vital within the biraderi: 'for fear of being ostracised within their tightly knit community, parents would not allow their child to do something not thought appropriate' (Lewis, 2007: 41). Such tradition-based community pressures can limit who young people can associate with and the educational and employment options they have, especially for young women, with marriage choices a particular source of conflict (Din, 2006; Lewis, 2007).

In light of these conflicts, the clear move by younger Pakistani- and Bangladeshi-origin young Britons to prioritise Muslim identity might be seen as a way of overcoming parochial and historical restrictions by emphasising the equality and openness inherent to Islam's teachings. This suggests that the growth of Muslim identity, including the increase in radicalism for a minority, is part of a generational 'de-coupling' of culture and religion to facilitate social change (Sanghera and Thapar-Bjorkert, 2007). Indeed, one of the attractions of Islamist groups for a minority of young Muslims has been their emphasis on Muslims of all national, ethnic and sect backgrounds coming together (Husain, 2007), with the facilitation of cross-sect 'love' marriages proving a key milestone in the alienation of the ringleader of the 7/7 bombings from his wider community (Malik, 2009). In this way, the very strong prioritisation of Muslim faith identity by young people in our survey can be understood as part of an embracing of a 'true' (Din, 2006) Islamic identity, free of caste, sect and cultural restrictions. Whilst an element of this identity is inevitably a defensive hardening in response to both profound economic change (May, 1999a) and to a very specific and racialised political and media scrutiny that some term 'Islamophobia' (Abbas, 2007b), this can also be understood as a way for young people to negotiate and understand their identity in a rapidly changing, multicultural society. The context for the criticisms of British foreign policy contained in the survey is the understanding of the global Muslim 'imagined community' (Shavit, 2009) or *Ummah* as central to their own identity. Understanding oneself as part of a global *Ummah* not only connects to a 'true', decultured Islamic identity, but enables British Muslims, as a migrant minority community often experiencing economic marginalisation as well as societal discrimination (Modood, 2005), a feeling of strength whereby they are part of a larger, worldwide community (Roy, 2004). Whilst the global growth in this identity, including in its minority and politicised radical Islamist form, can be understood as a reaction to the disjunctures and migrations connected to globalisation, it can also be seen as inherently part of globalisation, with the new technologies of globalisation enabling the rapid development of a new 'imagined community', and the creation of a virtual *Ummah*, albeit one that does not necessarily supplant existing national and ethnic identities (Shavit, 2009). Despite the limited impact on day-to-day life for most British Muslims discussed above, the concept of being part of the *Ummah* has facilitated a progressive, internationalist concern amongst some young British Muslims with poverty and suffering in other Muslim countries, such as the conflict in Palestine or the earthquake in Pakistan (McGhee, 2008).

However, the embracing of the 'true' (Din, 2006) version of an overtly religious identity, especially in an era when conservative and literalist understandings have been heavily promoted by the Saudi government in particular (Malik, 2009), can arguably result in the sort of prejudiced moral judgements on the lives and values of non-Muslims found in our survey, and echoed by another survey by right-of-centre think-tank Policy Exchange:

> When young Muslims complain about the lack of values, they reveal a remarkable intolerance for other peoples' personal behaviour. The overwhelming concerns for the more religious Muslims we spoke to were homosexuality, the overt sexuality of women, drugs and binge drinking.
>
> (Mirza et al., 2007: 49)

The very similar comments made by a minority of our respondents and reported above can be seen as one facet of such a strong, faith-based identity. Both partially a product of, and combining with, the common reality of ethnically segregated 'parallel lives' (Cantle, 2001), such moral judgements of the 'other' can interact dialectically with the racist prejudices held by some of the white young people surveyed and discussed in the following chapter.

The nature of the strong Muslim identity reported here and confirmed by other surveys, and the way young people understand and deploy it has been seen as highly gendered by some commentators. Previous research into an increase in violent street activity and protest by Muslim young people in Bradford (Sanghera and Thapar-Bjorkert, 2007) has identified a hardened and defensive religious identity in the face of media and political scrutiny, with a minority moving towards political radicalism that decouples culture and religion. Within this, researchers identified a clear gender difference, with the identity of young men being about territory, control and confrontation, whilst for young women, an increased Muslim identity being much more about a progressive social change that chooses to negotiate with, rather than overtly challenge, patriarchal controls within the community. Another piece of Bradford-based research suggested that control is central to the Muslim identity of some young men, with public discussion ignoring 'the use to which Islam is put in the control of women and the maintenance of traditional cultural practices to oppress them' (Macey,

1999: 846). This perspective would suggest that the overwhelmingly male deployment of moral judgementalism within our survey is part of a larger and gendered moral control, with young men policing the dress and behaviour of young women, as they do in other communities (Macey, 1999). Here, the strong Muslim identity for many young men allows them to exercise patriarchy in the name of community whilst at the same time portraying a strong masculinity that can 'resist stereotypes of weakness and passivity' (DCLG, 2007c: 5). In contrast, young women's deployment of Muslim identity may be more about inclusion and equality, strategically (Lewis, 2007) using understandings of 'true' Islam to question cultural norms and practice that hold them back: 'young women talked about how education was important Islamically and therefore used this strategically' (Sanghera and Thapar-Bjorkert, 2007: 185). In contrast to many uninformed, external criticisms of heightened religiosity amongst Muslim young women, this Bradford-based research found that faith identity was a source of empowerment, not limitation for the young women, allowing them to criticise the hypocritical and patriarchal behaviour of young men. Here, the increased wearing of the 'Hijab' headscarf can be understood as part of that assertive independence, with many families actually disapproving.

These understandings of the significantly increased Muslim faith identification amongst Pakistani- and Bangladeshi-origin young people, which this Oldham and Rochdale-based survey has confirmed, would suggest that, far from representing a reactionary and melancholic look back, this Muslim identity represents a modernist development (Malik, 2009; Roy, 2004) that is actually about personal assertiveness and identity, rather than communal conformity (Mirza et al., 2007). In contrast to the simplistic polarity of either being 'caught' between two cultures or moving effortlessly between them (Lewis, 2007), the evidence around the construction and use of this heightened Muslim identity amongst young people suggests that most young Muslims are somewhere in the middle, with identity developed dialectically through their negotiation of the conflicts and tensions. Much political attention has been paid to the small, radical Islamist minority amongst young British Muslims, but, arguably, a more significant development is the emergence of a genuinely European/British Muslim identity which, in the view of one of its key advocates, needs to take the next step to enable Muslims to be truly at home in multicultural society of multiple identities:

> European societies must reach this new perception of themselves; of people who are equal before the law, developing multidimensional

identities which are always in motion and flexible enough to defend
shared values.

(Ramadan, 2009: 15)

Conclusion

This empirical data from Oldham and Rochdale has highlighted the
extent to which moral panics around the national loyalty of young
British Muslims are misplaced, with a significant majority 'proud to be
British', and recent foreign policy decisions only having a marginally
negative impact. This recent data confirms similar findings of other
research (DCLG, 2007c; Din, 2006). Nevertheless, religious faith is by far
the most important form of identity for these Pakistani and Bangladeshi
young people, something again confirmed by other surveys (Mirza et al.,
2007). Whilst some would say that this is a timely revelation of 'true'
identity, it is suggested here that this identity preference is to a significant extent the product of policy approaches of 'ethnicism' that
has then been exploited by Islamist political groups to reify and priv-
ilege Muslim identity within political and popular discourse (Kundnani,
2007; Malik, 2009) as well as being a defensive response to clear societal prejudice (Abbas, 2007b). Young people have been an active part
of this development process, with Muslim affiliation representing an
attempt to overcome the barriers and limitations stemming from cultural norms of the parental generation (Din, 2006). Here, enhanced
Muslim identity amongst young people, although arguably significantly
gendered (Sanghera and Thapar-Bjorkert, 2007), can be seen as an
attempt to negotiate modern complexity. It also suggests a tension over
whether government policy is supporting the development of the more
nuanced, 'cooler' and complex identities needed to facilitate a successful multicultural society (McGhee, 2006) through the ethnic mixing
inherent to the community cohesion practice described in Chapter 4, or
instead working with simple, monocultural understandings of Muslim
identity as 'Prevent' has done (Thomas, 2009, 2010), and analysed in
Chapter 8. The following chapter looks at how we might understand
empirical research data around the identities favoured by white young
people, and what this suggests about policy attempts to engage with the
attitudes and values of white communities.

7
White Young People and Community Cohesion – Refusing Contact?

Introduction

Chapter 6 discussed how we might understand the strong preference for religious faith forms of identity amongst the Muslim young people surveyed in light of the political and media discourses that have portrayed Muslim youth identities as highly problematic and potentially dangerous to society. The thesis of community cohesion (Cantle, 2001, 2005) has suggested that ethnic segregation and a one-sided policy focus on separate ethnic identities, rather than on commonality, can create exclusive and oppositional identities and attitudes amongst all communities, including majority white communities. Indeed, the events of the 2001 riots in Oldham, Burnley and Bradford, as discussed in Chapter 1, suggested widespread, taken for granted attitudes of racial exclusiveness and antagonism to local Asian communities amongst white communities in those areas. The existence of such attitudes nationally has arguably been confirmed by the significant growth and move towards the political mainstream of the British National Party, a far-right party with overtly racist policies and roots in fascist ideologies (Copsey, 2008), and the rise of the English Defence League (Eatwell and Goodwin, 2010). Accompanying this political development of the past decade has been increasing claims that some people, especially the white working class, are the 'real' victims of racism within a policy regime of one-sided bias towards ethnic minorities, prompting both a 'white backlash' (Hewitt, 2005) and claims of actual racial inequality for white people (Gilborn, 2009). This chapter discusses these issues, and understandings of white 'identities' in modern Britain that underpin them. To do so, it draws on empirical research data relating to white young people's understandings of identity and their attitudes to, and experiences of, ethnic diversity from the Oldham and Rochdale Youth Identity Project discussed in Chapters 5 and 6. Understandings of the attitudes revealed in the data are discussed in relation to key academic perspectives. In light of the fact that some of this data is negative about ethnic diversity, and contains significant elements of overt racism, the chapter goes on to discuss the appropriacy of community cohesion's apparent move away from the priorities, language and operations of 'anti-racism' (Back et al., 2002), discussing whether this policy shift represented by community cohesion is a backward step in the face of these white identities and attitudes, or whether it is actually a potentially helpful way forward that enables the positive engagement of white young people in processes of cohesion and cross-ethnic contact.

Field research data

The data below relates in particular to responses by white young people surveyed to key sections of the questionnaire, particularly the statements 'Britain is a stronger country because of difference' and 'Britain is stronger if groups live separately', which respondents were asked to agree or disagree with on a three-point scale. It also presents material from group and individual interviews and word association/sentence completion exercises. In all cases, the names and neighbourhood localities of respondents have been removed, with this not seen as relevant to the discussions. The abbreviation 'WYP' is used to denote 'white young person'.

Some of the data relating to white young peoples' experiences of ethnic diversity could be seen as positive, with the minority of young people of all ethnic backgrounds who attended ethnically mixed schools and colleges saying that they did have friends of a different ethnic background. However, these friendships existed only in the educational setting, with virtually no cross-ethnic contact outside of that environment. Within one white background youth group, 100 per cent of the young people had 'friends' of a different background that they talked to in school/college, but only 10 per cent had any contact with such friends away from that site. Both white and Asian young people surveyed blamed the attitudes and prejudices of their own families and peers, and associated fears about entering 'unsafe' territory, for this lack of contact. One 13-year-old young man in Rochdale explained why he never invited Asian friends to visit him: 'my mates and stuff...'

[it would] 'start fighting and got mates who don't like 'em'. This leads to a reality that mirrors the 'parallel lives' picture painted in the community cohesion reports (Cantle, 2001; Ritchie, 2001), with white young people both pessimistic about the possibility of cross-ethnic contact, or not even seeing the point: 'If they spoke to me I would [talk to them] but I wouldn't go up to them and start talking to them' (WYP, Rochdale). It is clear nationally that young people of all ethnic backgrounds often feel that some areas or 'territory' are unsafe for them with clear 'mental maps' of which areas and routes are safe or not (Kintrea et al., 2008). The research found that the significant physical ethnic segregation and the racialised environment in Oldham and Rochdale led to an overlap between 'race' and territory found in other locality-based research (Webster, 1995). For instance, the significant Asian populations of the actual town centres of Oldham and Rochdale led many white young people from suburban areas or satellite townships to see the whole town centre and its amenities as unsafe for white young people: 'If I like went to hang around with my friends, like meet other people, I wouldn't feel safe' (WYP). This racialisation of the main towns by white young people included wild exaggerations about the ethnic minority population of the town. This racialisation, and the fact that many white young people see 'Oldham' or 'Rochdale' as the town, rather than the wider local authority area, helps to explain the noticeably more negative response of white young people to the questionnaire assertion that 'Different sorts of people get on well in (name of town)?'

Respondent group	Definitely agree (%)	Definitely disagree (%)
Muslim	25	20
Non-Muslim	14	40

For a significant number of the young people surveyed this lack of cross-cultural contact and the resulting ignorance allowed insults and stereotypes, some of them overtly hostile and racist in tone. Both white and Asian respondents expressed crude stereotypes and insults about each other, suggesting that the lack of contact made such positions easier to hold. The views expressed by some white young people supported the notion of a 'sense of unfairness' (Hewitt, 2005) amongst white

working-class young people who feel that other, ethnic minority, groups
have been prioritised and favoured by policy-makers: 'They [Asians] get
everything they want' (WYP), whilst they are looked down upon by the
rest of society, contrary to past notions that white racist prejudices are
about 'superiority': 'I don't mind them being Asian if they didn't look
down on us and take over; I wouldn't be bothered but everywhere you
go you get looked down on by them, and it's your country, it's our
country' (WYP, Rochdale). It was indeed true that a minority of Asian
respondents, especially, young men, were highly judgemental about
white young people, using religious terminology in describing them as
'immoral', 'godless' and 'drunken'. For some white young people, prejudices were expressed in crude racist terms, such as 'Muslim people are
money-grabbers', 'Rochdale is Pakistan now' and 'Multicultural means
bombers'. In this context, the strong preference amongst white young
people for 'English' as their favoured form of identity shown in the data
presented in Chapter 6 might be understood as a racialised and exclusive
form of nationality, a view expressed by the Asian young people surveyed who overwhelmingly saw 'English' as an exclusively white form
of identity (Thomas, forthcoming).

Young people were asked for their views regarding diversity in society, and whether they regarded this as a positive development. Attitudes
to a range of factors associated with living in a multicultural society
were explored using a three-point attitude scale. While a large number of respondents indicated they were 'not sure' about many of the
statements (often as large a proportion as 30 per cent), there were
still notable differences between the groups self-identifying as Muslim
and white young people. Sixty per cent of the group self-identifying
as 'Muslim' agreed that 'Britain is a stronger country because of difference' as opposed to 23 per cent white young people. In response
to the converse statement that 'Britain is stronger if groups live separately', only 16 per cent of the Muslim population definitely agreed
and 71 per cent definitely disagreed, as opposed to 36 per cent of the
white group definitely agreeing and 30 per cent definitely disagree-
ing, so displaying a small but significant white majority in support
of the idea that even greater ethnic segregation would be better for
all concerned, a highly pessimistic conclusion some years after the
promotion of community cohesion had supposedly become a major
policy priority. This pessimism about the possibility of a more successful multicultural future was shown in the qualitative comments of some
individual white young people: 'People don't want to mix with different
people' (WYP);

Q Why do you think young people from different backgrounds
don't mix?
A Don't know, it's never happened has it.

(WYP, Rochdale)

Not all white young people were so negative or pessimistic about ethnic diversity, and young people of all ethnic backgrounds who had
experienced significant ethnic mixing wanted more of it, and made
proposals around the sort of practices and sites that could encourage
it (Thomas and Sanderson, 2009). However, there is no escaping the
fact that this empirical field research data shows white young people
to be significantly more negative and resentful about the reality of ethnic diversity, and pessimistic about its future. Here, the openness and
'matter of factness' of racism within some predominantly white communities nationally is highly relevant. Whilst such white racism has
been a reality throughout the history of modern race relations (Solomos,
2003), prejudice is not necessarily an inevitable generational inheritance
in monocultural communities. It can also be generated independently
by young people (Back, 1996) partly as a 'counter-narrative' (Hewitt,
2005) to perceptions of 'unfair' anti-discriminatory policy initiatives, as
well as through racist media coverage, or through political campaigning
by far-right, racist groups who deliberately distort facts and inflame local
feelings through the production of racist narratives (Copsey, 2008), the
reality of which can be seen as directly causal to the 2001 Oldham riots
(Kalra and Rhodes, 2009). The existence of such a racialised reality in
some white communities was highlighted by a number of respondents,
including Deborah:

Growing up in Oldham I don't remember anyone being openly
racist...but when I started working in Branton [white working-class
area], people were, 'I'm racist and?? What of it??'

For Michael, some white people are increasingly willing to see everything that happens to them in terms of 'race'. He described tensions
over the local authority's introduction of quality Asian park wardens
to parks within a white-dominated area of Oldham:

Whether it had been White or Asian security guards, it would have
been young people winding them up, trying to get a rise, a response
out of them. But then one or two young people have gone home and
complained, the response that's come from the parents has been a

racist one, that 'I'm not having any Asians, any Pakis, telling my kids what to do.'

Having returned to Oldham after a long absence, Jennifer sees community identity within areas of Oldham as stronger and increasingly problematic, compared to the past:

> I think there's a greater focus on maintaining your cultural identity and there are stronger characters as well now who are pushing for that...I don't think it's just the Asian community, I think it's the white community as well.

The empirical data outlined above, and the ways in which we might understand and interpret these findings in relation to the focus and priorities of community cohesion activity, are discussed below.

Discussion: Refusing Contact?

In some ways the noticeably more negative attitude of white young people to ethnic diversity and cross-ethnic mixing found in this research data is hardly surprising, given certain demographic realities, and so questions even more why some community cohesion discourses apparently put so much stress on Asian communities to integrate. Given that the UK non-white ethnic minority population is currently only 8–9 per cent (Finney and Simpson, 2009) and that those communities are heavily concentrated in certain English conurbations (Modood et al., 1997), it inevitably means that the communities most 'segregated' and most conditioned to living within monocultural norms are white communities: 'it is the majority white populations that are the most isolated and least engaged with communities other than their own' (Finney and Simpson, 2009: 111). This demographic reality and the clear statistical data showing that no electoral wards in England can be called monocultural ethnic minority 'ghettos' in the American sense (Kalra and Kapoor, 2009) immediately suggests caution about some of the 'taken for granted' popular discourses in the wake of community cohesion's emergence. This picture is true even in apparently multicultural local authority areas like Oldham and Rochdale; in both cases the principal towns themselves have significant ethnic minority concentrations in certain electoral wards whose populations nevertheless do not contain more than 60 per cent of non-white ethnic minorities, but the wider local authority areas have suburban and rural areas that are overwhelmingly white (Oldham MBC, 2006). This relative ethnic isolation of white young people in itself, even in what are, statistically, 'multicultural' local authority areas, might well in itself partially explain the less positive attitudes of white young people to diversity, and this explanation is supported by a University of Lancaster study commissioned by the Home Office in which 'results show that white children who are segregated from other races have far more intolerant attitudes than schools where whites mix with others' (Dodd, 2006: 13). That survey examined the attitudes of 435 15-year-olds in the northwest of England on race, religion and integration, and found that belief in racial superiority was much higher in white majority schools than in Asian majority or ethnically mixed schools (Dodd, 2006). Such realities stemming from white monocultural isolation provide some explanation for the data presented above, but there are arguably a number of other reasons why many white young people such as those surveyed in Oldham and Rochdale currently feel negative and resentful about ethnic diversity and the prospects for a multicultural society. These are discussed below, and include the problematic impact of anti-racist educational efforts aimed at such young people, the profound social and cultural changes wrought on many white (and non-white) communities by de-industrialisation, the loss of focus on class in society as concern with ethnic equality has grown, and the resulting and highly questionable representation of the white working class as an 'ethnically disadvantaged' group.

The failure of anti-racism?

Firstly, there is long-term academic evidence around the decidedly mixed impacts of anti-racist educational work aimed at white young people through schools and youth work. Coming out of the early 1980s' frustration with the limitations of bland and apolitical multiculturalism (Thomas, 2007a), such anti-racist educational approaches were part of a wider drive for more meaningful ethnic equality and tangible progress against racism, and have so contributed to real progress on racial tolerance and equality (Modood, 2005). However, such anti-racist approaches have been far from universally successful with white young people. Whilst acknowledging that there has been a 'white backlash' (Hewitt, 2005) against every race equality measure in Britain (Law, 1996), it is clear that anti-racist educational measures have been unsuccessful, and even counterproductive, amongst some white young people, especially those from disadvantaged economic class backgrounds. Some of this has been about the clumsy implementation of rules within formal educational settings historically resented by many working-class young people (Cohen, 1988; Macdonald, 1989). Allied to this has been the nature of anti-racism itself, with some white young people perceiving such anti-racist rules as a one-sided policing of their language and behaviour with no matching focus on those of ethnic minority young people, leading to a 'white backlash' (Hewitt, 2005) from young people who feel that they are the ones discriminated against, often by (white) professionals who look down on their language, culture and community as 'racist' and ignorant. Indeed, research amongst youth workers attempting anti-racist work with white young people found that workers understood anti-racism as representing the sanctioning of the language and behaviour of white young people, closing down discussions of difference rather than exploring them for fear of perpetuating a 'racist incident' (CRE, 1999). Such approaches have built on the multicultural content of education, where education has become much better at acknowledging and celebrating 'difference', but has often done this through presentation of essentialised versions of different ethnicities, their faiths and foods, a stereotyping perpetuated by anti-racism (Bhavnani, 2001). Whilst there are undoubted positives about such work, their effect has not only been to highlight difference rather than commonality (Cantle, 2005) but to leave many white young people unsure about what 'their' culture and tradition is, in this differentiated and essentialised understanding of culture. This is partially because white Britishness is all around us as an uninterrogated norm (Bonnett, 2000), with Christian festivals setting the rhythm of the year and alcohol a key form of socialising, but it is also about the long-term decline of religious observance within many white communities and the wider loss of community focus and institutions brought about by profound economic change and explored below.

In that context, an educational approach to diversity that focuses on 'religion', 'traditions' and 'ceremonies' is highly likely to marginalise many white young people, and research amongst young people in the north-east of England, an overwhelmingly white area of the country, shows white young people the least clear and confident as to what their 'ethnic background' and 'traditions' are (Nayak, 1999). Indeed, our research found that some Asian young people were highly judgemental about white peers:

> White people: Shameless, not believing in God, no respect for other people.
>
> (AYP, Rochdale)

This focus on essentialised ethnic cultures has been exacerbated by the common failure to mark or celebrate symbols of Britishness or Englishness outside of short-lived football tournaments, whether flying national flags or marking St George's Day. A view that such behaviour would be 'racist' or exclusionary to ethnic minorities has fuelled the feelings of some white young people and their communities that they are 'not allowed' to celebrate their own identity, so handing the initiative to far-right racist organisations prepared to do so (Bragg, 2006). The strong support for 'English' as the preferred form of identity by the white young people surveyed in Oldham and Rochdale shows the importance of addressing such issues, particularly as further progress on devolution within the UK means that there *must* be more discussion around meaningful and inclusive understandings of 'Englishness' (Thomas, forthcoming).

The lost class?

The, arguably one-sided, concern with ethnicity discussed in the previous section developed at the same time as profound changes happened to class structures in Britain and so the way that class was viewed. Central to this has been the large-scale de-industrialisation that has had profound effects on former manufacturing areas like Oldham and Rochdale, and the very patchy development of a post-industrial, service sector-led economy. Portrayed as an inevitable development of globalisation that will ultimately benefit everyone, other commentators have seen this economic change, and the very significant accompanying social marginalisation known as 'social exclusion', as a deliberate development of a reserve army of labour by unregulated monopoly capitalism (Byrne, 1999). Beyond dispute is the fact that these changes have greatly undermined the stability and structures of working-class communities in former industrial areas, having a profound impact on the identities of the inhabitants, with class- and employment-based identities weakening, and identities more based on ethnicity and cultural norms inevitably moving into the vacuum (Collins, 2004). Here, 'whiteness' (Bonnett, 2000) had not previously been interrogated because secure working-class employment, stable communities and associated cultural institutions supplied identity, but 'working-class' communities increasingly no longer have common experiences, or even work at all. At the same time, the way class itself is viewed in society has changed profoundly, with the language of class studiously ignored even by Labour Party politicians who prefer phrases like 'hard working families', and the social exclusion prism of viewing social inequality arguably having a strong focus on individual responsibility and agency (Levitas, 2005). The result has been that disdain for the poorest sections of the working class, or 'chavs', has become publicly acceptable (Collins, 2004), and that significant sections of former Labour voters have been appealed to by the racial narratives of the far-right British National Party (Copsey, 2008; Eatwell and Goodwin, 2010). This and the continuation of an essentialised ethnic equality policy agenda at a time when life chances and experiences for different ethnic minority communities are increasingly diverse (Modood et al., 1997) goes some way to explain why some of the white young people we surveyed feel negatively judged by ethnic minorities as well as by other people in society. This can be seen in the way that the 'white working class' have been discussed in relation to educational achievement.

The real losers?

Historically, the close correlation between educational success and economic background in Britain has been explained by some as being due to the antipathy of the working class to formal education, with this traditionally right of centre class bias even deployed by champions of multiculturalism:

> There has been an alarming disregard for the obvious key connections between how the white working classes regard education in this country and how this affected the many bright and eager children of immigrants who found themselves both in competition with, and in need of approval from, these white children.
>
> (Alibhai-Brown, 2000: 166)

However, more recently, the 'white working class' have had their cause advocated from unlikely quarters, as a number of newspapers and political commentators have claimed that the white working class are the group really ethnically disadvantaged within educational achievement. This provides insights both into the very specific ways that class is now deployed to attack diversity measures in political discourse (Sveinsson, 2009) and to why some white young people and communities offer such a racialised understanding of their disadvantage, as our survey data indicates. The claim that the educational achievement of the 'white working class' is poorer than ethnic minorities is actually based on a highly misleading use both of 'working class' as a concept, and of the actual data (Gilborn, 2009). Achievement data shows that young people in poverty from all ethnic backgrounds achieve poorly. Media claims about the 'white working class' are actually about the 13.2 per cent of pupils that are on Free School Meals (FSMs) (the best available school measure of poverty), but any reasonable understanding of 'working class' would see that group as much larger, even allowing for the profound economic changes discussed above, and possibly as much as 50 per cent of the population (Bottero, 2009). The actual achievement gap between pupils of different ethnic backgrounds who receive FSMs is small, but media claims are actually comparing white young people on FSMs with ethnic minority young people of all social backgrounds, a clear manipulation of the data (Gilborn, 2009). Not only are such claims used to implicitly attack the 'unfairness' of multiculturalist policies of monitoring and achievement raising, echoing the political strategies of far-right political groups (Copsey, 2008), but they also contain a judgementalism about the lack of success of the 'white working class': 'By presenting the white working class in ethnic terms, as yet another cultural minority in a (dysfunctional) "multicultural Britain", commentators risk giving a *cultural* reading of inequality' (Bottero, 2009:7).

This has been exacerbated by the fact that the very genuinely redistributive educational measures introduced by the New Labour government, including extra funding for poor pupils, the Sure Start early years initiative and learning mentors attached to pupils struggling at school, were studiously *not* badged as redistributive or support for the working-class measures; instead opaque terms like social exclusion have been deployed (Levitas, 2005). As this data and other field-based research (Hewitt, 2005) indicate, this racialised picture of policies unfairly disadvantaging the 'white working class' has gained significant traction within white communities. Such discourses of unfairness around regeneration funding were seen as a significant trigger for the 2001 disturbances (Cantle, 2001), and around housing, with modern, equality-driven rules seen as responsible for housing shortages that have broken up traditional white communities in east London (Dench et al., 2006). That sympathetic narrative of 'white flight' flies in the face of evidence about how increasing affluence leads to housing drift towards suburban and semi-rural areas for *all* ethnic groups (Finney and Simpson, 2009), but also racialises much more profound structural changes in the housing market and associated policy (Garner, 2009). In particular, they gloss over the large reduction in the quantity and variety of social housing stock since the 'right to buy' policy changes of the 1980s and the subsequent failure to build new stock that has resulted in social housing being available only to the poorest and most needy, rather than those with historic family ties to an area (Garner, 2009). The inevitable resentment that broader sections of the (white) working class feel about their constrained housing options, with ownership often beyond their reach, has increasingly focused on minority 'others', egged on by political and media discourses from both right and left that have focused on 'race' and ethnic difference whilst ignoring class and social inequality: 'people see themselves engaged in struggles over culture, accommodation, language and benefits with minorities and immigrants, as well as with other white working class people seen as scroungers, but not with the middle classes' (Garner, 2009: 47).

Arguably, our survey area of Oldham and Rochdale is one of the 'hotspots' where this racialisation of social inequality issues, in a societal context where class is routinely denied, has increasingly influenced people's lived experiences (Ritchie, 2001), partially because of deeply unhelpful media coverage and opportunistic inflammation by far-right parties (Copsey, 2008):

> Feelings of injustice over inequality and material disadvantage have become focussed on opposition to multiculturalism as the only site where more wide-ranging issues and grievance around equality, identity and belonging can be articulated in public debate.
>
> (Wetherell, 2008: 309)

Such apparent manifestations of support for or tolerance of 'racism' has led supposedly anti-racist commentators to suggest that the white middle class are 'better' at ethnic diversity than the white working class (Ware, 2008), with working-class whites exclusively cast in the role of villain (Collins, 2004: 247). The evidence from working-class-based youth cultures that have embraced ethnic diversity clearly gives the lie to this (Hebdidge, 1979), and it is white working class, rather than white middle class, communities who have actually shared at first hand communities, schools and employment with non-white ethnic minorities over the past 60 years (Collins, 2004). Indeed, despite the significantly more negative and pessimistic views of ethnic diversity amongst the white respondents, and the virulent racism that some of them expressed, there were still grounds for optimism. Firstly, all the white respondents who attended ethnically mixed schools or colleges said that they had 'friends' of a different ethnic background within that environment, with issues of family and peer pressure and associated issues of territorial safety being the constraints on meeting outside, rather than personal preferences. Secondly, the majority of young people of all ethnic backgrounds in our survey wanted more opportunities and sites to meet people of a different ethnic background, as shown in Chapter 4.

A backwards step from anti-racism?

The data presented above, and the significant negativity to ethnic diversity amongst many white young people contained within it, could easily be seen as requiring an enhanced 'anti-racist' effort to change these attitudes and prejudiced behaviour based upon them. However, the chapter has already suggested that the way anti-racist educational efforts have often been implemented, and certainly understood by some young people, is a significant part of this white negativity. This chimes with the key themes of community cohesion outlined in Chapter 1, whereby previous policy approaches of political multiculturalism have inadvertently encouraged feelings of separation and ethnic antagonism. The result has been that community cohesion has involved an overt move away from the language and stated priorities of anti-racism in favour of cohesion, integration and commonality. Inevitably, this has attracted a very mixed response. Chapter 3 highlighted how this shift of language and focus has been seen as a diminution of concern with racism and the need to oppose it (Back et al., 2002; Pilkington, 2008) by many academic commentators. The majority of youth work practitioners surveyed in Oldham about their community cohesion practice (Thomas, 2006, 2007a) were positive about the shift and saw it crucially as incorporating a continued anti-racist concern within a new practice approach, as outlined in Chapter 4, but a minority of practitioners strongly disagreed. They were much more concerned that community cohesion may represent not only a moving away from the language of anti-racism but from a concern with racism itself, and the need for educational activity to oppose and challenge it. Mary sums up this move away from the language, if not the assumptions, of anti-racism contained within the development of the new community cohesion approach:

> We don't use the words [anti-racism], I suppose…everything we do has this…embedded within community cohesion, so that its part and parcel. In terms of using words like anti-racism….I guess we sort of don't use those words….community cohesion is such a nicer, softer…word, isn't it, than anti-racism?

The concerns regarding the implications of community cohesion as a dominant term and concept expressed by Mary were explored much more comprehensively by a number of other respondents. Their concern was that community cohesion was not just a 'nicer, softer' term, but represents a watering down, a stepping back from the harsh realities of challenging and exposing racism. From that perspective, whatever the shortcomings, or unintended consequences, of anti-racism explored earlier in the chapter, there remains a pressing need for explicitly anti-racist educational work with white young people. Is community cohesion enabling educationalists and their agencies to 'slip backwards' on these issues of racism and anti-racism? Some workers felt so. Salma, who has experienced racial abuse from white young people during her youth work practice, was concerned that anti-racism is being downplayed:

> I would say that cohesion is an easy option because you can get negatives and positives out of it, but when you talk about racism, you do get a lot of hatred and a lot of negativity out of it … but then I think that it needs to be talked about so that you can get solutions out of it as well … it needs to be questioned, if it's not questioned, then it will be carrying on.

For Salma, this downplaying of anti-racism suits some practitioners because they are not confident in engaging with and challenging the (often virulent) racist attitudes of some young people that they work with. The confidence expressed in community cohesion as a new paradigm of educational practice by many youth workers, and especially by more experienced staff, may well be based on the confidence that, for them, this new paradigm builds on and takes helpful understandings from the previously dominant anti-racism paradigm. That is to say, their belief that the language and assumptions of anti-racism can be left behind is based on the confidence that any helpful understandings and skills have already been imbibed and integrated from anti-racism; there is no longer a need to focus explicitly on anti-racism, as its (helpful and necessary) practices and assumptions are already inherent to professional practice. From this perspective, community cohesion has offered a way out from anti-racism's cul-de-sac analysed earlier in this chapter and in Chapter 1, and a positive move forward. However, is it right to assume that a proper concern with challenging racism, if not using anti-racist approaches, is successfully mainstreamed, implicit in the professional educational practice and understandings now guiding community cohesion? For Imran, the answer is 'no', and he believes that community cohesion has led to a clear downplaying of anti-racism as an important focus and priority:

> It's [community cohesion] put race equality on the back burner because in this town you see the term 'cohesion' bandied around all over the place, but as soon as you mention race equality, it's like saying, 'no you're going back five years, no, you're going back ten years'...but you can't realistically ignore race equality...it's not divided on cohesion grounds, it's based on racial grounds.

Habib shares this concern:

> You've got to educate people about those issues, and not simply say, 'well, community cohesion is an issue that we all need to face'...that's something that I think community cohesion might dilute, that you'll get absolutely no racism and anti-racism work with young people in general.

This perspective suggests that 'anti-racism' has (rightly) involved facing up to the harsh realities of where racism has come from and what impact it has on some people (Solomos, 2003), whereas community cohesion could allow a simplistic and apolitical 'positivity' reminiscent of previous approaches to multiculturalism (Chauhan, 1990). These views, and those expressed earlier by Salma, were representative of a general concern amongst a number of ethnic minority background professionals that anti-racism and race equality may be downplayed within the wider community cohesion agenda. White background workers also have this concern, with David commenting that:

> I think there are people who would say, and people have said to me, including young people in the Asian community, that it [anti-racism] is being neglected.

For some youth workers and people generally less experienced and politically motivated than David, the threat of continuity between anti-racism and community cohesion may not be obvious. For some, the failure to continue to use the terminology and key phrases of anti-racism and 'race equality' may seem a self-evident backward step, made all the more incongruous by the continued reality of day-to-day racial tensions and barriers in many communities. Nevertheless, other respondents saw the community cohesion practice approach analysed in Chapter 4 as the only effective way forward in terms of engaging white young people and their communities who have felt marginalised and negatively judged by previous policy approaches. This is articulated by Rafiq:

> I think the distinction between anti-racist work in its historical sense and community cohesion work in its contemporary sense is that anti-racism work historically was always about trying to get white people to understand black issues...the community cohesion issue, agenda, I think, is also about trying to recognise that white working class and non-working community's needs, and to try and deliver their needs in an inclusive manner alongside the needs of the Black communities.

Conclusion

This chapter has argued that the popular view of community cohesion as being, and needing to be, solely about encouraging Muslim communities to integrate more and so to break out of 'self-created segregation' is misplaced. Not only is that view a partial and one-sided reading of the more nuanced and balanced arguments put forward by the authors of the community cohesion and 'parallel lives' thesis (Cantle, 2001; Ouseley, 2001), but it runs counter to the empirical research data from Oldham and Rochdale presented over the preceding two chapters that shows white young people to be significantly less supportive of and negative about ethnic diversity and the future prospects for Britain's multicultural society. It is argued here that a number of wider structural and political factors can be understood as feeding in to the sort of white fears and attitudes that this survey uncovered and which have been mirrored in other studies (Hewitt, 2005). Firstly, white people, even in 'multicultural' local authority areas, are more likely to have 'segregated' experiences, and live in overwhelmingly monocultural white areas, so limiting experience of, and learning about, the realities, rather than the myths, of ethnic diversity (Finney and Simpson, 2009). Secondly, 'anti-racist' educational efforts aimed at white young people have had mixed results, provoking a 'backlash' from some, particularly working-class white young people who have felt judged and policed by the middle-class professionals implementing such work (CRE, 1999; Hewitt, 2005). The underpinning policies of ethnicism have ignored both white identities (Bonnett, 2000; Nayak, 1999) and class identities generally (Collins, 2004), leading to white reactions that can be understood as a racialisation of social inequality realities in a political and societal context where the reality and meaning of class is increasingly denied (Garner, 2009; Sveinsson, 2009). Despite such problematic and racialised responses from white young people, there are grounds for optimism, both in this survey data and from Chapter 4's evidence around the implementation of community cohesion work with young people. That evidence showed young people of all ethnic groups positive about work that gave them the chance to meet across ethnic divides in safe and well-planned circumstances, but it is far from clear how much such meaningful work is being replicated by educational agencies in other parts of the country (Green and Pinto, 2005). Such cohesion activity that focused on the active involvement of white young people and their communities in the process as much as that of ethnic minorities would not 'solve' the problems of areas like Oldham and Rochdale, but would contribute positively to getting 'race' out of the way, and challenge the white young people displaying overt prejudices to re-think their attitudes and assumptions (Hanley, 2008). It would also allow a collective focus on the profound, class-based social and economic inequalities discussed in Chapter 5, and which are currently limiting the potential of young people of all ethnic backgrounds.

8
A Contradiction to Community Cohesion? The 'Preventing Violent Extremism' Agenda

Introduction

Chapter 1 highlighted the main themes and concerns of the post-2001 community cohesion policy agenda, and Chapter 4 outlined how those themes and concerns have been supported and operationalised by educational practitioners at ground level. Central to community cohesion's analysis of problematic and separate ethnic identities has been how past policies have focused on the needs, equality and identities of each separate ethnic group, at the expense of a focus on commonality of concern and identity (Cantle, 2005). The suggestion here is that such policy approaches have made real progress in addressing the marginalisation of, and inequalities faced by, many non-white ethnic minority groups (Modood et al., 1997), but that this one-sided concern on difference has had unintended and negative effects on the bonds between groups. As a result, overcoming physical and cultural ethnic divisions and re-emphasising commonality has been the key focus for community cohesion practice, focused on 'direct contact' across ethnic divides and on policy approaches that enable and encourage it. Chapter 3 examined concerns that such community cohesion practice is a new phase of assimilationism (Alexander, 2007; Back et al., 2002), a forcible attempt to make minorities forsake their separate identities and cultural traditions in the interests of national unity, but the empirical evidence offered in Chapter 4 suggested that, in fact, community cohesion practice accepts and works with distinct ethnic and social identities, whilst augmenting them with overarching identities based on common connections, needs and experiences. Such evidence suggests that claims of community cohesion representing the 'death of multiculturalism' (Kundnani, 2002) are misplaced.

This chapter explores this further by focusing on an additional and important post-2001 British policy initiative, 'Preventing Violent Extremism' (PVE) (DCLG, 2007b) that is arguably in stark contradiction to the policy priority of community cohesion, and which, ironically, suggests that the traditional, highly problematic and much criticised pre-2001 understanding of multiculturalism (Phillips, 2005) is far from dead. The allegation here is that the approach of PVE has left it 'between two stools' (Thomas, 2009), neither working in harmony with community cohesion nor effectively addressing the roots of the domestic Islamist terrorist threat that undoubtedly exists. The contradictions between PVE and community cohesion have become increasingly politically contentious as a result (House of Commons, 2010). The chapter first provides a brief factual overview of the PVE agenda and its aims. This is then followed by explanation and a discussion of four key identified problems with PVE activity to date, all of which support the view of a fundamental tension between PVE as it has been implemented to date and community cohesion.

Preventing violent extremism

The emergence of the PVE policy agenda has obviously been closely related to the very serious domestic terrorism threat that the UK has faced over the past decade. The 7/7 bombings of July 2005, when 52 commuters were killed in four co-ordinated suicide bomb attacks on London's public transport, carried out by four young Muslims brought up in the north of England, marked the start of a new phase for UK policy. The fact that these attacks were not a one-off aberration was confirmed by further failed suicide attacks two weeks later, an attack on Glasgow airport in 2007 and a number of other foiled plots leading to convictions. In the majority of cases, these attacks and plots have involved young Muslim men educated, and often born, in Britain, whilst the deliberate targeting of civilians by such plots arguably represents a new terrorist challenge for the country (English, 2009). In fact, whilst the announcement of the PVE programme in October 2006 (DCLG, 2006b) created the impression that it was simply a response to the terrorist events of July 2005, the government had previously mapped out the key elements of the PVE strategy (FCO/Home Office, 2004), as well as identified key dilemmas over it that remain and which are implicit in the discussions below. This suggests that the 9/11 attacks on New York of September 2001, the riots in northern England the same summer and intelligence highlighting the involvement of British Muslims in Jihadist training camps in Afghanistan from the late 1990s onwards (Burke, 2007) had all combined to convince the government that it had a significant 'Muslim problem' (Masood, 2006) in relation to attractions to violent extremism.

An initial £6 million 'Pathfinder', or pilot, fund for the 70 local authorities in England having Muslims as 5 per cent or more of their populations was announced in 2007 (DCLG, 2007c); this was subsequently expanded significantly in 2008 as a three-year £45 million fund for all local authorities with 2000 or more Muslims (Thomas, 2009, 2010). In parallel, further development came through significant funding to local youth offending teams through the Youth Justice Board, and to the Prison Service, both reflecting well-founded concerns that radicalisation of individual Muslims was taking place during incarceration (Warnes and Hannah, 2008). The important role played for radical Islamist political groups by further and higher education settings also led to a funding focus on universities and colleges (DIUS, 2008), whilst PVE funding led to 300 new dedicated police posts nationally, some of them attached to the newly established regional Counter-Terrorism Units (CTUs). This all added up to a 2008–11 PVE budget of £140 million, some £85 million of which came from the local government-focused Department for Communities and Local Government (DCLG), and the security-focused remainder from the Home Office. Pressure came on local authorities through the Local Area Agreements under the Common Spending Assessment to adopt 'National Indicator 35' around developing 'resilience to violent extremism'; some local authorities refused to adopt it initially, but all were required to report on it to the regional government offices (DCLG, 2008a).

Many local authorities were deeply anxious about PVE from the start, seeing it as damaging to their relations with local Muslim communities, and contradictory to their attempts to develop community cohesion strategies (Turley, 2009). However, pressure from government saw PVE continue to grow to the point where all local authorities with significant Muslim communities were involved, although a number of national and local Muslim community groups refused to participate in PVE-funded activity. A summary of PVE activities funded by the initial 'Pathfinder' pilot year (DCLG, 2008a) claimed that over 44,000 people, almost all of them Muslim young people taking part in broad and unfocused activities, had been engaged with nationally, but admitted that little independent evaluation had taken place. An exception was Kirklees in West Yorkshire (home of two of the 7/7 bombers), where independent evaluation identified a lack of clarity over the aims of the well-meaning work with young people and its relationship to community cohesion. This evaluation highlighted an uncertainty and lack of confidence amongst professional practitioners involved as to whether they were supposed to engage directly in discussions around the causes of terrorism and associated political issues (Thomas, 2008). The national expansion of PVE did lead to new guidance over evaluation approaches, but this was confined to vague suggestions that local authorities 'might' decide to develop external evaluation of programmes (DCLG, 2009b). The significant evidence generated through the Parliamentary Select Committee Inquiry into PVE (House of Commons, 2010) highlighted how difficult it is to quantify success, especially if this is seen as a longer-term approach rather than concerned with the prevention of terrorist plots now. Indeed, oral evidence to the Inquiry from the Association of Chief Police Officers (ACPO) suggested that PVE represented a 'generational' struggle to influence young Muslims (House of Commons, 2010). That Inquiry process acknowledged that PVE had enabled stronger relationships between local authorities and Muslim communities in some areas, had strengthened the organisation and transparency of some Muslim community organisations, promoted the voices of women and young people within community processes, and had highlighted the need for more open debates within Muslim communities around the causes of domestic violent extremism. However, it concluded that the impact of the problems and contradictions of PVE outweighed any positive impacts, and so called for significant reshaping of the programme, including for DCLG and local authorities to focus solely on community cohesion, rather than PVE (House of Commons, 2010). The Coalition government elected in May 2010 moved in that direction by scrapping the local authority element of PVE funding in favour of a youth volunteering initiative, and focusing on a reduced PVE security approach.

The PVE policy agenda of the Labour government has to be understood within the wider context of broader UK anti-terrorism policies. The Initial CONTEST strategy (Home Office, 2003b), subsequently updated by CONTEST 2 (Home Office, 2009), outlined four distinct but interrelated elements: Pursue, Prevent (PVE), Protect and Prepare. Government acknowledged that, in the original strategy, 'Prevent' was the least developed element, and it was subsequently prioritised (House of Commons, 2010). Here, PVE can be understood as a 'hearts and minds' approach aimed at people seen as vulnerable to persuasion to support terrorists and who might 'reject and undermine our shared values and jeopardise community cohesion' (Home Office, 2009: 15). Such a prioritisation of community engagement within the overall strategy acknowledged that 'Intelligence is the most vital element in successful counter-terrorism' (English, 2009: 131). This approach focuses both on increasing the resilience and addressing the grievances of communities, and on identifying vulnerable individuals, as well as challenging and disrupting ideologies sympathetic to violent extremism (Home Office, 2009). Here, 'resilience' can be understood as resisting the appeal of, or even standing up to, extremist political activity and terrorist recruitment attempts within Muslim communities. Largely operationalised through education and welfare-based state agencies, and through support for community organisations, PVE can be seen as a relatively restrained and preventative anti-terrorism approach in comparison to other Western states facing a similar threat both now and in the recent past (Gupta, 2008). Nevertheless, PVE has been criticised from a number of different quarters, and these criticisms are discussed below. The four key concerns with PVE policy activity to date are that it has involved an unhelpful and contradictory focus on Muslims only; that the manner of this focus on and interventions in Muslim communities has been counterproductive and has risked repeating the mistakes of anti-racist interventions in white communities; that PVE has involved an unhelpful blurring of the distinction between the legitimate roles of educational and community-focused practitioners, on one hand, and policing and security practitioners, on the other, that may have resulted in inappropriate surveillance; and that the actual policy design and implementation mechanisms of PVE have exacerbated these problems. Each of these concerns is discussed below, enabling a concluding discussion that focuses on the interrelationship between PVE and attempts to develop community cohesion strategies and practice at a local level.

An unhelpful Muslim focus?

From the start, PVE has focused exclusively on Muslim communities, and particularly on young Muslims. This focus might appear self-evident given the serious Islamist threat faced, but it is argued here that this monocultural approach has been wrong, counterproductive and in flat contradiction to community cohesion principles and policies. Whilst the terrorist bombings and other plots quoted above are clearly serious, they have involved very small numbers of individuals. This was apparently acknowledged by government in introducing PVE: 'There has always been a tiny minority who oppose tolerance and diversity' (DCLG, 2007c: 2), but the same document baldly stated that 'the key measure of success will be demonstrable changes in attitudes among Muslims' (DCLG, 2007c: 7). This impression that government was concerned with Muslim communities in general was confirmed by the broad brush targeting of PVE funding at all significant Muslim communities even though there is no evidence from plots to date that terrorists are more likely to emerge from 'dense' Muslim communities (Finney and Simpson, 2009). Whilst a number of DCLG PVE documents talk about extremism in other communities,

> We have been unable, however, to document any practical Prevent work in the community that is not directed in some way at Muslim communities, and we have been unable to find any examples of work that focuses substantially on far-right extremism.
>
> (Kundnani, 2009: 24)

This focus on Muslims per se is also highlighted by the large-scale engagement with Muslim young people (DCLG, 2008a), and the clear emphasis of Muslim community capacity building of civic infrastructure locally (Thomas, 2008) and nationally (DCLG, 2009b), such as enhanced training and support for mosque schools. The nature of this PVE engagement with Muslim communities has proved controversial. Shortly after the 7/7 bombings, the government established seven working groups under the collective title 'Preventing Extremism Together' (PET), whilst also establishing the Commission on Cohesion and Integration (DCLG, 2007a), whose subsequent report re-energised many of the original community cohesion recommendations (Cantle, 2001). The PET process had significant Muslim involvement, and ranged across issues of economic, social and educational experiences, creating an expectation that it would lead to an explicit focus on 'Muslim' disadvantage (Kundnani, 2009). In fact, the government was already focused on educational and economic social exclusion of Pakistani- and Bangladeshi-origin young people and communities (SEU, 1999), so, arguably addressing underlying root problems (English, 2009), but showed no inclination to integrate this as an explicitly holistic Muslim policy initiative. As a result, PVE emerged from the beginning very much as a 'Muslim' agenda concerned with radicalisation, and issues of 'values' and community organisation that might be contributing to it (DCLG, 2007b).

Whilst highly contested (Flint and Robinson, 2008), there is clear evidence, as shown in the empirical data presented in Chapter 4, that community cohesion has been understood and supported by educational practitioners. This meant that the explicitly monocultural focus of PVE was immediately identified at ground level as problematically at odds with community cohesion (Thomas, 2008). The government was adamant that PVE 'is not the same as a wider concern for community cohesion' (DCLG, 2007c: 2), but consistently struggled to clarify this distinction. One of the key conclusions of community cohesion in relation to the 2001 disturbances was that ethnic tension had built up in towns such as Oldham because of funding schemes targeted at specific ethnic and geographical communities (often the same thing in a reality of ethnic housing segregation) and the associated myth that some (ethnic) communities were being favoured over others (Ritchie, 2001). This led to an emphasis, reinforced by the recommendations of the Commission on Cohesion and Integration (DCLG, 2007a), that policy and funding should work across ethnic groups, so building shared identities. The design and implementation of PVE has been in clear contradiction to that approach and has had the predictable results of creating suspicion, competitive claims and 'virulent envy' (Birt, 2009) from other ethnic minority faith groups, who are envious of the very considerable government support for Muslim faith organisations and infrastructure (House of Commons, 2010), whilst vehemently denying that their faiths have any problems with extremism.

A more worrying envy comparison has come from certain white communities, particularly those white working-class communities who have been marginalised by post-industrial re-structuring and the dominant neo-liberal political responses to it (Byrne, 1999). A 'white backlash' (Hewitt, 2005) against the implementation of anti-racist measures and the fact that such perceptions contributed to urban unrest (Cantle, 2001; Ritchie, 2001) has already been identified and community cohesion was meant to offer a holistic solution. However, it is far from clear how much that new vision has been operationalised, judging by the monocultural focus of PVE. The result has been two-way envy and resentment, with Muslim communities asking why extremism, including its violent political form of far-right activists (Eatwell and Goodwin, 2010), was not being addressed in some white communities, whilst non-Muslims questioned why such significant public resources were being directed towards often bland and generalised youth and community activities for Muslims only. The growing political strength of the British National Party did lead the Labour government to establish a short-lived 'Connecting Communities' fund (DCLG, 2009c), aimed at certain white working-class areas, in practice witnessing far-right-related political tensions, but described by DCLG as being 'communities under pressure'.

However, despite the impression created, this fund was *not* part of PVE, and had modest resources attached to it.

This policy expansion to white areas was accompanied by explicit guidance by DCLG Minister John Denham that 'cross-community activities could form a legitimate part of Prevent activities' and the promise of money to support it (DCLG, 2009c). Both these initiatives went some way to answer the criticisms of PVE as monocultural, and Denham also explicitly refuted the allegations of PVE as surveillance of Muslim communities, or as an attempt to change the values and leadership of Muslim communities, both of which allegations are discussed below. However, the amendments to the Muslim-only focus of PVE were minor at best, and the interpretation of purpose by Denham suggested more questions than answers. For Denham, PVE was a 'crime prevention programme', and claimed that a distinction from cohesion needed to be maintained:

> community cohesion – building a strong society with shared values and a strong sense of shared identity – is a broader and more ambitious aim, involving every part of every community equally, not just the Muslim communities. Prevent needs to remain focussed on preventing crime.
>
> (DCLG, 2009c)

Whilst addressing discussions around surveillance and political interference, this crime prevention formulation is highly problematic for two reasons. Firstly, assuming the crime to be prevented is terrorist activity, why had PVE activity worked with such large numbers of Muslim young people, yet focused so little on political, social and individual/psychological factors likely to make at least some young Muslims at risk of being involved in violent extremism? The evaluation evidence available suggests that engagement with such issues has been studiously avoided for a number of reasons, leaving PVE activity as bland and generalised youth activities for Muslims only (DCLG, 2008a; Thomas, 2008, 2009, 2010). In contrast, crime prevention youth activities have worked with smaller numbers of carefully targeted young people, often referred by relevant agencies. The 'Channel' programme element of PVE has worked with 200–300 young people to date (ACPO, 2009), and would seem to fit the 'crime prevention' understanding well, but the broader PVE activity to date simply doesn't fit any meaningful understanding of that concept.

Secondly, it avoids discussion of how the monocultural approach of PVE discussed above may actually be re-enforcing the likelihood of some young Muslims being attracted to violent extremism. The community cohesion analysis of ethnic relations in Britain (Cantle, 2001) was precisely that 'parallel lives' had encouraged tensions between communities, and separate, oppositional identities, as discussed in Chapters 6 and 7. Denham (DCLG, 2009c) focused on how building resilience against extremism amongst Muslim communities was a key aim of this 'crime prevention' PVE policy, but arguably you cannot build resilience against intolerance and racism without individuals and their communities having the confidence, skills and links, the 'bridging social capital' (Putnam, 2000), or cross-community links that comes from meaningful and ongoing cross-ethnic contact. Indeed, Denham himself said in the government's response to the 2001 urban disturbances that the areas of the country not experiencing racial tensions were those who had 'succeeded in uniting diverse groups through a shared sense of belonging to, and pride in, a common civic identity' (Denham, 2001: 11). The Labour government's consistent defence of why a PVE policy separate to community cohesion is needed was that terrorists can emerge from cohesive communities, with the ACPO (2009) supporting this because of 'the fact that the four suicide bombers in 2005 were nurtured in cohesive communities'. However, this is simply not true – three of the bombers grew up in the highly ethnically segregated and racially tense Leeds suburb of Beeston, an area which very much fits the theory of 'parallel lives' (Cantle, 2001). From that perspective, attractions to violent extremism whether radical Islamist or racist white extremism are likely to be stronger in isolated and monocultural communities where ethnic segregation and singular identities are the norm (Thomas, 2009, 2010), yet PVE has done exactly that, work with Muslims only, thereby giving the message that their Muslim faith is the *only* form of identity and experience that is of importance.

Clumsy social engineering?

It is not only this monocultural focus per se within PVE that has been problematic but the manner in which it has attempted to engage with Muslim communities, and the impression that it has often given of trying to 'engineer' different forms of leadership and religious practice within those communities. The discussions above around the emergence of PVE highlighted how PVE has offered Muslim community organisations funding for capacity building and youth activities through an explicitly anti-terrorism agenda. The labelling of an entire community as susceptible to terrorist involvement that is arguably inherent in this approach was exacerbated by the way the Labour government went about this. Birt (2009) identifies a tension in government's approach between 'values-based' and 'means-based' strategies, with the pragmatism of the 'means-based' approach being sidelined by an inherently judgemental and interventionist 'values-based approach'. The former sees Islamist terrorism in the UK as largely a socio-political phenomenon and so focuses on the personal and political factors attracting some young Muslim men to radicalisation, and engages with groups and individuals who can work constructively with such young men. This approach is favoured by professional practitioners on the ground being asked to operationalise PVE, including the Metropolitan Police's Muslim Contact Unit, which has worked constructively with Islamist groups who dislike British society but who vehemently oppose violence (Birt, 2009), and is supported by strong empirical evidence (University of Central Lancashire, 2009).

However, the 'values-based' approach has dominated government's view of PVE and the way they have shaped it nationally. It has arguably given the impression that government is overtly intervening to shape religious practice and to promote new types of community leadership within Muslim communities. This 'values-based' approach sees a problem with the way Islam itself is being understood and practised by many second- and third-generation Muslims, leading to a need to promote and develop a more moderate and progressive British Islam (Birt, 2009). Whilst President Obama has initiated a move in the USA towards the 'means-based' approach, the British government has gone the other way since the 2006 airliners plot towards the 'values-based' approach through PVE, an approach confirmed by recent refinements: 'As part of CONTEST 2, the revised Prevent strategy reflects this shift in emphasis and works out its rationale in greater detail' (Birt, 2009: 54). One approach has been to fund new organisations, promoting them as the voice of modern and moderate British Islam. This approach saw The Quillam Foundation, headed by ex-Islamist radical Ed Husain (2007), receiving over £1 million, the Sufi Muslim Council over £200,000 and the Radical Middle Way almost £400,000 (Kundnani, 2009). This has been supported by explicit guidance to local authorities and others receiving PVE funding to prioritise work with Muslim women and young people as under-represented voices and experiences within Muslim communities (DCLG, 2007c, 2009b). Together, this can be seen as an attempt by government to engineer different types of leadership and representation from Muslim communities, with the assumption that this will lead to more progressive attitudes, values and behaviour. This has been supported by withdrawal of funding and engagement with national umbrella Muslim organisations, such as the Muslim Council of Britain (MCB), not seen as taking a sufficiently robust enough position against Islamist terrorism at home or abroad. Ironically, the MCB's formation and development in the 1990s was encouraged by both Conservative and Labour governments as a clear national voice for 'moderate' Muslims, even though the MCB was always led by Islamist activists whose overtly political perspectives were at odds with the vast majority of practising British Muslims (McRoy, 2006). The MCB had considerable success in lobbying for state support for Muslim faith schools and more policy focus on religious affiliation (such as a question on faith in the 2001 Census), but their relationship with government came under increasing strain as the 'values-based' approach became predominant, with contact cut over the pro-Hamas views of a MCB leader (McRoy, 2006). The Labour government's attempt to create a new generation and type of 'community leaders' can be seen as a parallel of policy approaches to ethnic minority communities in the wake of serious urban disturbances in the early 1980s (Kundnani, 2009), and clearly provoked resentment from more established Muslim community groups (House of Commons, 2010).

Ironically, the PVE funding approach sometimes resulted in working with exactly the sort of traditional Muslim community leaders, many of them MCB affiliates, that the 'values-based' approach had tried to move away from, as evidenced with the considerable support for mosque schools (Thomas, 2008). At the local level, Muslim organisations have often felt that they are being treated as clients and service deliverers, rather than strategic partners, either playing no role in delivery (Thomas, 2008), or having to compete with each other for funding and overtly 'sign up' to government positions against terrorism (which virtually everyone opposes) and 'extremism' (which no one can agree a definition of). The danger of this 'values-based' approach, and the fact that funding is contingent on its acceptance, is that it closes down the open debates and involvements needed to undermine the appeal of violent extremism: 'One effect of Prevent is to undermine exactly the kind of radical discussions of political issues that would need to occur if young people are to be won over and support for illegitimate political violence diminished' (Kundnani, 2009: 35). Here, in such a broad focus on Muslim communities as a whole as discussed in the previous section, whilst prioritising the acceptance of certain 'values', PVE has

represented the worst of all worlds, approaching an entire faith community as being at risk of terrorist involvement, whilst forcing particular
political and doctrinal issues that have only limited meaning to most
Muslims going about their ordinary, day-to-day lives. In fact, the ruling out under the PVE 'values-based' approach of certain legitimately
established Muslim organisations would seem to play into the hands
of certain Islamist groups, such as Hizb-Ut-Tahir, who demand that
Muslims have nothing to do with any democratic, secular processes
within wider society. For Birt (2009: 54), the fundamental difficulty
of PVE, 'is an over-emphasis upon counter-terrorism without engaging
Muslims as citizens, rather than as an "at risk" set of communities'.

In this way, PVE has risked repeating some of the unintended mistakes
of earlier attempts to develop anti-racist educational initiatives in white
communities. An additional facet of the 'political multiculturalism'
or anti-racism race relations policy approaches increasingly dominant
post-1981 was anti-racist educational approaches operationalised in
schools, colleges and youth work settings. Whilst well intentioned,
and sometimes successful with young people of particular social backgrounds, these anti-racist educational approaches involved inherent
problems and unintended consequences that should act as salutary
warnings for those designing PVE programmes, as Chapter 7 highlighted. An immediate problem is the way young people from disadvantaged backgrounds understand and interpret any educational agenda
designed and enforced by those in power and concerned with changing
behaviour (Cohen, 1988). Anti-racist rules and programmes introduced
by schools from the 1980s onwards came up against this problem, with
white working-class pupils often rejecting these new anti-racist norms as
part of their wider rejection of compulsory schooling that felt irrelevant
to their lives and experiences. The extension of the PVE programme
to youth offending teams, schools and the police has risked a similar
rejection by Muslim-origin young people selected for involvement, particularly if implementation is as clumsy as anti-racism implementation
sometimes was. The most graphic example of this was the racist murder
in Manchester of a young Bangladeshi man by a fellow pupil in 1986,
with the independent inquiry identifying the clumsy implementation
of anti-racist policies as having strongly contributed to the context of
the murder (Macdonald, 1989).

Central to the rejection by many white working-class young people of
'anti-racism', as it was often implemented educationally on the ground,
was the perception that these anti-racist norms were explicitly critical of the assumptions, attitudes and cultures of white working-class

communities by outsiders (including middle-class white people). As discussed in Chapter 7, this led to feelings of 'unfairness' amongst white working-class young people (Hewitt, 2005), fuelled by the perception that their attitudes and behaviour were judged more harshly than similar behaviour by other ethnic communities. Such a clear focus within PVE on Muslim communities and the associated lack of focus on racist extremism within white communities could well have had the unintended consequence of hardening a defensive and antagonistic 'Muslim' identity amongst those involved in response to a perception that their whole identity and community lifestyle is being implicitly criticised and scrutinised. Arguably, post 9/11 popular media coverage has already had this effect, as witnessed by more overt displays of Islamic dress by many young Muslims (Lewis, 2007), and PVE activity could further exacerbate this trend. Associated with the 'white backlash' by some white working-class young people against anti-racism was the perception that they were viewed as 'all racist', even though many vehemently denied that their *motivations* during inter-racial conflicts were actually racial. A concern with the PVE agenda would be that at least some of the practitioners involved in its delivery carried similar assumptions about Muslim young men, fuelled by some media coverage and popular prejudices concerning religiously observant young men with beards. Within this are problematic issues of targeting. Youth offending teams have been allocated PVE funds, yet few if any young offenders are likely to be referred to youth offending teams for involvement in violent extremist activity, as numbers associated with such plots are small. This suggests that PVE activity through youth-offending teams might be extended to all those seen as 'racially motivated offenders'(RMO) even though 'RMO' programmes are only slowly developing within the youth justice system, and identification of which offenders are genuinely 'racially motivated', and should so be on a RMO programme, is far from straightforward. This leads to the question of whether 'racial motivation' can really 'read across' to support for 'violent extremism'. An even more questionable alternative would be to 'profile' Muslim young offenders more generally for PVE activity.

A programme of surveillance?

Perhaps the most heated criticism of PVE has been that its significant growth has been cover for the development of surveillance of Muslim communities, with claims that 'there is evidence that the Prevent programme has been used to establish one of the most elaborate systems of surveillance ever seen in Britain' (Kundnani, 2009: 8). Whilst this has been strongly denied by the government (DCLG, 2009c), there has been a very significant growth in police and security service involvement in PVE, and, arguably, an associated blurring of roles, between education and policing, between security apparatus and local democratic account-ability, and between the Prevent and Pursue arms of CONTEST 2 (Home Office, 2009). Such blurring of roles is arguably inevitable within a counter-terrorism strategy that attempts to include community develop-ment aspects as well as policing and security functions (English, 2009). The resulting allegations of covert surveillance and intelligence gather-ing are discussed below, and whilst the actual evidence of them is very limited, the impression of it has taken firm hold (House of Commons, 2010), fuelled by political campaigning and media coverage (Kundnani, 2009; *Guardian*, 2009b).

The basis of these claims has been an increased focus on policing, identification of threats and monitoring/information sharing within the 2008–11 expansion of the PVE programme, with the Home Office 'pro-viding additional funding to establish over three hundred new Police posts across the country dedicated to Prevent' (DCLG, 2009b: 25), and additional money for police forces to work with schools, universities and colleges on PVE. The context for this has been the establishment in 2007 of the Office for Security and Counter-Terrorism (OSCT), designed to overcome cross-departmental confusion, and the resulting development of regional CTUs, to which some of these new police posts have been attached. This has been mirrored by the security service MI5 develop-ing regional offices for the first time. These very significant policing and security developments have fuelled fears of surveillance for some, and prompted conflicts around power, information and appropriate roles at a local level. The reality of police officers playing prominent roles in local Prevent boards 'has raised questions of police interference in the political relationships between Local Authorities and Muslim com-munities' (Birt, 2009: 8). Indeed, some agencies feel that the police are actually in charge of this supposedly 'hearts and minds' programme at the local level:

> The police are such key drivers at a local level together with your counterterrorism officers and the intelligence services, they become the funnel through which what is happening in the community is funnelled back to the government . . . it is the police who are leading the agenda.
>
> (Lachman, 2009)

This is confirmed by Birmingham City Council (2009), the largest single recipient of PVE funding nationally: 'Our delivery plan utilises intelligence from West Midlands Police (e.g. Counter-Terrorism local profile) in order to target funding and provision as necessary.' Critics (Kundnani, 2009: 6) identify growing concerns from both Muslim community organisations and public sector professionals that involvement in PVE required them to pass on information to the police, whilst at the same time local authorities felt that information flows within PVE were one way only, with them expected to pass intelligence on, but CTUs and police not willing to pass anything the other way, often claiming that local authority chief executives did not have the right 'clearance' (Turley, 2009). Arguably, these concerns demonstrate a naivety about the way community interaction and security aspects of counter-terrorism strategies will inevitably interact, as the Northern Ireland experience indicates (English, 2009). This misunderstanding has perhaps been unhelpfully fuelled by the PVE label being used for such a wide range of policy functions (House of Commons, 2010).

This fear of surveillance has been heightened by the increased involvement of police officers in education-based PVE activities that would be normally seen as the territory of teachers and of youth and community workers:

> A significant part of the prevent programme is the embedding of counter-terrorism police officers within the delivery of other local services. The implication of teachers and youth, community and cultural workers in information-sharing undercuts professional norms of confidentiality.
>
> (Kundnani, 2009: 28)

The argument here is not that the police do not have a legitimate counter-terrorism role to play but whether that such an overt involvement in funding and monitoring PVE activity, and increasingly even directly delivering it to young people and community groups, is effective, or rather whether it is counterproductive through the unhelpful blurring of professional roles and their proper boundaries. Local authorities clearly feel that this police involvement has unhelpfully blurred the distinction between 'Prevent' (education and community development-based activity) and 'Pursue' (necessary surveillance and policing interventions) with this having a counterproductive effect: 'there is a danger that the levels of suspicion and mistrust around Prevent could be used as a tool by those elements who seek to undermine cohesion' (Turley, 2009: 12).

The more recent development of the 'Channel' initiative within PVE is seen as progress at the local level. Channel works with much smaller numbers of 'at risk' young people identified through multi-agency partnership mechanisms, and utilises both diversionary and de-radicalisation approaches, tailored to the individual (House of Commons, 2010). However, this may well simply be a smaller-scale surveillance or 'fishing expedition' in that there is little evidence as to how those genuinely at risk of involvement in 'violent extremism' can be identified in advance, so casting doubt over the whole role of and significant resource allocation to the police within PVE. Despite very close government investigation of those Britons to date involved in Islamist terror plots, 'the security services can identify neither a uniform pattern by which a process occurs nor a particular type that is susceptible' (Bux, 2007: 269). The danger here is that 'fact'-based profiles of susceptibility underestimate the process of relationships and peer group operation that can tip individuals towards violence, and that predicting this in advance is very difficult. Clearly, high levels of vigilance are needed against further Islamist terror plots, but the question here is whether a crude focus on Muslim communities as a whole, steered overtly by the police and security forces in an effort to 'spot' likely terrorists will really be effective, or may even be counterproductive because of the suspicions and distrust this approach engenders amongst ordinary Muslims. The term 'hearts and minds' originates in counter-insurgency campaigns and was based on isolating insurgents through winning the support and trust of the majority (English, 2009). On that basis, the success or otherwise of PVE is unclear, as the appearance and partial reality of state surveillance that is central to its operationalisation has seriously damaged the prospect of community partnership. In contrast, moving towards community cohesion-based approaches 'would create the space and legitimacy for a more sophisticated, intelligence-led approach to tackling specific local threats as and when they occur' (Turley, 2009: 22). Such an approach would suggest a clear separation between policing and cohesion-based community development activities, as highlighted by the overwhelming majority of submissions to the Parliamentary inquiry and their subsequent recommendations (House of Commons, 2010).

Problematic policy design?

Over and above the fundamental flaws and contradictions of PVE that have been explored above, there have been a number of problematic features of the way that the policy has been organised and implemented.

These have included misleading titles, a lack of meaningful evaluation, significant tensions between central and local government and tensions between different parts of central government over the proper focus for PVE activity. The disquiet from Muslim community groups over the focus of PVE and worries from local government around the lack of congruence with community cohesion, both discussed above, have led central government to connive in the use of misleading titles without any fundamental changes to PVE. Local evaluation of the initial phase of PVE (Thomas, 2008) found the bland title 'Pathfinder' being used, whilst government formally dropped 'Preventing Violent Extremism': 'This term is no longer used to describe that funding' (DCLG, 2009b: 34), in favour of the enigmatic 'Prevent'. This was in recognition of the fact that many Muslims felt stigmatised as potential terrorists by the PVE title. More serious has been the lack of independent and robust evaluation, with few exceptions (Thomas, 2008; University of Central Lancashire, 2009). Whilst government seemed relaxed over the need for such evaluation (DCLG, 2009b), ACPO (2009) acknowledged the effects of this absence: 'the apparent lack of evaluation of Prevent initiatives has made the "value for money" assessment of Prevent difficult.'

It is likely that such evaluation would reveal significant disparities between what central government has claimed for PVE and the reality of much of its operation on the ground. Consistent with wider Labour policy approaches, PVE was supposedly a locally determined policy but was actually strongly driven from the centre through use of NI35 and monitoring/pressure from local government offices. Despite substantial initial misgivings (Thomas, 2008), local authorities have formally cooperated, but in practice have demonstrated a wide range of responses. A small minority, some of which have received very substantial funding, have been vociferous in their support for PVE (Birmingham City Council, 2009), but a large number seem to have subverted the funding to a significant extent, 'many statutory and community partners have been uncomfortable with direct counter-terrorism work and have sought to employ the funds for other ends' (Birt, 2009: 54). The result, as discussed above, has usually been bland and unfocused youth activities (DCLG, 2008a; Thomas, 2008), with the Association of Police Authorities (APA) (2009) commenting that 'many Police Authorities question whether, in practice, there is any real difference between Prevent and community cohesion.' The problem here, though, has been that this activity is monocultural and so ineffective in terms of cohesion, just as it has little demonstrable focus on factors and issues likely to lead some individuals towards violent extremism. For APA, the solution is a tighter focus on Muslim 'extremism', with some recent evidence that police influence is being used to block PVE support for more general youth activities (Birt, 2009).

What this reality on the ground exposes is the biggest tension within PVE – the tension between the two government departments delivering PVE under the Labour government, DCLG and the Home Office. Each department contributed some of the overall budget, with DCLG 'owning' some of the PVE strategy objectives, whilst OSCT/Home Office 'owned' the others (APA, 2009). This might not be problematic in itself, but it is clear that the operationalisation of PVE was built on real inter-departmental tensions over purpose and priority, as identified by the Local Government Association (2009): 'Tension between OSCT and CLG on the nature of the focus of Prevent, and the activity which should flow from that, can be a problem at times', with lack of consistency identified as a result. It is clear that a 'turf war', something far from new in the history of counter-terrorism policies (English, 2009), has been taking place, based on significantly different views of effective ways forward:

> We in local government support John Denham's view of Prevent as distinct but necessarily situated within the broader context of community cohesion and equalities.... Police and the security services will necessarily see things from a different perspective...these messages need to be properly aligned across government.
>
> (LGA, 2009)

From this perspective, the very limited and nuanced changes made to PVE prior to the 2010 general election (DCLG, 2009c) could actually be understood as hard-won concessions in the right direction by a minister with a clear track record of support for community cohesion (Denham, 2001), and the Inquiry by the Communities and Local Government Select Committee (House of Commons, 2010) as an attempt to bolster such support from a minister, whilst the Home Office 'wing' of PVE demanded more robust scrutiny and surveillance of, and judgements on, Muslim communities and organisations (APA, 2009). This suggests that PVE, as it developed, had few genuine friends even within government, with both DCLG and the Home Office profoundly dissatisfied with it, but for very different reasons, so introducing instability in local policy design and delivery.

Conclusion

It is beyond dispute that the UK has faced a very serious Islamist terror threat over the past decade, a threat unlikely to diminish in the
near future (Burke, 2007; English, 2009). In the face of that, the Labour
government deserves significant credit for attempting to implement preventative 'hearts and minds' programmes through PVE, rather than
simply focusing on repressive policing and surveillance approaches, as
many states have counterproductively done when facing home-grown
terrorism (Gupta, 2008). However, the design and implementation of
PVE to date has been highly problematic in relation to the focus of,
and the arguments developed by, this book. The broad but unfocused
PVE concern with Muslim communities only is in flat contradiction
to community cohesion, and has provoked exactly the sort of envy
and suspicion from other communities that community cohesion perceived to be an inevitable outcome of ethnic specific social policies
(Cantle, 2001; Ritchie, 2001). Similarly, this focus runs a real danger
of re-enforcing the Islamist threat by privileging Muslim faith identity, engaging with 'Muslim' communities unproblematically, whilst at
the same time antagonising many Muslims through the clumsy social
engineering of the 'values-based' approach (Birt, 2009) and giving the
appearance, if not the reality, of widespread surveillance (House of Commons, 2010; Kundnani, 2009). Here, there is evidence of PVE working
counter to community cohesion, and growing concerns that the central
government demands for rapid action on PVE have sidelined progress
on community cohesion at the local level (Monro et al., 2010). Not
only has this PVE approach struggled for success on its own terms
(DCLG, 2007b) and in so doing worked contrary to the community
cohesion approaches that many policy-makers and practitioners want
to develop further at the local level (Thomas, 2008), but it has appeared
to be a continuation of the worst sort of unreconstructed 'multiculturalist' policies, whereby ethnic-specific funds and facilities are distributed
through a layer of 'community leaders', some old, some newly hand-
picked, in order to achieve central government's stated outcomes. Here,
PVE has appeared to take 'Muslim' identity as an essentialised and reified given, not as the sort of dynamic and contested identity discussed
in Chapter 6. This PVE experience suggests that, to date, the community cohesion analysis and approach has only partially been accepted
by British policy-makers at the national level.

9
Conclusion: Community Cohesion as a New Phase of British Multiculturalism

It is beyond dispute that 2001 marked a significant watershed in British policy approaches to 'race relations'. The Inquiries prompted by the riots in Oldham, Burnley and Bradford led directly to a new policy priority of community cohesion, and the associated concern with the 'parallel lives' apparently produced by ethnic segregation, and with the separate ethnic, rather than shared common, identities and values created and maintained as a result. This new focus has subsequently been sharpened by the shocking events of the 7/7 terrorist attacks in July 2005, and by other plots, all seemingly confirming that Britain faces a significant Islamist terror threat from a small minority of young British Muslims apparently growing up with an ideology violently oppositional to the values and identity shared by the wider population. Past policy approaches of multiculturalism have been blamed by commentators from across the political spectrum for these developments, suggesting that such multiculturalist approaches have disastrously fostered division and separate values, rather than commonality, a development mirrored by political debates of the past 15 years in the Netherlands (Sniderman and Hagendoorn, 2009).

The result has been that the new post-2001 policies of community cohesion have focused on commonality and shared identities, supported by a renewed debate over the meaning of an overarching Britishness, and have superseded the previous concentration on equality and diversity for each separate and distinct ethnic and faith communities. Arguably, the 2001 riots and subsequent terror threats have merely provided the opportunity for a policy re-think that was already underway, prompted by the findings of the Commission on the Future of Multi-Ethnic Britain (2000), as Chapter 1 suggested. That perspective is supported by the very limited focus in the community cohesion reports (Cantle, 2001; Denham, 2001; Ritchie, 2001) on the actual triggers and events of the Oldham, Burnley and Bradford riots, with factors of far-right political agitation, clumsy policing and provocative media coverage all being downplayed in a process that suggested such events were symptomatic of much wider deeper fissures within Britain's multicultural society.

The key themes and concerns of community cohesion, as outlined in Chapter 1, give considerable grounds to suggest that this post-2001 British policy shift has been a reactionary and backwards one towards a new assimilationism that rejects the multiculturalist progress of the previous three decades. In portraying ethnic segregation as problematic and implicitly suggesting that it is actively getting worse, both highly contested positions, community cohesion has arguably focused on symptoms rather than causes, whilst its concern with the agency of communities, and with the problematic bonding capital of those communities, has implied for some that structural forces of racism or economic inequality have little to do with the ethnic tensions that undoubtedly exist. Above all, it is community cohesion's critique of previous race relations policy approaches that condemns it as reactionary for critics. Cantle (2001, 2005) suggests that the policies emphasised in the wake of previous urban disturbances of the early 1980s focused exclusively on equality and the needs of each separate ethnic community, rather than on commonality or relations between different ethnic communities. That policy focus, popularly known in Britain as 'anti-racism' or equal opportunities, led to significant reductions in ethnic inequalities but arguably at the cost of deeper divisions between different ethnic and faith communities and much weaker bonds across communities. In itself, the new cohesion policy prescription of re-emphasising commonality rather than distinctness was questionable to some, but the emergence of community cohesion has been accompanied by overt attacks on multiculturalism itself, suggesting that ethnic difference per se is no longer accepted or tolerated by British policy. Such perspectives portray community cohesion as a lurch back to the British assimilationist policies of the early 1960s, an understandable accusation if a selective reading of parts of the community cohesion reports and accompanying political pronouncements is employed. Furthermore, Chapter 2 highlighted the extent to which previously multiculturalist model, the Netherlands has indeed also appeared to significantly re-think its policy stance, whilst France has hardened its colour-blind, republican model of citizenship into a shrill and alarmist 'debate' around the supposed dangers of Muslim identity.

Does community cohesion represent a similar reactionary move in Britain?

This book's position has been that the many critical interpretations of community cohesion are understandable but misplaced. It has suggested that, rather than representing the 'death of multiculturalism', community cohesion actually can, and does on the ground, represent a new and positive, 'critical' phase of multiculturalism that attempts to engage with the complexity of identity and experience of young Britons, and which potentially offers a way forward out of the cul-de-sac of ethnicism that previous policy approaches had clearly become stuck in. In doing so, it supports the position of Joppke (2004) that this 'new assertiveness' of the liberal state in both Britain and the Netherlands is *not* a reversion to a reactionary assimilationism, but rather a re-balancing of multiculturalism towards a more overt and proactive commitment to liberal citizenship and democracy for all citizens, of whatever ethnic background. In the context of increasing and progressively more diverse immigration within a European Union of open borders, the hyper-diverse societies that are resulting, and in an increasingly uncertain economic world, multiculturalist policies that only stress ethnic differences and distinctions within society are not sustainable and will not win support from majority groups who *perceive* their own identity to be threatened. Instead, a policy focus on commonality, and a climate of more limited live and let live tolerance, rather than overt demands for and celebration of difference, are likely to prove a more productive way forward.

Here, community cohesion is not a 'lurch backwards' but a move forward beyond superficial politeness towards a genuinely open and multicultural society. In this way, community cohesion has also represented coherence with wider recent British governmental approaches to social policy, in its recognition of the dangers to national cohesion of separate experiences and identities, whether ethnic or social/spatial, and the importance of agency and community responsibility in overcoming those dangers. The book has argued for that positive interpretation through drawing on significant empirical evidence around how community cohesion has actually been understood and articulated on the ground, how young people of different backgrounds living in the sort of segregated and tense areas policy has been particularly concerned with understand their identity, and on how associated policies such as Preventing Violent Extremism have been implemented. The approach here has not been one of a case study, but instead to use a variety of empirical evidence to support wider discussion of how we might understand interrelated policy questions around youth, multiculturalism and community cohesion in Britain.

The evidence drawn on has come from Oldham and Rochdale, Greater Manchester. Whilst Oldham was one of the northern towns witnessing riots in 2001, it is clear that the issues of ethnic segregation, racial tension and problematic youth identities found in Oldham and Rochdale are also found across many 'multicultural' towns and cities in Britain. Therefore, the book does *not* imply that Oldham and Rochdale are particularly noteworthy or negative, as although measures of physical ethnic segregation do highlight their problems (ODPM, 2006), the serious inter-ethnic rioting in Birmingham in 2005 and periodic tensions between different ethnic communities in a number of Britain's largest cities supports the community cohesion notion that policy has badly neglected community relations *between* different ethnic and social communities nationally, and the importance of nurturing and maintaining those relations. Indeed, the book in many ways suggests Oldham and Rochdale as positive national examples. The community cohesion-based practice with young people developed post-2001 in Oldham and analysed here is one of the few documented examples nationally of good community relations practice in the name of community cohesion. Similarly, given the very substantial criticisms outlined in Chapter 8 of the way PVE has been designed and implemented, the Rochdale Pride Partnership deserve great credit for using PVE resources to work positively with young people of all ethnic backgrounds, and to actually gather real data about young peoples' experiences and aspirations, rather than simply imposing a questionable national agenda on them. The positive evidence from this research, and from other sources (Phillips et al., 2008) shows that there are considerable grounds for optimism around cohesion in Oldham and Rochdale.

Much of the criticism of the move towards community cohesion in Britain has not drawn on any empirical evidence, and this book has attempted to redress this by drawing on examination of how community cohesion has actually been understood and practised in work with young people. This evidence has highlighted the very considerable support educational policy-makers and practitioners at ground level have for the analysis of damaging ethnic segregation, and the limitations it places on young people's aspirations, possibilities and identity development. With the 2001 riots and the resulting national focus acting as a spur, youth work agencies in Oldham have significantly altered the shape, priorities and content of their professional practice as a result. Meaningful direct contact between young people of different ethnic and social backgrounds has been made a priority of all youth work activity, with this approach 'mainstreamed' through youth project linking schemes used as a basis for regular activities, and joint events and residential conferences in neutral space that have brought young people together using informal methods, supported by ethnically mixed teams of youth workers willing to use their own identity and background as a learning resource with young people. The key approach here has been one of fun, that young people get the chance to enjoy being together and take part in shared activities, rather than a more formal educational focus on 'learning' about racism or diversity which has been experienced by educational practitioners and young people (CRE, 1999) as a counterproductive approach.

This community cohesion-inspired new youth work approach can be understood as an operationalisation of 'contact theory', a social psychology-based approach to overcoming deep divides and fears between identifiable communities in situations of tension and mutual fear. The youth work practice in Oldham analysed meets the key principles of this in that contact is carried out in groups, over time, in enjoyable and informal ways, and no existing identity is under criticism or threat. This enables a 'transversal' politics of 'rooting and shifting' (Yuval-Davis, 1997) of identities to take place, whereby individuals are willing to amend their prejudices and assumptions about others, and so their own 'identity', because they do not feel under threat. This practice emphasises that the Commission on Integration and Cohesion (DCLG, 2007a) was badly wrong in arguing against a continuation of 'single group' funding, because preparatory work in young people's own monocultural and geographical groups is a vital stage of this cohesion contact approach. This also suggests that allegations of community cohesion representing the 'death of multiculturalism' (Kundnani, 2002) are misplaced, with this practice seeking to augment existing ethnic or social identities with common and overarching identities, rather than replace them. This community cohesion practice has a continued awareness of 'race' and the need to combat it, but also accepts that in strengthening shared identities and experiences, there will be a 'cooling' (McGhee, 2005) of existing ethnic identities, something essential if a complex, multicultural society is to operate peacefully and successfully. Research in the Netherlands similarly shows the need for policy there to focus more on commonality within a relaxed framework of tolerance, rather than overtly emphasising difference in the way multiculturalist approaches have done in the past (Sniderman and Hagendoorn, 2009).

What this empirical evidence of British community cohesion in practice does suggest is genuine dilemmas over the extent to which young people's identities and the tensions many of them experience in areas like Oldham are genuinely only about 'race' and ethnic divisions, or whether wider 'social' understandings of cohesion should be employed. The latter position suggests that youth tensions over 'territory' (Kintrea et al., 2008), the resulting impact of youth perceptions, often well founded, of 'safe' and 'unsafe' space, the social exclusion and economic marginalisation that many young people of all ethnic backgrounds increasingly experience, and the gendered performance of youth roles on the streets should all be considered as part of the cause of the racialised tension experienced by young people and manifested in the 2001 riots. Whilst seeing 'race' and ethnicity as central to the lived experiences of young people in Oldham, youth workers surveyed were also working on these wider 'social' causes of experience and identity in their policy and practice responses, so arguably deploying a more 'critical' form of multiculturalism (May, 1999a), whereby ethnicity and the continuing reality of racism is addressed without essentialising or reifying ethnic identity, and the complex interplay of influences on identity and experience is also recognised. Such doubts around how much 'race' truly explains events and identities in places like Oldham perhaps explains the 'slipperiness' (Worley, 2005) of the way government has used community cohesion, with a clear reluctance to accept this solely as a 'race' agenda. Chapter 2 suggested that France currently has the opposite problem – a policy approach that gives no credence to differentiated ethnic identity or experience whatsoever.

Nevertheless, the data presented in this book suggests that in Oldham and Rochdale, and many other parts of multicultural Britain, 'race' and ethnicity are perceived to be the main determinant of experience in the context of highly racialised environments. Here, ideas of increasing 'hybridity' (Hall, 2000) or 'convivial cosmopolitanism' (Gilroy, 2004) seem a long way off. As Modood (2005) suggests, we may indeed have multiple identities but some identities are perceived to be more important than others, and this is graphically illustrated by the data presented here on how young people understand their national, ethnic and local identity. Young people of Pakistani and Bangladeshi origin overwhelmingly prioritise a Muslim faith identity, as confirmed by other surveys. Contrary to alarmist suggestions, this Muslim identity is *not* in conflict with British identity, although 'English' is clearly perceived by young Muslims as being the preserve of white people. There are differing views on how this increasingly strong Muslim identification can be understood, with this book suggesting that it should be seen partly as a result of policy approaches that have essentialised and reified first ethnic and now Muslim faith identity, seeing such young people and their communities as 'Muslims' and nothing else. This understanding has been operationalised by the Preventing Violent Extremism counter-terrorism strategy (DCLG, 2007b), a counterproductive and monocultural approach flatly in contradiction to community cohesion. It would be wrong to see this growth in Islamic identity amongst young people as reactionary, however, with a reinterpretation of 'true Islam' (Lewis, 2007) helping many young Muslim constructively negotiate with older generations over the possibilities of identity and experience (Din, 2006). A similar debate about the positive social potential of Islamic identity is taking place in other European countries, such as the Netherlands (Buruma, 2006). However, the overwhelming focus on this faith identity allows a minority of young Muslims, particularly men, to make highly negative judgements about non-Muslims, arguably a step on the road that a small number then travel towards Islamic extremism (Malik, 2009).

Whilst this strong preference for Muslim identity is arguably problematic in some ways, young Muslims surveyed are clearly positive about both British identity and ethnic diversity in society. White young people were much less positive about ethnic diversity and the desirability of cohesion, and often expressed this opposition in overtly racist terms, as Chapter 7 shows. Such negativity is partially understandable, given that the most segregated and monocultural communities in Britain, even in local authority areas viewed as 'multicultural', are white communities, with many white young people having no experience of contact with ethnic minorities in or out of school (Finney and Simpson, 2009). However, white negativity of the type reported here can also be understood as resulting from processes of clumsy multicultural and anti-racist education that have made some white young people feel cultureless, inferior and negatively judged (Hewitt, 2005), and from a broader lack of focus on, or respect for, class identities in society. This has both made it acceptable to mock elements of the poor working class as 'chavs' in an era when is almost 'to mdotal a since is whumd as erumph it it ju numer quabih. Tuu has also created a vacuum of explanation for experience in society, a space filled by the racialised explanations provided by elements of the media and egged on by racist political groupings. As a result, increasing numbers of white people blame ethnic minorities and immigrants for social problems whose origins lie in the profound economic changes driven by neo-liberal policy approaches (Byrne, 1999), as shown by the white resentment over regeneration funding and spurious claims of 'no go' areas for whites seen as triggers of the 2001 riots in Oldham (Ritchie, 2001). Here, it is clear that white young people and their communities need to be more central to the focus of community cohesion policy initiatives that have too often been concerned primarily with supposedly 'self-segregating' Asian communities. Debates in the Netherlands suggest that there is a more general problem of well-intentioned policies of multiculturalism actually stoking fears around perceived threats to the cultural identity of white majority groups (Sniderman and Hagendoorn, 2009), and such a response of racialised perceptions can be seen within the attitudes of some young white Britons.

Such racialised understandings of experience help to explain community cohesion's focus on physical and cultural segregation. Critics use demographic data to challenge the implicit suggestion that this is actually getting worse (Finney and Simpson, 2009), but it is clear that many people *perceive* ethnic relations to be getting worse, and hence that community cohesion is concerned with these perceptions, with the psychology of ethnic relations (Cantle, 2005), as much as the 'facts'. This can be seen in the ways that youth 'turf' disputes are understood solely as racial conflicts in many towns and cities (Webster, 1995), in the growing number of white people who perceive the crime they have been the victim of to be 'racially motivated' and the increasing way that areas of towns and cities are simplistically understood as 'white' or 'Asian', regardless of the demographic facts (Kalra and Rhodes, 2009). The post-2001 changes to youth work practice in Oldham as a result of community cohesion analysed in Chapter 4 are centrally concerned with building support and commitment for ethnic diversity and direct contact amongst young people in the face of social forces and structures that militate against it. This can be seen as consistent with the proactive 'Bradfordian Peoples Programme' suggested by Ouseley (2001), and the approach of measuring, and hopefully steadily improving, how people nationally feel about cohesion and 'how different people get on' in their local area (LGA, 2002). These attempts to develop, operationalise and then measure the perceptions resulting from community cohesion programmes can be seen as a policy attempt to turn ethnic diversity and a multicultural society from a perceived negative to a perceived positive (McGhee, 2005). This is a considerable challenge in many areas, as the data presented here indicates, but the empirical evidence from community cohesion's implementation with young people in Oldham also shows that real and tangible steps forward have been taken, and young people surveyed here and elsewhere (Phillips et al.,

2008) were clear that more cross-community contact and housing is needed.

The empirical evidence summarised above around community cohesion in practice suggests that it is 'an exercise in avoiding the term "multiculturalism", rather than moving away from the principles of multiculturalism altogether' (McGhee, 2008: 85). The suggestion here is that community cohesion practice, regardless of intemperate attacks on multiculturalism from people who should know better (Phillips, 2005), actually continues to respect and work with the reality of distinct ethnic, faith and social identities, seeking to augment them and create positive contact and dialogue between them, rather than replace them. This confirms that its goal is *not* assimilationism, but that it recognises that the post-1981 phase of multiculturalism in its form of anti-racism or equal opportunities has done considerable, unintended damage to 'multiculturalism' through its one-sided focus on distinct ethnic communities and their needs, whilst not focusing on relations between communities or on how white communities, and their perceptions and identities, fit into this model. Accordingly, the term multiculturalism has become tainted and unhelpful, no longer offering constructive ways forward. Whilst the term community cohesion has only limited meaning and purchase (Robinson, 2005), the approach it represents of a renewed focus on both commonality and on community relations is recognised and supported on the ground. This can actually be understood as a reversion to Roy Jenkins's original conception of multiculturalism as individuals and communities having rights and responsibilities to ensure social cohesion within a diverse society (Cantle, 2005), underpinned by a new, human rights-based approach to identity that is essential to peacefully manage the increasing complexity of identity within society (McGhee, 2006).

This understanding means that policy and its practitioners, as well as writers who criticise racial stereotyping but use terms like 'Muslim' and 'Asian' unproblematically, have to stop essentialising and reifying ethnicity as the main creator of experience, as has arguably been done since the early 1980s. However, despite the understandable concerns of critics, who view the commonality or cohesion requirements that community cohesion's change of language and priorities represents an end of concern with 'race' and ethnic inequality, the 'death of multiculturalism' per se, the evidence suggests otherwise. The case study evidence of continued respect and acceptance for distinct identities has been summarised above. Nationally, the embedding of community cohesion within overarching race equality strategies (Home Office, 2005, 2009), the continued use of ethnic monitoring data to close achievement gaps in education (Gilborn, 2009), and the ongoing development and implementation of race equality and diversity strategies locally all highlight the continuity of this agenda, albeit within the context of changed language and approaches. Whilst the relationship between race equality and community cohesion at the level of local policy operation needs to be developed further (Monro et al., 2010), it is clear that community cohesion co-exists with equality and diversity strategies, impacting on their approach but not replacing them. Indeed, the PVE policy approach outlined in Chapter 8 suggests that community cohesion has only had limited impact on national policy approaches, given the way that PVE has represented some of the most unhelpful facets of old-style multiculturalism in its monocultural focus on essentialised Muslims and its implementation through a client layer of 'community leaders' (Kundnani, 2009).

Community cohesion has represented a significant change to the language, priorities and approaches of 'race relations' policies in Britain since 2001 but claims of multiculturalism's 'death' are therefore much exaggerated. Here, it needs to be accepted that a 'shift' in policy is not the same as a retreat (Meer and Modood, 2009), and the empirical evidence of community cohesion in practice presented here suggests that the largely negative characterisations of the aims, content and assumptions of community cohesion are significantly misplaced. Such localised evidence as that offered here cannot speak to what community cohesion practice has been to date in different localities, but given the very limited evidence available around community cohesion's implementation, it does suggest what community cohesion *could* represent nationally. Such positive, direct contact between young people of different ethnic backgrounds has not 'solved' the problem of youth racial tension and oppositional identities in Oldham. However, what it has contributed to, and what such community cohesion practice nationally has the potential to offer, is to get 'race' out of the way in situations where people are currently 'seeing' and talking about little else, as then CRE Chief Trevor Phillips (2005) observed in one of the more thoughtful passages of the speech that generated counterproductive controversy: 'contact won't necessarily make you like someone, but it may stop you fearing them and regarding them as an enemy'. Bringing young people together, as community cohesion youth work practice in Oldham has done, and focusing on what they have in common offers the potential for a focus on the *real* issues and challenges facing a growing number of young people from all ethnic backgrounds as Britain returns to recession: the lack of jobs, access to quality further and higher education and training, and affordable housing, without racialised explanations being as effective in dividing young people as they are at present in areas like Oldham and Rochdale. By enabling young people to come together within carefully planned and managed processes and to recognise and experience their commonality and shared humanity, community cohesion practice offers the potential for divisive understandings of 'race' and ethnicity to be seen as the limited and outdated road to nowhere that they are.

Bibliography

Abbas, T. (2005) (ed.) *Muslim Britain: Communities under Pressure*, London: Zed Books.
—— (ed.) (2007a) *Islamic Political Radicalism: A European Perspective*, Edinburgh: Edinburgh University Press.
—— (2007b) 'Muslim minorities in Britain: integration, multiculturalism and radicalism in the post 7/7 period', *Journal of Intercultural Studies*, 28:3, pp. 287–300.
Albrecht, T., Johnson, G.M. and Walther, J.B. (1993) 'Understanding communication processes in focus groups', in D.M. Morgan (ed.) *Successful Focus Groups*, pp. 51–63, Newbury Park, CA: Sage.
Alexander, C. (2000) *The Asian Gang: Ethnicity, Identity, Masculinity*, Oxford: Berg.
—— (2004) 'Imagining the Asian gang: ethnicity, masculinity and youth after "the riots"', *Critical Social Policy*, 24:4, pp. 526–49.
—— (2007) 'Cohesive identities: the distance between meaning and understanding', in M. Wetherell, M. Lafleche and R. Berkley (eds) *Identity, Ethnic Diversity and Community Cohesion*, pp. 115–26.
Alibhai-Brown, A. (2000) *Who Do We Think We Are? Imagining the New Britain*, London: Penguin.
Amin, A. (2003) 'Unruly strangers? The 2001 urban riots in Britain', *International Journal of Urban and Regional Research*, 27:2, pp. 460–63.
Anderson, B. (1991) *Imagined Communities: Reflections on the Origin and Spread of Nationalism* (2nd edn), London: Verso.
Association of Chief Police Officers (2009) *Submission to Communities and Local Government Select Committee PVE Inquiry* (PVE 60).
Association of Police Authorities (2009) *Submission to Communities and Local Government Select Committee PVE Inquiry* (PVE 28).
Back, L. (1996) *New Ethnicities and Urban Culture*, London: UCL Press.
Back, L., Keith, M., Khan, A., Shukra, K. and Solomos, J. (2002) 'New Labour's white heart: politics, multiculturalism and the return of assimilationism', *Political Quarterly*, 73:4, pp. 445–54.
Bagguley, P. and Hussain, Y. (2005) 'Flying the flag for England? Citizenship, religion and cultural identity among British Pakistani Muslims', in T. Abbas (ed.) *Muslim Britain: Communities under Pressure*, pp. 208–21, London: Zed Books.
Bagguley, P. and Hussain, Y. (2008) *Riotous Citizens?*, Aldershot: Ashagte.
Bagley, C. (1973) *The Dutch Plural Society: A Comparative Study in Race Relations*, London: Institute of Race Relations.
Beaumont, P. (2010) 'Geert Wilders, the ultra-right firebrand, campaigns to be Holland's Prime Minister', *Guardian*, 16 May.
Bertossi, C. (2007) *Distant Neighbours: Understanding How the French Deal with Ethnic and Religious Diversity*, London: Runnymede Trust.
Bhavnani, R. (2001) *Rethinking Interventions in Racism*, Stoke-on-Trent: Trentham Books.

Birmingham City Council (2009) *Evidence Submission to Communities and Local Government Select Committee PVE Inquiry* (PVE 25).

Birt, Y. (2009) 'Promoting virulent envy – reconsidering the UK's terrorist prevention strategy', *RUSI Journal*, 154:4, pp. 52–8.

Blunkett, D. (2004) *New Challenges for Race Equality and Community Cohesion in the 21st Century: Speech to the Institute of Public Policy Research*, 7 July 2004, London: Home Office.

Bonnett, A. (2000) *Anti-Racism*, London: Routledge.

Bottero, W. (2009) 'Class in the 1st century', in Runnymede Trust, *Who Cares about the White Working Class?*, pp. 7–14.

Bourne, J. (2007) 'In defence of multiculturalism', IRR Briefing Paper no. 2, Institute of Race Relations, London.

Bragg, B. (2006) *The Progressive Patriot*, London: Bantam Press.

Brown, G. (2007) 'We need a United Kingdom', *Daily Telegraph*, 13 January.

Brown, R. (1995) *Prejudice: Its Social Psychology*, Oxford: Blackwell.

Bujra, J. and Pearce, J. (2009) 'Police on the line: between control and correctness in multi-ethnic contexts of urban unrest', in D. Waddington, F. Jobard and M. King (eds) *Rioting in the UK and France: A Comparative Analysis*, pp. 56–70.

Burgess, S., Wilson, D. and Lupton, R. (2005) 'Parallel lives? Ethnic segregation in schools and neighbourhoods', *Urban Studies*, 42:7, pp. 1027–56.

Burke, J. (2007) *Al-Qaeda* (3rd edn), London: Penguin.

Burnett, J. (2004) 'Community, cohesion and the state', *Race and Class*, 45:3, p. 18.

Buruma, I. (2006) *Murder in Amsterdam: The Death of Theo Van Gogh and the Limits of Tolerance*, London: Atlantic.

Bux, S. (2007) 'Muslim youths, Islam and violent radicalisation: addressing some myths', *The Police Journal*, 80, pp. 267–78.

Byrne, D. (1999) *Social Exclusion*, Oxford: Blackwell.

Campbell, B. (1993) *Goliath: Britain's Dangerous Places*, London: Routledge.

Cantle, T. (2001) *Community Cohesion – A Report of the Independent Review Team*, London: Home Office.

——— (2004) *The End of Parallel Lives? The Report of the Community Cohesion Panel*, London: Home Office.

——— (2005) *Community Cohesion: A New Framework for Race Relations*, Basingstoke: Palgrave.

——— (2007) Speech to Europe and Its Established and Emerging Immigrant Communities Conference, De Montfort University, Leicester, 10–11 November.

Carling, A. (2008) 'The curious case of the mis-claimed myth claims: ethnic segregation, polarisation and the future of Bradford', *Urban Studies*, 45:3, pp. 37–53.

Chauhan, V. (1990) *Beyond Steel Bands 'n' Samosas'*, Leicester: National Youth Bureau.

Clarke, T. (2001) *Burnley Task Force Report on the Disturbances in June 2001*, Burnley: Burnley Borough Council.

Cohen, P. (1988) 'The perversions of inheritance', in P. Cohen and H.S. Bains (eds) *Multi-Racist Britain*, pp. 9–118, London: Macmillan.

Cohen, S. (1972) *Folk Devils and Moral Panics*, London: MacGibbon and Kee.

Collins, M. (2004) *The Likes of Us: A Biography of the White Working Class*, London: Granta.

Commission for Racial Equality (CRE) (1999) *Open Talk, Open Minds*, London: CRE.

––––– (2001) *A Place for Us All – Learning from Bradford, Oldham and Burnley*, London: CRE.

Commission on the Future of Multi-Ethnic Britain (CFMEB) (2000) *The Future of Multi-Ethnic Britain: The Parekh Report*, London: Profile Books.

Community Relations Council (1976) *Seen But Not Served*, London: CRC.

Copsey, N. (2008) *Contemporary British Fascism: The British National Party and the Quest for Legitimacy*, Basingstoke: Palgrave.

CRE/Ethnos (2005) *Citizenship and Belonging: What is Britishness? And the Decline of Britishness (Surveys conducted by Ethnos)*, London: CRE.

Davies, B. (1999) *A History of the Youth Service in England and Wales*, Leicester: Youth Work Press.

––––– (2005) 'Youth work: a manifesto for our times', *Youth and Policy*, 88, pp. 5–27.

Dench, G., Gavron, K. and Young, M. (2006) *The New East End: Kinship, Race and Conflict*, London: Profile Books.

Denham, J. (2001) *Building Cohesive Communities – A Report of the Inter-Departmental Ministerial Group on Public Order and Community Cohesion*, London: Home Office.

Department for Communities and Local Government (DCLG) (2007a) *Commission on Integration and Cohesion: Our Shared Future*, London: DCLG.

––––– (2007b) *Preventing Violent Extremism – Winning Hearts and Minds*, London: DCLG.

––––– (2007c) *Preventing Violent Extremism Pathfinder Fund: Guidance Note for Government Offices and Local Authorities in England*, London: DCLG.

––––– (2007d) *The Role of Muslim Identity Politics in Radicalisation (A Case Study in Progress)*, London: DCLG.

––––– (2008a) *PVE Pathfinder Fund – Mapping of Project Activities 2007/08*, London: DCLG.

––––– (2008b) *Guidance for Local Authorities on Community Cohesion Contingency Planning and Tension Monitoring*, London: DCLG.

––––– (2009a) *Improving Opportunity, Strengthening Society: A Third Progress Report on the Government's Strategy for Race Equality and Community Cohesion*, London: DCLG.

––––– (2009b) *Delivering the Prevent Strategy: An Updated Guide for Local Partners*, London: DCLG.

––––– (2009c) Rt. Hon. John Denham, MP, Ministerial Speech to National Prevent Conference, Birmingham, 8 December.

Department for Education (1982) *Experience and Participation: Report of the Review Group on the Youth Service in England (Commonly Known as the Thompson Report)*, London: HMSO.

Department of Innovation, Universities and Skills (DIUS) (2008) *Promoting Good Campus Relations, Fostering Shared Values and Preventing Violent Extremism in Universities and Higher Education Colleges*, London: DIUS.

Din, I. (2006) *The New British: The Impact of Culture and Community on Young Pakistanis*, Aldershot: Ashgate.

Dodd, V. (2006) 'White pupils less tolerant, survey shows', *Guardian*, 21 October.

Donald, J. and Rattansi, A. (eds) (1992) *Race, Culture and Difference*, London: Sage.

Dorling, D. (2009) 'From housing to health – to whom are the white working class losing out? Frequently asked questions', in Runnymede Trust, *Who Cares about the White Working Class?*, pp. 59–65.

Eatwell, R. (2006) 'Community cohesion and cumulative extremism in contemporary Britain', *The Political Quarterly*, 77:2, pp. 204–16.

Eatwell, R. and Goodwin, M. (eds) (2010) *The New Extremism in Twenty-first Century Britain*, London: Routledge.

English, R. (2009) *Terrorism: How to Respond*, Oxford: Oxford University Press.

Etzioni, A. (1995) *The Spirit of Community: Rights, Responsibilities and the Communitarian Agenda*, London: Fontana.

Farrar, M. (2002) 'The northern "race riots" of the summer of 2001 – were they riots, were they Racial? A case study of the events in Harehills, Leeds', Paper given to 'Parallel Lives and Polarisation', BSA 'Race' Seminar at City University, London, May.

Fekete, L., Bouteldja, N. and Muhe, N. (2010) *Alternative Voices on Integration*, London: Institute for Race Relations.

Fenton, S. (2007) 'Indifference towards national identity: what young adults think about being English and British', *Nations and Nationalism*, 13:2, pp. 321–39.

Finney, N. and Simpson, L. (2009) *'Sleepwalking to Segregation'? Challenging Myths about Race and Migration*, Bristol: Policy Press.

Flavell, A. (2001) *Philosophies of Integration: Immigration and the Idea of Citizenship in France and Britain* (2nd edn), Basingstoke: Palgrave.

Flint, J. and Robinson, D. (eds) (2008) *Community Cohesion in Crisis?*, Bristol: Policy Press.

Foreign and Commonwealth Office and Home Office (2004) *Draft Report on Young Muslims and Extremism*, London: FCO.

Forrest, R. and Kearns, A. (2000) 'Social cohesion, social capital and the neighbourhood', Paper presented to ESRC Cities Programme Neighbourhoods Colloquium, Liverpool, 5–6 June.

Garner, S., (2009) 'Home truths: the white working class and the racialisation of social housing', in Runnymede Trust, *Who Cares about the White Working Class?*, pp. 45–50.

Geaves, R. (2005) 'Negotiating British citizenship and Muslim identity', in T. Abbas (ed.) *Muslim Britain: Communities under Pressure*, pp. 66–77.

Giddens, A. (1998) *The Third Way: The Renewal of Social Democracy*, Cambridge: Polity.

Gilborn, D. (2009) 'Education: the numbers game and the construction of White racial victimhood', in Runnymede Trust, *Who Cares about the White Working Class?*, pp. 15–21.

Gilroy, P. (2000) *Between Camps: Nations, Cultures and the Allure of Race*, London: Penguin.

—— (2002) *There Ain't No Black in the Union Jack: The Cultural Politics of Race and Nation*, London: Routledge.

—— (2004) *After Empire: Melancholia or Convivial Culture?*, Abingdon: Routledge.

Goodhart, D. (2004) 'Discomfort of strangers', *Guardian*, 24 and 25 February.

Green, R. and Pinto, R. (2005) 'Youth related community cohesion policy and practice: the divide between rhetoric and reality', *Youth and Policy*, 88, pp. 45–61.

Greener, I. (2002) 'Agency, social theory and social policy', *Critical Social Policy*, 22:4, pp. 688–705.

Grieve, D. (2009) 'Multiculturalism: A Conservative Vision of a Free Society', The Lord Smith Annual Lecture, London, 4 March.

Guardian (2009) *MPs Investigate Anti-extremism Programme after Spying Claims*, 18th October, available at http://www.guardian.co.uk/uk/2009/oct/18/prevent-extremism-muslims-information, accessed 18 January 2010.

Guardian (2010) Editorial, 'Netherlands election: austerity with a conscience', 12 June.

Guene, F. (2010) 'In search of Frenchness', *Guardian: Comment is Free*, 28 January.

Gunaratnam, Y. (2003) *Researching 'Race' and Ethnicity*, London: Sage.

Gupta, D. (2008) *Understanding Political Violence*, Abingdon: Routledge.

Hall, S. (1992) 'New ethnicities', in J. Donald and A. Rattansi (eds) *'Race', Culture and Difference*, pp. 252–9, London: Sage.

—— (2000) 'Conclusion: the multicultural question', in B. Hesse (ed.) *Un/Settled Multiculturalisms*, pp. 209–41, London: Zed Books.

Hamidi, C. (2009) 'Riots and protest cycles: immigrant mobilisation in France 1968–2008', in D. Waddington, F. Jobard, and M. King (eds) *Rioting in the UK and France: A Comparative Analysis*, pp. 15–146.

Hanley, L. (2008) 'This white working class stuff is a media invention', *Guardian*, May 30.

Hebdidge, D. (1979) *Sub-culture – The Meaning of Style*, London: Routledge.

Hesse, B. (ed.) (2000) *Un/Settled Multiculturalisms: Diasporas, Entanglements, Transruptions*, London: Zed Books.

Hewitt, R. (1996) *Routes of Racism – The Social Basis of Racist Action*, Stoke-on-Trent: Trentham Books.

—— (2005) *White Backlash: The Politics of Multiculturalism*, Cambridge: Cambridge University Press.

Hewstone, M., Tausch, N., Hughes, J. and Cairns, E. (2007) 'Prejudice, inter-group contact and identity: do neighbourhoods matter?', in M. Wetherell, M. Lafleche and R. Berkley (eds) *Identity, Ethnic Diversity and Community Cohesion*, pp. 102–12.

Hills, J., Le Grand, J. and Piachaud, D. (eds) (2002) *Understanding Social Exclusion*, Oxford: Oxford University Press.

Home Office (2003a) *Building a Picture of Community Cohesion – A Guide for Local Authorities and their Partners*, London: Home Office.

—— (2003b) *Community Cohesion Pathfinder Programme: The First Six Months*, London: Home Office.

—— (2004) *Community Cohesion Pathfinder Dissemination Programme – Report of National Conference of November 2003*, London: Home Office.

—— (2005) *Improving Opportunity, Strengthening Society: The Government's Strategy to Increase Race Equality and Community Cohesion*, London: Home Office.

—— (2007) *Improving Opportunity, Strengthening Society: A Two Year Review*, London: Home Office.

—— (2009) *CONTEST 2 –The United Kingdom's Strategy for Countering International Terrorism*, London: Home Office.

House of Commons (2010) *Communities and Local Government Select Committee: Preventing Violent Extremism: Sixth Report of Session 2009–10*, London: House of Commons.

Husain, E. (2007) *The Islamist*, London: Penguin.

Hutnik, N. and Coran-Street, R. (2010) 'Profiles of British Muslim identity: adolescent girls in Birmingham', *Journal of Adolescence*, 33:1, pp. 33–42.

Ipsos Mori (2007) *Young People and Britishness: Survey for Camelot Foundation*, London: Ipsos Mori.

Ismail, S. (2008) 'Muslim public self-presentation: interrogating the liberal public sphere', *Political Studies*, 41:1, pp. 25–9.

Jan-Khan, M. (2003) 'The right to riot?', *Community Development Journal*, 38:1, pp. 32–42.

Jeffs, T. and Smith, M. (eds) (1988) *Welfare and Youth Work Practice*, Basingstoke: Macmillan.

Joppke, C. (2004) 'The retreat of multiculturalism in the liberal state: theory and practice', *British Journal of Sociology*, 55:2, 237–58.

Kalra, V.S. (2000) *From Textile Mills to Taxi Ranks*, Aldershot: Ashgate.

––––– (2002) 'Extended view: riots, race and reports: Denham, Cantle, Oldham and Burnley inquiries', *Sage Race Relations Abstracts*, 27:4, pp. 20–30.

Kalra, V.S. and Rhodes, J. (2009) 'Local events, national implications: riots in Oldham and Burnley', in D. Waddington, F. Jobard and M. King (eds) *Rioting in the UK and France: A Comparative Analysis*, pp. 41–55.

Kalra, V. and Kapoor, N. (2009) 'Interrogating segregation, integration and the community cohesion agenda', *Journal of Ethnic and Migration Studies*, 35:9, pp. 1397–415.

King, M. (2009) 'From rumour to riot: the 2005 Lozells disorders', in D. Waddington, F. Jobard and M. King (eds) *Rioting in the UK and France: A Comparative Analysis*, pp. 94–104.

King, M. and Waddington, D. (2004) 'Coping with disorder? The changing relationship between police public order strategy and practice – a critical analysis of the Burnley riot', *Policing and Society*, 14:2, pp. 118–37.

Kintrea, K., Bannister, J., Pickering, J., Reid, M. and Suzuki, N. (2008) *Young People and Territoriality in British Cities*, York: Joseph Rowntree Foundation.

Kokeroff, M. (2009) 'The political dimension of the 2005 riots', in D. Waddington, F. Jobard and M. King (eds) *Rioting in the UK and France: A Comparative Analysis*, pp. 147–56.

Kundnani, A. (2001) 'From Oldham to Bradford: the violence of the violated', in *The Three faces of British Racism*, London: Institute of Race Relations, available at http://www.irr.org.uk/2001/october/ak000003.html.

––––– (2002) *The Death of Multiculturalism*, London: Institute of Race Relations, available at http://www.irr.org.uk/2002/april/ak000001.html.

––––– (2007) *The End of Tolerance? Racism in 21st Century Britain*, London: Pluto Press.

––––– (2009) *Spooked: How Not to Prevent Violent Extremism*, London: Institute of Race Relations.

Lagrange, H. (2009) 'The French riots and urban segregation', in D. Waddington, F. Jobard and M. King (eds) *Rioting in the UK and France: A Comparative Analysis*, pp. 107–23.

Law, I. (1996) *Racism, Ethnicity and Social Policy*, London: Prentice Hall.

Levitas, R. (2005) *The Inclusive Society? Social Exclusion and New Labour* (2nd edn), Basingstoke: Palgrave.

Lewis, P. (2007) *Young, British and Muslim*, London: Continuum.

Local Government Association (LGA) (2002) *Guidance on Community Cohesion*, London: Local Government Association.

—— (2004) *Community Cohesion – An Action Guide: Guidance for Local Authorities*, London: Local Government Association.

—— (2009) *Submission to Communities and Local Government Select Committee PVE Inquiry* (PVE 30).

Lowndes, V. and Thorp, L. (2010) ' "Preventing violent extremism" – why local context matters', in R. Eatwell and M. Goodwin (eds) *The New extremism in 21st Century Britain*, pp. 123–41.

Macdonald, I. (1989) *Murder in the Playground – The Report of the Macdonald Inquiry*, Manchester: Longsight Press.

Macey, M. (1999) 'Class, gender and religious influences on the changing patterns of Pakistani Muslim male violence in Bradford', *Ethnic and Racial Studies*, 22:5, pp. 845–66.

—— (2007) 'Islamic political radicalism in Britain: Muslim men in Bradford', in T. Abbas (ed.) *Islamic Political Radicalism: A European Perspective*, pp. 160–72.

Macpherson, W. (1999) *The Stephen Lawrence Inquiry: Report of an Inquiry by Sir William Macpherson of Cluny (Cm 4262)*, London: The Stationery Office.

Malik, K. (2009) *From Fatwa to Jihad: The Rushdie Affair and Its Legacy*, London: Atlantic.

Mason, J. (2002) *Qualitative Researching*, London: Sage.

Masood, E. (2006) 'British Muslims – ends and beginnings', Open Democracy, available at http://www.opendemocracy.net/globalization/british_muslims_4048.jsp.

May, S. (ed.) (1999a) *Critical Multiculturalism – Rethinking Multicultural and Anti-racist Education*, London: Falmer.

—— (1999b) 'Critical multiculturalism and cultural difference: avoiding essentialism', in S. May (ed.) *Critical Multiculturalism*, pp. 11–41, London: Falmer.

—— (2002) 'Multiculturalism', in D.T. Goldberg and J. Solomos (eds) *A Companion to Racial and Ethnic Studies*, pp. 124–44, Oxford: Blackwell.

McGhee, D. (2003) 'Moving to "our" common ground – a critical examination of community cohesion discourse in twenty first century Britain', *Sociological Review*, 51:3, pp. 366–404.

—— (2005) *Intolerant Britain: Hate, Citizenship and Difference*, Maidenhead: Open University Press.

—— (2006) 'The new Commission for Equality and Human Rights: building community cohesion and revitalising citizenship in contemporary Britain', *Ethnopolitics*, 5:2, pp. 145–66.

—— (2008) *The End of Multiculturalism? Terrorism, Integration and Human Rights*, Maidenhead: Oxford University Press.

McRoy, A. (2006) *From Rushdie to 7/7: The Radicalisation of Islam in Britain*, London: Social Affairs Unit.

Meer, N. and Modood, T. (2009) 'The multicultural state we're in: Muslims, "multiculture" and the "civic re-balancing of British multiculturalism" ', *Political Studies*, 57:3, pp. 473–97.

Mirza, M., Senthilkumaran, A. and Ja'far, Z. (2007) *Living Apart Together: British Muslims and the Paradox of Multiculturalism*, London: Policy Exchange.

Mizen, P. (2004) *The Changing State of Youth*, Basingstoke: Palgrave Macmillan.

Modood, T. (1994) 'Political blackness and British Asians', *Sociology*, 28:4, pp. 859–76.

——— (1997) ' "Difference", cultural racism and anti-racism', in T. Modood and P. Werbner (eds) *Debating Cultural Hybridity*, pp. 154–172, London: Zed Books.

——— (2005) *Multicultural Politics: Racism, Ethnicity and Muslims in Britain*, Edinburgh: Edinburgh University Press.

Modood, T. and Werbner, P. (eds) (1997) *Debating Cultural Hybridity*, London: Zed Books.

Modood, T., Berthoud, R., Lakey, J. et al. (1997) *Ethnic Minorities in Britain – Diversity and Disadvantage*, London: PSI.

Monro, S., Rafiq, U., Thomas, P. and Mycock, A. (2010) *Regional Improvement & Efficiency Partnerships (RIEPs) Community Cohesion (PREVENT) Pilot: A Report Prepared for Local Government Yorkshire and Humber*, Huddersfield: University of Huddersfield.

Nayak, A. (1999) 'White English ethnicities; racism, anti-racism and student perspectives', *Race, Ethnicity and Education*, 2:2, pp. 177–202.

Office of the Deputy Prime Minister (2006) *State of the English Cities*, London: ODPM.

Oldham Metropolitan Borough Council (2004) *Oldham Youth Service Strategic Plan*, Oldham: OMBC.

——— (2005) *Population Forecasts for Oldham*, Oldham: OMBC.

——— (2006) *Population Forecasts for Oldham: Children and Young People*, Oldham: OMBC.

Ouseley, H. (2001) *Community Pride, Not Prejudice – Making Diversity Work in Bradford*, Bradford: Bradford Vision.

Parekh, B. (2006) *Re-thinking Multiculturalism: Cultural Diversity and Political Theory* (2nd edn), Basingstoke: Palgrave Macmillan.

Perryman, M. (ed.) (2008) *Imagined Nation – England after Britain*, London: Lawrence and Wishart.

Phillips, T. (2004a) 'Multiculturalism's legacy is "have a nice day" racism', *Guardian*, 28 May.

Phillips, T. (2004b) *The Observer*, 'Race in Britain', p. 24, November.

——— (2005) 'After 7/7: sleepwalking to segregation', Speech given to the Manchester Council for Community Relations, 25 September.

Phillips, D., Simpson, L. and Ahmed, S. (2008) 'Shifting geographies of minority ethnic populations: re-making communities in Oldham and Rochdale', in J. Flint and D. Robinson (eds) *Community Cohesion in Crisis?*, pp. 81–98.

Pilkington, A. (2008) 'From institutional racism to community cohesion: the changing nature of racial discourse in Britain', *Sociology Online*, 13, available at http://www.socresonline.org.uk/13/3/6.html.

Popple, K. (1997) 'Understanding and tackling racism among young people in the United Kingdom', in J. Hazekamp and K. Popple (eds) *Racism in Europe*, pp. 13–38, London: UCL Press.

Prins, G. and Salisbury, R. (2008) 'Risk, threat and security: the case of the UK', *RUSI Journal*, 153:1, pp. 6–11.

Putnam, R. (2000) *Bowling Alone – The Collapse and Revival of American Community*, London: Touchstone.

Ramadan, T. (2009) 'Muslims and European policies: the way forward', in C. Howson and M. Sallah (eds) *Europe's Established and Emerging Immigrant*

Communities: Assimilation, Multiculturalism or Integration, pp. 11–18, Stoke-on-Trent: Trentham Books.

Ramdani, N. (2010) 'Laicite and the French veil debate', *Guardian: Comment is Free*, 23 May.

Rattansi, A. (1999) 'Racism, "postmodernism" and reflexive multiculturalism', in S. May (ed.) *Critical Multiculturalism – Rethinking Multicultural and Anti-racist Education*, pp. 77–112, London: Falmer.

Ray, L. and Smith, D. (2002) 'Racist offending, policing and community conflict', Paper presented to the British Sociological Association Conference, Leicester, April.

Rendeiro, M.F. (2010) 'Keep the PVV's Dutch gains in perspective', *Guardian*, 4 March.

Ritchie, D. (2001) *Oldham Independent Review – One Oldham, One Future*, Manchester: Government Office for the Northwest.

Robinson, D. (2005) 'The search for community cohesion: key themes and dominant concepts of the public policy agenda', *Urban Studies*, 42:8, pp. 1411–27.

Rochdale Metropolitan Borough Council (2009) *Rochdale Borough Profile 2009*, Rochdale: Rochdale MBC.

Roy, O. (2004) *Globalised Islam: The Search for a New Ummah*, London: Hurst.

Runnymede Trust (2000) *Report of the Commission into the Future of Multi-ethnic Britain (The Parekh Report)*, London: Profile Books.

——— (2009) *Who Cares about the White Working Class?* London: Runnymede Trust.

Saeed, A., Blain, N. and Forbes, D. (1999) 'New ethnic and national questions in Scotland: post-British identities among Glasgow Pakistani teenagers', *Ethnic and Racial Studies*, 22:5, pp. 821–44.

Sanghera, G. and Thapar-Bjorkert, S. (2007) ' "Because I am Pakistani and I am Muslim . . . I am political" – gendering political radicalism: young feminities in Bradford in 2007', in Tahir Abbas (ed.) *Islamic Political Radicalism: A European Perspective*, Edinburgh: Edinburgh University Press, pp. 173–91.

Scarman, L. (1981) *A Report into the Brixton Disturbances of 11/12th April 1981*, London: Home Office.

Schalk-Soekar, S., Breugelmans, S. and van de Vijver, F. (2009) 'Support for multiculturalism in The Netherlands', *International Social Science Journal*, 59:192, pp. 269–81.

Scheffer, P. (2000) 'The multicultural drama', *The Weekly Standard*, 29 January.

Sen, A. (2006) *Identity and Violence: The Illusion of Destiny*, London: Norton.

Shavit, U. (2009) *The New Imagined Community: Global Media and the Construction of National and Muslim Identities of Migrants*, Eastbourne: Sussex Academic Press.

Sibbit, R. (1997) *The Perpetrators of Racial Harassment and Racial Violence (Home Office Research Study 176)*, London: Home Office.

Silvestri, S. (2010) 'French parliament approves ban on face veils', *Guardian*, 13 July.

Simpson, L. (2004) 'Statistics of racial segregation: measures, evidence and policy', *Urban Studies*, 41:3, pp. 661–81.

Sivanandan, A. (1981) *A Different Hunger*, London: Pluto Press.

——— (2004) 'Our common values are brought about by a clash of cultures', *Guardian*, 26 February.

——— (2005) *Its Anti-racism That Was Failed, Not Multiculturalism That Failed*, London: Institute of Race Relations, available at http://www.irr.org.uk/2005/october/ak000021.html.

Smith, M. (1982) *Creators Not Consumers: Rediscovering Social Education*, London: NAYC.

Sniderman, P. and Hagendoorn, L. (2009) *When Ways of Life Collide: Multiculturalism and Its Discontents in The Netherlands*, Woodstock: Princeton University Press.

Social Exclusion Unit (SEU) (1999) *Bridging the Gap – New Opportunities for 16–18 Year Olds*, London: SEU.

Solomos, J. (1988) 'Institutionalised racism: policies of marginalisation in education and training', in P. Cohen and H.S. Bains (eds) *Multi-Racist Britain*, pp. 156–94, London: Macmillan.

——— (2003) *Race and Racism in Britain* (3rd edn), Basingstoke: Palgrave Macmillan.

Sutcliffe, H. (2003) *The Oldham Riots – What Happened, Why and What Next?* Oldham: Newton and Freehold Community Partnership.

Sveinsson, K.P. (2009) 'The white working class and multiculturalism: is there space for a progressive agenda?', in Runnymede Trust, *Who Cares about the White Working Class?*, pp. 3–6.

Thomas, P. (2002) 'Youth work, racist behaviour and young people – education or blame?', *Scottish Journal of Youth Issues*, 4, pp. 49–66.

——— (2003) 'Young people, community cohesion, and the role of youth work in building social capital', *Youth and Policy*, 81, pp. 21–43.

——— (2006) 'The impact of community cohesion on youth work: a case study from Oldham', *Youth and Policy*, 93, pp. 41–60.

——— (2007a) 'Moving on from "anti-racism"? Understandings of community cohesion held by youth workers', *Journal of Social Policy*, 36:3, pp. 435–55.

——— (2007b) 'Community cohesion, "the death of multiculturalism" and work with young people', Paper presented to the Europe and Its Established and Emerging Immigrant Communities Conference, De Montfort University, Leicester, 10–11 November.

——— (2008) *Evaluation of the Kirklees Preventing Violent Extremism Pathfinder: Issues and Lessons from the First Year*, Huddersfield: University of Huddersfield.

——— (2009) 'Between two stools? The government's Preventing Violent Extremism agenda', *The Political Quarterly Journal*, 80:2, pp. 282–91.

——— (2010) 'Failed and friendless – the government's Preventing Violent Extremism agenda', *British Journal of Politics and International Relations*, 12:3, pp. 442–58.

——— (forthcoming) 'All white? Englishness, 'race' and ethnic identities', in A. Aughey and C. Berberich (eds) *These Englands: A Conversation on National Identity*, Manchester: Manchester University Press.

Thomas, P. and Sanderson, P. (2009) *The Oldham and Rochdale Youth Identity Project Final Report*, Huddersfield: University of Huddersfield.

Travis, A. (2001) 'Blunkett in race row over culture tests', *Guardian*, 10 December.

Travis, A. (2006) ' "Summer of race riots" feared after clashes in 2001', *Guardian*, 28 December.

——— (2010) 'Time for new approach to race relations, minister urges', *Guardian*, 14 January.

Traynor, I. (2009) 'Profile: Geert Wilders', *Guardian*, 16 October.

Turley, A. (2009) *Stronger Together: A New Approach to Preventing Violent Extremism*, London: New Local Government Network.

University of Central Lancashire (2009) *Submission to Communities and Local Government Select Committee PVE Inquiry*, Preston: University of Central Lancashire.

Vasagar, J. and Dodd, V. (2001) 'Poverty and racism create an explosive mix', *Guardian*, 9 July.

Vink, M. (2007) 'Dutch "multiculturalism" beyond the pillarisation myth', *Political Studies Review*, 5, pp. 337–50.

Waddington, D. (2010) 'Applying the flashpoints model of public disorder to the 2001 Bradford riot', *British Journal of Criminology*, 50, pp. 342–59.

Waddington, D., Jobard, F. and King, M. (eds) (2009) *Rioting in the UK and France: A Comparative Analysis*, Cullompton: Willan Publishing.

Ward, D. (2001) 'Nine hours on the Bradford front-line', *Guardian*, 9 July.

Ward, L. and Carvel, J. (2007) 'Growing sense of Englishness explains why less than half the country feel British', *Guardian*, 24 January.

Ware, V. (2008) 'Towards sociology of resentment: a debate on class and whiteness', *Sociological Research Online*, 13:5, available at http://www.socresonline.org.uk/13/5/9.html.

Warnes, R. and Hannah, G. (2008) 'Meeting the challenge of extremists and radicalised prisoners: the experiences of the UK and Spain', *Policing Journal*, 2:4, pp. 402–411.

Watson, C.W. (2000) *Multiculturalism*, Buckingham: Open University Press.

Webster, C. (1995) *Youth Crime, Victimisation and Racial Harassment – The Keighley Survey*, Bradford: Bradford College.

——— (1996) 'Local heroes – violent racism, localism and spacism among Asian and white young people', *Youth and Policy*, 53, pp. 15–27.

——— (2001) 'Race, space and fear – imagined geographies of racism, crime, violence, and disorder in northern England', Paper submitted to the Oldham Independent Review into the Oldham Disorders of 26–29 May 2001, University of Teesside, Middlesbrough (reproduced in *Capital and Class*, January 2002).

Wetherell, M., Lafleche, M. and Berkley, R. (eds) (2007) *Identity, Ethnic Diversity and Community Cohesion*, London: Sage.

——— (2008) 'Speaking to power: Tony Blair, complex multicultures and fragile White English identities', *Critical Social Policy*, 28:3, pp. 299–319.

Williams, L. (1988) *Partial Surrender: Race and Resistance in the Youth Service*, London: Falmer.

Willsher, K. (2010) 'France to issue citizen's handbooks to every child', *Guardian*, 8 February.

Winder, R. (2004) *Bloody Foreigners: The Story of Immigration to Britain*, London: Abacus.

Worley, C. (2005) ' "It's not about race, it's about the community": New Labour and "Community Cohesion" ', *Critical Social Policy*, 25:4, pp. 483–96.

Young, K. (1999) *The Art of Youth Work*, London: Russell House.

Yuval-Davis, N. (1997) 'Ethnicity, gender relations and multiculturalism', in T. Modood and P. Werbner (eds) *Debating Cultural Hybridity*, pp. 193–208, London: Zed Books.

Index